Family Life and
School Achievement

Reginald Clark

Family Life and School Achievement
Why Poor Black Children Succeed or Fail

The University of Chicago Press
Chicago and London

THE UNIVERSITY OF CHICAGO PRESS, CHICAGO 60637
THE UNIVERSITY OF CHICAGO PRESS, LTD., LONDON

LIBRARY OF CONGRESS CATALOGING IN PUBLICATION DATA

Clark, Reginald M.
   Family life and school achievement.

   Bibliography: p.
   1. Afro-Americans—Education. 2. Home and school—
United States. 3. Family—United States. 4. Academic
achievement. I. Title.
LC2801.C56   1983   370'.890973   83-3481
ISBN 0-226-10769-8 (cloth); 0-226-10770-1 (paper)

To Robin

Contents

Acknowledgments

This book is the product of a research project started over ten years ago at the University of Wisconsin, Madison. I have nurtured this project with the sustained collaboration and invaluable conceptual contributions of Professor Bert Adams. Bert has supported me in many ways over the last ten years—first as one of my advisors in graduate school and later as an active mentor—collaborating with me to move this book along to its completion. It was Bert who kept insisting that "his book absolutely has to see the light of day." As a prominent contemporary figure in the field of American family sociology (and a uniquely caring individual), Bert is indeed one of the finest gentlemen that I've had the opportunity to work with. We continue our work together on a major study of the communication patterns between families and schools, and the effect of these patterns on family processes.

A number of people have contributed to the ideas in this book. I want particularly to thank my family for providing many opportunities to learn about family interaction. I also want to acknowledge the special response and support received from Robin Jarrett, Joan Roberts, Vernon Haubrich, Herbert Kliebard, Silas Purnell, James Conyers, Edgar Epps, John Hope Franklin, Kenneth Prewitt, Clarence Olsen, Chad Gordon, Conrad Briner, Malcolm Douglass, John Regan, Philip Dreyer, Gwendolyn Baker, Walter Allen, Robert K. Murphy, James Baugh, Howard Taylor, Doris Wilkerson, Hubert Blalock, Jeffrey Baker and other friends who must remain nameless because of space limitations.

My students and colleagues at Chicago State University and my colleagues, students, and office staff at Claremont Graduate School also contributed precious wisdom and support to the production of this book. Of course, the parents and adolescents who agreed to tell their stories were simply fantastic in their cooperation and assistance. Finally, I want to thank the University of Wisconsin Institute for Research on Poverty for providing funds to conduct the early pilot study that led to this book.

Foreword

The family is the basic institution through which children learn who they are, where they fit into society, and what kinds of futures they are likely to experience. One's ethnic group membership determines much of the content and flavor of interaction within the family. If one is Black, Puerto Rican, or Chicano, he or she will be exposed to parental values and priorities that differ in important ways from those experienced by white children. Within each ethnic group, values and priorities are also influenced by the family's social status. While distinguishing ethnic influences from social status influences is extremely difficult, it seems clear that among oppressed minorities, families face great problems in their efforts to shape their children's futures so that they will experience a reasonable degree of success in school and in adult life. Different ethnic groups inhabit different cultural niches; thus, they face different subsistence demands, provide different role models, and have different conceptions of adult success. In *Family Life and School Achievement*, Professor Clark has done an excellent job of describing those aspects of family life in one particular cultural niche that have important influences on children's school success. Perhaps the most important contribution of the book is the way it clearly and vividly makes the point that even within the confines of one narrowly restricted cultural niche, poor urban Black families differ substantially in the quality of family life they are able to provide, and these differences are reflected in their children's school achievement. Possibly of equal importance is the fact that differences in quality of life are not explained by such family composition variables as marital status of parents, income, or amount of parents' formal education.

During the past twenty years, a fair amount of agreement has developed among sociologists that educational achievement and educational attainment can be predicted rather successfully by social background characteristics of families of origin. The family background factors studied typically include parental occupation, education, and income. Some studies also include such compositional variables as marital status (intact two-parent families versus families containing one parent), number of children, number of adults in the household, and whether or not the mother works outside the home. Recent studies tend to include a measure of the student's ability (aptitude test score); however, I perceive this to be an outcome of family experience rather than a background characteristic.

Generally speaking, investigations of the influence of social background (excluding ability) on Black students' achievement have found that such "surface" family characteristics provide very little help in explaining variations in achievement. Family socioeconomic characteristics are usually found to be positively and significantly related to educational aspirations and expectations, but the strength of the relationships is modest and leaves much room for additional inquiry into the processes by which families encourage their children to develop high educational aspirations and expectations.

A family's ability to provide a home environment that prepares its children for future success, including success in school, develops out of past experiences with cultural tasks and social rewards. The values and emphases derived from past experiences are either reinforced or altered by current experiences and by perceptions and interpretations of available opportunity structures. There is a long history of survey research that indicates that Black low-income families have high educational aspirations for their children. The experiences of Blacks in American society have convinced the majority of parents that their children's chances for occupational success and a comfortable life-style are extremely limited if they are not able to attain considerably more education than their parents.

The fact that education is highly valued among Black families is not at issue. What the typical study of the relation of family background to children's educational achievement has failed to tell us is why some Black families with high aspirations for their children are able to translate their aspirations into reality through their children's school success whereas others with equally high aspirations are unable to achieve the desired outcomes. In other words, these studies tell us nothing about the specific aspects of family organization, interaction, and cohesiveness that contribute to high attainment. It is this gap in our knowledge that is the focus of *Family Life and School Achievement*.

Professor Clark's study will become, in my opinion, an important addition to our knowledge of how families contribute to their children's success or failure in school. What this book contributes, in contrast to other studies, is a specification of the attitudes, knowledge, skills, and behaviors that students must develop if they are to succeed in school. In addition, it describes in detail the types of activities, interactional styles, and support systems that are found in the homes of successful students and contrasts these with the home life of unsuccessful students. The information from the ten case studies on low-income Black families provides strong support for Clark's contention that it is by looking at family socialization processes, not compositional properties, that school personnel, developmental psychologists, and sociologists will acquire a better understanding of the content of the "hidden curriculum" of the home that results in children reaching the school years with vastly different levels of preparation for the challenge of schooling. The case studies of the families of successful achievers include many illustrations of explicit literacy nurturing activities including reading, writing, topical dialogues, and explicit practice in social etiquette as well as indirect literacy-enhancing activities such as word games and hobbies. Other important aspects of supportive family systems include interactive communication styles that provide opportunities for direct instruction, feedback opportunities, and reinforcement opportunities. Affect, or emotional climate, is also important. It is crucial that the child can be afforded opportunities to develop academic and social skills through personally satisfying activities. Throughout the case studies of the families of high achievers there are examples of supportiveness and a type of social control or discipline that can be characterized as "firm but not harsh." The results of this study confirm some of the findings of my survey studies of Black high school students. For example, using student self-report questionnaires, we found that in addition to firm but not harsh disciplinary practices, some aspects of discipline that are positively related to academic achievement include willingness to explain decisions and willingness to involve students in the decision-making process. These are essentially the same qualities that Clark observed in his case studies. This convergence of results involving different methodologies and different locations lends additional credibility to Clark's research.

If the results of this qualitative research can be consistently replicated with similar or dissimilar methodologies, it will help us to come closer to an explanation of why some families provide better support for school achievement than others. Socieconomic status and ethnicity are types of measures that can tell us that a relationship between variables is present and the direction of that relationship as well as its strength as determined by the set of indicators used in a specific study. By looking at family internal structure, we will be able to examine the actual processes involved in the family background effect.

It has been observed in other research that for low-income urban Black children the school experience is often discontinuous with early childhood development. Teacher expectations, and the culture of the school, often conflict with home experiences; competencies acquired in the home may not be valued in the classroom. The interface between home and school learning environments is an important area of inquiry. Clark's study is suggestive in that he found the parents of high achievers to be assertive in their efforts to attain information about their children's progress in school. The parents of low achievers, in contrast, tended to avoid contact with school personnel unless they were summoned to the school by the authority figures. Again there is convergence with previous research. Studies of adult alienation and sense of control over the environment have consistently found that less alienated persons and persons who exhibited internal locus of control are more assertive and acquire more knowledge of how organizations work. In this case, these personal qualities of parents result in successful advocacy for children in the school setting.

Clark has noted that parents of high achievers appear to be more optimistic than parents of low achievers and that they seem to perceive themselves as persons who can cope with the current exigencies of life. The parents of low achievers do not perceive themselves as copers, and they tend to see the world around them as unmanageable and devoid of opportunities for self-improvement. This agrees with results of my survey research which show that both parents and students who perceive the opportunity structure to be closed have relatively low educational aspirations. The policy implication of this finding is that it will not be enough to enhance interactional styles and educational skills of families of low achievers; these families must also be provided with realistic opportunities for improvement in living conditions. They must be enabled to perceive a bright future for themselves and their children.

While he studied only low-income families in Black urban ghettoes, Clark appears to be convinced that the qualities identified as being characteristic of the families of high achievers are generalizable across racial, ethnic, and social status groups. This is probably true in a broad sense, but I suspect that careful attention to cultural differences in child-rearing practices among groups that have had vastly different experiential histories might turn up some important group differences. At any rate, this issue is one that should be a focus of future research. Some authors also contend that there are cognitive style differences associated with membership in different ethnic groups. Clark's study does not address that possibility. It will require careful systematic research to resolve the question of cognitive style differences.

The case studies presented here provide an illuminating snapshot of family interaction among urban Black Americans. Clark's analysis presents researchers with a provocative set of hypotheses about how families prepare their children for success or failure in school. It is gratifying to note that the qualities of family life that lead to school success may be found among low-income Black families whether or not the family includes both parents. Much has been written about the possible emergence of a permanent underclass comprised largely of single-parent families dependent upon public welfare. This research, which contrasts competent intact and single-parent families with comparable less successful families, provides a basis for determining the kinds of social policies that would be needed to enhance the educational capabilities of the less successful families. If the educational capacities of these families can be strengthened and they are helped to perceive actual opportunities for improving their way of life, the cycle of intergenerational inheritance of poverty may be broken.

Clark's study does not inform us about the distribution of educationally competent families within the stratification system. It is likely that the distribution will be found to conform to expectations from earlier studies of the relation of family background to educational achievement. That is, more educationally competent families will be found among the higher social strata than among lower social strata. However, we can infer from this research that educationally competent or incompetent families will be found at every social class level. This research makes it very clear that it is not class position that determines a family's educational competence; rather it is the quality of life within the home that makes a difference. Most important, there is a strong suggestion that the educational competence of a family can be enhanced through direct intervention. That is certainly a strong challenge for policymakers and policy-oriented researchers.

Edgar G. Epps

1. The Issue

Studies of the poor American family's role in children's achievements have often focused on household composition, specifically the presence or absence of the father in the home, as the major factor. These studies have argued that the two-parent intact family has a positive effect on the child's school performance, whereas the one-parent broken family has a negative effect. Those studies not emphasizing family personnel have given attention to a specific family process, such as encouragement, or to such status variables as parental income and education, as the key to children's academic success. In the present study I will demonstrate that it is the overall *quality* of the family's life-style, not the composition, or status, or some subset of family process dynamics, that determines whether children are prepared for academically competent performance in the classroom.[1]

My basic contention is that the family's main contribution to a child's success in school is made through parents' dispositions and interpersonal relationships with the child in the household. Children receive essential "survival knowledge" for competent classroom role enactment from their exposure to positive home attitudes and communication encounters. I am interested in the *way* in which this knowledge is organized and passed on to youths through home interaction—that is, with how activities and events are organized in the family unit to stimulate youth's acquisition of academic and social communication skills. My argument is that a family's ability to equip its young members with survival and "success" knowledge is determined by the parent's (and other older family members') own upbringing, the parents' past relationships and experiences in community institutions, the parents' current support networks, social relationships and other circumstances outside the home, and, most centrally, the parents' current social relationships in the home, and their satisfaction with themselves and with home conditions.

I do not agree with the claims and implications of previous studies that the family unit's personnel and role properties (number of parents in the home, parent's marital status, family size, maternal employment status, maternal educational status, migration patterns, ethnic background, income, and so forth) are the source of children's school behavior or learning outcomes. Rather, it is the family members' *beliefs*, *activities*, and overall *cultural style*, not the family units' composition or social status, that produces the requisite mental structures for effective and desirable behavior during classroom lessons.

This is a critical point, since much official and informal school and governmental policy toward children and their families is based on the misleading assumption that the source of many youth needs and problems is their participation in family groups with one or more of the following demographic characteristics:

divorced parents (or "missing parents")
working mothers (of "latch-key" children)
young mothers
households functioning on limited incomes
poorly educated mothers
recently migrated to American cities
racial or ethnic minority
residing in depressed urban neighborhoods

Invariably these sociodemographic characteristics of family units provide only a thumbnail sketch of, or minimal insight into, the overall lifestyles of the children. Nevertheless, they are often portrayed as being indicative of an entire set of assumptions, often incorrect, about the mental capacities and activity patterns of the children and their parents. The ameliorative prescriptions and support programs that derive from these dubious assumptions, therefore, inevitably meet with limited success.

In my conception of life in families, parents employ one of two basic communication styles to prepare their progeny for life's major roles. The first is a "sponsored independence" style,[2] in which parents use their influence in a predominantly "authoritative" way (see Baumrind, 1971). The authoritative sponsorship variation tends to facilitate children's social competence most efficiently. It is characterized by the following behavior patterns: large amounts of parent involvement and interest in children's home activities; consistent parental monitoring of children's use of time and space; frequent, almost ritualistic, parent and child activities involving studying, reading, writing, conversing, and creating; regular parental explanation, advisement, and demonstration of everyday life skills to the child; consistent parental expectations and standards for responsible and restricted child behavior; regular praiseworthy sentiments expressed for the child's talents, abilities, and achievements; generally disciplined parental role behavior modeled to the child; and regular utilization of special parent-child role etiquettes to get the child's compliance with house rules. In contrast, the basic communication style in low achievers' homes is an "unsponsored independence" style of parent-child communication. This style is characterized by predominantly "permissive" or "authoritarian" parental behavior patterns such as: limited parent involvement and interest in child's home activities; inconsistent knowledge of child's in-home and out-of-home activities (these first two sometimes bordering on neglect); infrequent parent-child activities involving literacy tasks such as studying, reading, writing, information-sharing and creating; limited parental teaching, advising, and demonstrating of concepts and ideas to the child; inconsistent or non-existent parental expectations and standards for "responsible" child behavior in home, classroom, and neighborhood settings; frequent criticism and dissatisfaction expressed to the child about his or her worth and ability; inconsistent discipline or irresponsible role behavior modeled before the child, and frequent disagreement and conflict over the legitimacy of enforcing parental authority. The particular form of the parent-child communication style in any given household is guided by those psychological orientations that parents and children developed through social encounters with relatives, friends, co-workers, colleagues and strangers. These social encounters can have a positive carryover effect or a negative carryover effect on interactions between family members.

By distinguishing these styles at the outset, I wish to draw the reader's attention to the quality of interaction in the home. To focus our attention exclusively on family sociodemographics is to miss the essential point: *psychological processes and social communication patterns of family life come closest to capturing the essence of human learning experiences in homes.* Social scientists and educators who use the surface characteristics of family composition and status to explain outcomes in children's school behavior are ignoring the essential character of the family environment. For example, although much of the explanation for Black family limitations in the marketplace has in past years been laid to "family structure disorganization," there is little evidence to support this position. Blacks and other low-status minorities have little opportunity for developing aims and ambitions, this argument goes, because typically they come from disorganized and structurally inadequate families, with their matriarchs and either missing or shiftless, emasculated males.[3] In the advancement of this argument, little attention is given to what actually happens in the daily lives of families. When authors do discuss the interpersonal dynamics of home life, they are very often doing little more than perpetuating ideology about a particular ethnic group or, worse, engaging in wishful thinking. The truth is, previous studies have told us little about what happens educationally in American homes. Some of our guesses and hunches have been good, but not good enough. Consequently, we are not yet prepared to offer the schools useful data on family functioning that will enable curriculum planners, teachers, administrators, or parents to construct the most effective literacy nurturing lessons for school-age children.

This book describes how communication behavior in the family works to produce children's motivations, expectations, and social competence in student roles. The ethnographic case studies of ten Black families

reveal how parents may be predisposed by their good and bad life experiences to form family relationships and activities so that children learn, or
fail to learn, how to develop their intellectual skills and abilities for use in
school settings. We will see how parents establish role relationships within the home, how standards for "acceptable behavior" are set, and how
mothers and fathers manipulate affection and material resources in ways
which motivate the child rather routinely to do what the parents ask of her
or him.

I will contrast and compare the child development strategies used by
parents of five high achieving students with the strategies used by parents
of five pupils who are not as successful in classroom activities. It will
become apparent that a crucial factor affecting differences in knowledge
transmission in these homes is the parents' own psychological-emotional
state and coping ability. We shall see how parents' own life experiences
have had a profound influence on their current psychological-emotional
state and subsequently on the communication styles they use with their
children. Further, parents' particular approaches to organizing current
home learning activities will have been significantly influenced by their
past and contemporary experiences in the social world. This social world
includes public places such as occupational settings, school settings,
church settings, and other community settings.

The Role of Home Experiences in Pupils' Preparation for
School Learning

Many parents have assumed that the primary function of the school is to
make their children literate and successful. (Here I am defining literacy as
the general ability to speak, write, and understand at a level sufficient to
achieve communication goals in interpersonal encounters.) Yet our public
schools have only rarely performed that "producer" function.[4] Especially with ethnic minority groups and the poor, our schools have served as
institutions that select, sort, and control; that is, the schools have tended
to take most incoming ethnic students and teach them just enough to enter
occupational positions that parallel the status positions of their parents. In
this way, schools have functioned to reproduce the ethnic division of
labor between competing groups of families.[5]

While most of us agree that the purpose of schooling is to teach skills
and not just values (culture), the predominant trend has been for the
school to inculcate values and attitudes. Career-related technical skills or
literacy-based skills have not been imparted quite as efficiently as have
the cultural orientations preferred by school boards and school personnel.
Indeed, many millions of elementary and high school students do not read
or write at a level commensurate with their school grade. Whenever children do develop high levels of linguistic competence, the parents have

usually made the difference by guiding them *in the home* in academically enhancing encounters. Although no nationwide study has ever centered principally on the role of American parents in children's school performance, there is a substantial body of evidence that children's chances of school success throughout their educational career are significantly increased by a supportive home environment and, conversely, are significantly decreased by a "neutral" or nonsupportive family context.

Children spend most of the first five years of life in the home. After that, between the ages of five and seventeen, over 60 percent of the days in a child's life are spent moving from home to school and back again. How the child comes to perceive life in the classroom will be shaped by the messages the parent provides to the child about the parent's own experiences with school, the routine communications among parents, children, and teachers, and the academic information or experience the child acquires in the home which provides greater knowledge about various aspects of school subject matter. The most pedagogically effective instruction occurs when the role demands and cognitive functioning in the classroom are compatible with, or built upon, those in the home. To the degree that the activities and experiences in these two settings reinforce each other while facilitating mutual trust, mutual goals, and personal autonomy, the child will show a greater proficiency with the basic skills (academic knowledge and social skills) that schools are expected to teach.[6]

Most people would have no trouble agreeing that experiences in the home significantly shape their interpersonal competence (as indicated by their academic and interactive responses) in classroom settings and other out-of-home environments. After all, the home-community setting is where students first develop—or fail to develop—their social abilities to express themselves maturely and intelligently, be attentive, concentrate, volunteer, comply, engage in constructive self-directed activity, initiate work interactions, enjoy orderly social interaction, accept responsibility, carry through and complete tasks, hold positive concepts of "learning," manifest leadership skills, exercise self-control, show sensitivity to the needs of others, and enjoy a sense of accomplishment about goals achieved. It is these social "survival skills" that are basic to high quality student performance in learning classroom lessons.[7] The mechanisms for transmitting these skills are the preparatory tasks that take up the family members' use of time in the home.[8]

There are at least three types of home activity that prepare children for the competent performance of school responsibilities. These are home educational-instructional activities, such as deliberate teaching in the three Rs, home recreational activities, and health maintenance activities. During these activities parents and other family members may coach, nurse, guide, protect, and teach preschool children to care for themselves hygienically, to write important information such as their name, address, and telephone number, and to carry on civil conversation with adults and other children. Later lessons involve learning how to play complex verbal and social games, perform math computation exercises, solve riddles and reasoning problems, read and interpret challenging and interesting books, newspaper articles, and magazines, do creative art projects and hobbies, write about experiences and ideas, tell stories and share ideas, analyze the motivations of others, and interact with and enjoy relationships with kin, other adults, and peers. These are the kinds of preparation the child takes to school and uses to compete during his or her school career.

Previous Research on Families as Producers of Children's Achievement

There is virtually no disagreement among social scientists that family life plays a critical role in educational and social development. The disagreement concerns the specific family attributes considered most influential. In a content analysis that makes some general conclusions about families as educators, Trevor Williams reappraised the data sets from several sizable studies of family life in Canada, Australia, and the United States. He concluded that the three most significant inculcative functions of contemporary family life are its ability to stimulate, its reinforcement ability, and its ability to foster high expectations through encouragement.[9]

One of the major studies of the impact of American family environments on youngsters' life chances was the Blau and Duncan research on the American occupational structure. Concerned primarily with occupational mobility among American men, this research makes racial and social class comparisons based on a large sample (N=20,700) of men 25–64 years old. It concludes that a man's family of origin can be a benefit or a handicap. The authors state: "The family into which a man is born exerts a significant influence on his occupation in life, ascribing a status to him at birth that influences his chances for achieving any other status later in his career."[10] The authors specifically argue that unskilled and semi-skilled parents with low educational attainment and inferior career experiences provide a low quality of family experiences which tend to limit the skill development and life chances of their sons. Yet Blau and Duncan do not attempt to analyze *how* the total family environment functions to exert such an influence on the educational lives of its school-age members.

Practically all of the empirical research done to date has reported statistically significant relationships between "family background" and American children's school achievement levels.[11] Unfortunately, none of these studies analyzes the total form and substance of family life. Rather, they tend to focus on surface status characteristics (such as parents' occupation, education, family size, material possessions) or certain home dynamics while virtually ignoring the framework of psychological orientations and activity patterns that more closely represent the life blood of the family interpersonal experience.

The massive Coleman study, for example, used "objective" and "subjective" variables to represent family background and neighborhood life ("community input"): ratio of intact families in the school district, "urbanism" of the family, number of child's siblings, median occupational status of the father, parents' educational experience, parents' interest in child's school experiences, parents' expectations for child's success in school, number of reading items in the home (such as dictionary or newspaper), and other "home items."[12] The "home items" category concerned the presence of specific material items in the home, including a television set, automobile, vacuum cleaner, refrigerator, telephone, and record player. Taken together, these variables fall far short of capturing even *family input* (not to mention community input) because (1) they mainly refer to surface compositional properties of the family unit and ignore the internal structural and cultural patterns of the household, and (2) they say virtually nothing about *how* these surface variables reflect or shape behavior in the daily lives of the family members.

The Jencks study (which uses some of Coleman's data) claims that genes, economic background, race, and data taken from studies comparing identical twins reared together and apart gives us an estimate of the influence of "family background" on children's test scores. Although he admits that this notion of "family background" is "rather fuzzy,"[13] he uses it to make guesses about the degree to which his variables measure "family background." Like the Coleman report, the Jencks study measures surface compositional variables used to represent family environment.

At the Unversity of Wisconsin, the work of William Sewell and colleagues (which produced the Wisconsin model of family socialization) set out to include social-psychological variables in its conceptual framework, for example, parental encouragement. While this work did begin to look at parent's attitudes and values, it did not look at the internal structures and dynamics of home life at all. Indeed, none of these three major researches presents the entire *set* of home characteristics which tell us *how* home dynamics function to affect children's cognitive and behavioral reaction to school.

Nevertheless, these large pathbreaking studies and a fair number of smaller ones have made it clear that parents' family background (composition) and home interpersonal environment (home discourse events and psychological and cultural perspectives) play a major role—however little understood—in determining a child's school experience. Well-designed studies of the impact of home dynamics on American children's school performance are slowly beginning to emerge. Yet the current paucity of work in this area makes it necessary that we clarify the conceptual dimensions of family-school research through the use of empirical small-group data, small scale studies of family dynamics, and findings from exploratory research. Unfortunately, very few of the available comparative studies of American families have systematically looked at the entire family pedagogical environment in a reasonable number of homes. This I have attempted to do in the present research.

There are at least four conceptually comprehensive "total family environment" researches that have used smaller sample sizes in demonstrating how American family units function as agents of academic socialization. These studies are comprehensive because they try to conceptualize, measure and explain the role of the three major components of the family environment: its compositional properties (human, material, time, and space resources), social behavior patterns, and psychological patterns. Even these studies, however, do not examine how school-age children have been affected by the family environment at different stages in the life-cycle. Neither do these works say anything about intergenerational patterns of educational development in families. Of these four small-scale studies of American families as educators, three were done as parts of doctoral dissertations at the University of Chicago during the 1960s. Two of these studies, by Dave and Wolf, used the same sample (N = 60) of White junior high school youngsters. Dave identified home psychological and social patterns which measure (1) parents' press for achievement of family members, (2) parents' use of language models in the home, (3) degree of parents' academic guidance, (4) the quality of family routine activities, (5) the intellectual atmosphere in the home, and (6) the division of labor in the family. His main conclusion was that the family environment affects children's performance in certain academic subjects (e.g., arithmetic computation).[14]

Children's "intelligence" was the dependent variable of interest for Robert Wolf. Like his colleague, he sought to measure parents' press for children's achievement and parents' emphasis on language development. In a third category representing family environment, Wolf was concerned with "provisions for general learning" in the home. This last category corresponded closely with the patterns covered in Dave's final four categories (3–6 above). Wolf's three components of family educational environment explained approximately half of the variance in the children's intelligence test scores. It is interesting to note that in these studies family intactness (whether there were one or two parents in the home) and family size were not primary to parents' facilitation of children's "intelligence."[15]

A third key study of American family pedagogy using a nonrestricted conceptual framework of the total family environment was done by Joel

Weiss.[16] Weiss was interested in discovering how children's self-esteem and achievement motivation had been shaped by the family environment. Like his predecessors, Weiss selected a small sample ($N = 56$) of junior high students from one neighborhood in the State of Illinois. Family environment was viewed as being comprised of a subenvironment for achievement motivation and a subenvironment for self-esteem. He saw the subenvironment for achievement motivation as having three components: degree of parental generation of standards of excellence and expectations, independence training (role relations in activities), and parental support and approval. Pupils' self-esteem was measured by variables representing maternal role functioning ("maternal acceptance"), parent evaluations of the child's competence, and parentally encouraged opportunities for the child's self-enhancement. Weiss's principal finding was that there is a moderate but significant relationship between what happens in the child's family environment and his or her level of achievement motivation and self-esteem. The more recent work of Sigel and McGillicuddy-Delisi also establishes the utility of conceptualizing the role of the "total family environment" in producing particular communication styles among family members.[17] They use the concept of "representational competence" of preschoolers as their dependent variable and family size, parents' beliefs, and parents' "distancing behaviors" as their antecedents.

The most promising new research on the topic of "families as educators" is taking a more holistic view of family units as producers of knowledge. Most of this work is now underway at American universities with financial support from the National Institute of Education. The preliminary findings of one study being conducted by Hope Leichter, Ray McDermott, and others at Columbia University report that a wide variety of "naturally occurring occasions in family life, for example, shopping, cooking, note- and letter-writing, games, visiting, reading, television-viewing, homework tutoring, community involvement" may be responsible for children's acquisition of literacy. This work uses ethnographic field methods with six Irish-American families and six Afro-American families in New York City. Another research project being conducted with thirty-six low-income Cambridge, Massachusetts, primary school youngsters and their families is based at Harvard School of Education. This study by Jeanne Chall and Catherine Snow uses "observational and interview techniques" in order to determine "the constellation of factors which enable some low-income families to provide their children with experiences that contribute to reading success." At Harvard, the work of Deborah Belle and her colleagues, "Lives in Stress: Women and Depression," serves as a basis for explaining variations in parents' pedagogic styles. A very interesting aspect of this work is its concurrent emphasis on (a) parents' interaction patterns in job settings and other institutions, (b) the effects of these social patterns on parents' psychological orientations, and (c) parents' contact patterns with their own children in the home. This psychosocial approach promises to yield significant data on home activity structures and their social and psychological antecedents. Alonzo Anderson is looking at the aims and uses of print materials in the home and school environments of ninety-six Black, Anglo and Chicano five- and seven-year-olds in San Diego. This study endeavors to uncover the ways in which children use written materials in the home, thereby going beyond most previous studies of "family background" and children's school performance.

Perhaps the most expansive and promising of the new "family as educator" studies is the longitudinal work being undertaken by Lawrence Cochran, Urie Bronfenbrenner and others with 270 Syracuse, New York, families and their preschool (3–4 year old) children in 18 distinct urban and suburban neighborhoods. This Cornell University study looks at the home activity patterns of a random sample of families (in randomly selected neighborhoods), and assesses the effect of "middle-range" ecological support systems (e.g., work settings, health and welfare services, and neighborhood network patterns) on processes of socialization, education, and development in the home. These resultant home processes are presumed to "foster the development of the child's capacity to cope effectively with educational and social situations outside the home that require initiative, cooperation, and sustained effort in pursuit of a goal." Now that the children in this study have completed the first grade, the researchers will be able to make a careful assessment of the role of family socialization experiences in providing skills that pupils may transfer to classroom learning encounters.

In a 1979 review article, Boyd Rollins and Darwin Thomas distinguish among parental support, coercive control, and inductive control and relate these parental socialization techniques to outcomes in children.[18] One of the outcomes they review is academic achievement. They note, for example, that Heilbrun and Waters found in 1968 that when parental support is low, there is a negative relationship between control attempts and achievement, but when support is high, the relationship is reversed and is positive.[19] According to Rollins and Thomas, Diana Baumrind concluded in 1972: "that the parental behaviors associated with high achievement were high support and high control if of the inductive type and if accompanied by high power. However, she cautioned that this might not apply to girls or 'disadvantaged' families."[20]

Following their lengthy review of such research, Rollins and Thomas generalize about the difference between the academic achievement of girls and that of boys on the basis of parental variables. For girls, the *less* the parental support and the *greater* the control attempts, the greater the academic achievement. For boys, however, academic achievement occurs when both support and control attempts are high. They suggest that this difference may result from the fact that the typical support socialization of girls does not lead to assertiveness and achievement, and thus "a non-supportive environment best prepares females to succeed by making them 'tough' and 'hard,' therefore increasing their aggressive tendencies."[21] Such an explanation relies on differences in the typical socialization patterns for boys and girls and also on a quasi-biological explanation that boys are naturally more *aggressive* and success-oriented. Interestingly enough, Rollins and Thomas do not return to Baumrind's comment that the disadvantaged may also be different, and most of the research leading up to these sex distinctions comes from studies of the middle-class. Thus, our study of the Black ghetto family will be able to contribute by looking at achievement from the perspective of the disadvantaged family.

There are, in addition, a score of home learning environment studies that focus on a specific component or specific interactive process within the family.[22] And, besides the Rollins and Thomas review, there are several other good literature reviews of families as educators currently available.[23]

In large measure, the available American studies of family environments have made it clear that the student's family life plays a significant, perhaps an overwhelming, role in preparing the student to function well in settings outside the home. As a group, these studies discuss almost all aspects of life in families. When taken individually, however, it is hard to find studies of U.S. families that present a systematic conceptual model of academic socialization in the family unit and also explain specifically how family psychosocial dynamics function to produce academically useful skills and habits in its youth.

The Role of Ethnicity in Family Educational Life

> Every single American family is in some ways like *all* other American families, in other ways like *some* American families, and in still other ways like *no* other American family.

Perhaps the most critical single criterion that establishes the foundation of a family's standing in society is the parent's ethnicity or race. The ethnic background of parents is ordinarily an excellent gauge for predicting how family members have fared with other American families in the resource marketplace. To accept that this is true requires that we remember how closely one's family background is linked to the family's economic, occupational, and political status in the United States. Economic stratification in our society is, to a significant degree, distinguishable according to an ethnic division of labor. With this kind of economic and ethnic stratification pattern, social class and ethnicity become very closely linked for many ethnic groups.[24]

The theoretical basis for this ethnic, occupational, and economic tie is the notion that ethnic groups have always functioned more or less as economic and political competitors for the acquisition of prized resources in the society.[25] Each ethnic group came to America under relatively unusual circumstances. And each group brought with it a relatively unusual social experience from "the old country." Very simply, each ethnic group has had its own historical experience and has developed its own ideological posture, while being exposed to the same "Americanizing" influence.

An assumption of this study is that the family's ethnic or racial background has determined the way other groups have responded to them. Furthermore, differences between the particular social histories of ethnic groups in the United States have led to fundamental differences in the quality and level of knowledge acquired by particular ethnic groups. It is these life quality differences in (a) personal life histories, (b) opportunities for economic and knowledge resources, and (c) residential segregation over time that have produced different sensibilities in parents about how to organize their particular family unit for survival. Yet, despite unique ethnic and racial group experiences, this work will argue that many of the *same* communication dynamics and processes account for success or failure of offspring, regardless of ethnic, occupational, income, or structural differences between families.

Several studies have found that, racial and social class background notwithstanding, core dispositional and life-style differences do exist between families of high-achieving cohorts and families of low-achieving cohorts. When Cervantes studied White youths in Boston, St. Louis, New Orleans, Omaha, Denver and Los Angeles, he discovered that the family experiences of high school graduates produced (a) a strong adolescent self-concept, (b) intellectual alertness and vocabulary and competition, and (c) skill at engaging in "orderly" social relations.[26] One early comparative study of high and low achievers found that mothers of White high achievers were more authoritarian and restrictive with their children than were mothers of low achievers.[27] Still another study of British families found that the "good home" could aid school success. The "good" home was characterized as small with "emotionally bleak" home relationships and demanding (somewhat authoritarian) parents who have high ambitions for their children.[28] In a study of Swedish families, Torsten Husen documented a significant relationship between the mother's child-rearing ideology and the child's school behavior. He states that: "Children from homes with a consistent and established habit pattern exhibit 'better' ratings as to their school behavior. Children from homes where parents have difficulties in establishing or maintaining a regular habit pattern have 'worse' ratings by the teachers."[29]

Currently in the United States, a few academically successful poor and near-poor students annually emerge from urban neighborhood schools.[30] How did these students manage to achieve what most children in similar social and economic circumstances could not achieve? Why did these few achieve in the face of poverty? What were the functioning patterns within the families of these successful students? Hardly anything is known about the adaptive strategies and strengths of this group, because few research investigations have endeavored to study these strengths as they exist in the homes' psychosocial processes. In this book, we want to talk about the internal dynamics of these families.

The case studies in this book look at the way some ethnic parents have chosen to organize themselves in preparation for, and in conjunction with, their children's participation in one major social institution—the school. The question that concerns us is "How do parents prepare for and manage this home-school interface?" Case studies provide a descriptive and analytic interpretation of the quality of preparation for school involvement and explain the processes of this preparation.

Teacher Expectations and Student Learning Experiences

Let us now look at how classroom dynamics mediate between what skills students bring from home and their ultimate achievement. Much of what is considered appropriate or desirable classroom behavior is inductively learned by teachers and pupils as they routinely interact with others over time. For example, teachers come from home and earlier school experiences to their jobs with a set of learned predispositions about what "real knowledge" is and about what "promising" students *should* already know and how they should behave. These internalized predispositions are represented in the teacher's *expectations* of students. The ethos of the school site further wields its effect on teachers' dispositions about appropriate standards. Principals and other teachers play a dominant role in setting the tone for what is "appropriate" to expect from particular students. During classroom lessons, teachers tend to make higher evaluations and give greater pedagogic commitment to those students whose academic and social behavior is closest to the classroom standards and rules maintained by the teacher.[31] Some writers have referred to this match—mismatch between teachers' preferences for behavior and students' actual classroom behavior as an example of "value consensus" or "value dissensus." Others have used the notion of a "congruence-incongruence" in goals or cultural interests to explain the degree of "fit" between what teachers enter the classroom believing about themselves and their students and what their students come to the classroom believing about themselves and their circumstances.

The degree of symmetry (or asymmetry) between the set of literacy skills pupils acquire in the home and the set of communication skills teachers expect in the classroom does indeed have a direct impact on a teacher's performance expectations for pupils, on her classroom teaching practices, on her level of classroom control, and ultimately on her pupils' performance of school tasks. Students who demonstrate an ability to anticipate a person's behavior and prepare an appropriate response are seen as more "teachable." In other words, most teachers *prefer* to work with children whose conduct and appearance is in line with their perception of what is "appropriate." Once such behavior is exhibited by the student during classroom lessons, teachers will typically try to reinforce it while engaged in teaching activities by providing contingent rewards and corrective feedback. Usually, teachers are most pedagogically effective when they perceive cues or messages from the student which hint that certain "essential" academic and social lessons have already been learned in the home. To the extent that both the teacher and the student are able to understand, trust, and build on one another's communication cues they are likely to engage in growth-enhancing responses toward one another.[32]

Some of the most common behavioral signals (or social "etiquettes") that teachers expect to see are that the pupil can and will rather readily engage in quiet social interaction, ask questions and otherwise participate in class, be obedient, use standard English when speaking, accept personal responsibility for conduct, and be accountable for its consequences, be mindful of his or her appearance and hygiene, perform tasks actively and harmoniously interact with others in the classroom, and accept the teacher's right to treat her or him as a member of a category based on a few discrete personal characteristics (such as skin color, attractiveness, family background, classroom social personality, and previous teacher evaluations) rather than the full range of characteristics of the whole person.[33]

Inaccurate teacher assessments of student abilities tend to *nurture* student failure by reinforcing prejudicial, stereotypic attitudes and perceptions about the learning capability of the children and, ultimately, about their humanity. Under these circumstances, teachers do not get the opportunity to perceive the intellectual *diversity* in minority families. With standards and expectations for academic performance then lowered or fitted to a generalized stereotype, teachers tend not to teach effectively and pupils tend not to learn. The pupil is then evaluated or "graded" as having only "average" ability or as being "hopeless," and certain "low yield" pedagogic resources are provided to fit this diagnosis.[34]

Conclusion

The literature pertinent to family and school outcome falls primarily into two types. First, there are studies of achievement and success that focus on the family's sociodemographic characteristics, including intactness, size, occupation, income, education, and so on. These studies have ordinarily not tapped the internal dynamics of family life. Second, there are studies that illuminate family processes and culture, without referring directly to offspring achievement or success. The present study attempts to apply the methods and insights of the second approach to the issues raised by the achievement studies. It is hoped that our results, however tentative, may be the basis for further, more extensive, research into family dynamics and offspring outcomes. Let us now look at the research design and families to be investigated.

2. Research Methods

The Study Design

This study is similar in its conception to Elizabeth Bott's study of "whole families and their social networks" and to Hess and Handel's psychosocial study of "family worlds."[1] Both these studies treat the individual family as a "unity of interacting persons, each occupying a position(s) within the family to which a number of roles are assigned, i.e., the individual perceives norms or role expectations held individually or collectively by other family members for his attributes and behavior."[2]

Generalizations about all families cannot be made from studies of small groups of families, but we can uncover patterns of family organization and describe the social processes in *some* homes and, from such analyses, generate sound hypotheses about family behavior and influence for further research with larger family samples. With descriptive case study data we can also better understand the life perceptions, personal meanings, frustrations, concerns, hopes, and dreams of millions of American families through the personal experiences of a few.

Because individual families are unique social units with unique styles of communication, it is certainly important to conduct exploratory case studies of the social organization of these family units and their communication styles. Dr. Bott has discussed the problems and practice of doing intensive study with a few families in exploratory field studies: "The difficulties in applying this method to the study of families seems to lie in conventional selection of units for study. When familial affairs are concerned, the unit that springs to mind is the total society. It must be *the* family, not *some* families. We should therefore like to make it clear that we are discussing only some families, not all families or the family."[3]

The case studies in this book are not treated as a "sample" per se. Rather they are examples of ordinary family units residing in three low income urban communities. The structures and processes of these family units are the focus of our analysis. The specific categories of family structures and processes that guided the data collection and case interpretations in this study are the following:

Framework for Description, Coding, and Analysis of
Achievement-Related Functioning Processes in Whole Families

1. The Family Theme and Background—Background information, for example, names, ages, religion, ordinal position, group affiliation, residence, and the like; degree and kind of environmental stresses; house descriptions; general physical description of parents, of student; educational background; migratory patterns, and the like; social history of parent(s); family theme and context.
2. Early Child-rearing and Familial Practices—Events and effects of student's formative years; historical perspective of family transactions; early training and value orientation; socialization to norms; early family dynamics.
3. Mental Health: Student Values, Attitudes, and Personality—General personality characteristics of student; sex-role attitudes; racial attitude; level of altruism; trust; self-conception; attitude toward roles; social outlook; self-awareness.
4. Home Living Patterns—All routine living patterns, for example, housekeeping and living arrangements, money handling, and the like; family relations, that is, interaction between any family members; rules of the house (e.g., role expectations); power relations, for example, authoritarian, permissive, share-oriented; child-rearing practices, for example, methods of discipline and control, duties and responsibilities; division of labor; parental approach to time and space; parental approach to student's time and space.
5. Intellectuality in the Home, Past and Present—Family members' intellectual orientations; educational aids; parent and student academic values; student occupational goals and aspirations; approach to homework, study, and other potentially educational activities, for example, reading, working on hobbies, and so forth; monitoring and instructional activities of parents; parental school aspirations and expectations; contact with child's school, teacher, and the like; educational rituals performed.

The first category includes the family orientation toward life; this involves those key stresses and pursuits that tell us what the family is "about." The second category provides data concerning those antecedent familial practices and patterns which were experienced by the student during his formative elementary school years. An attempt was made to capture the dominant personality traits and general psychological orientation of the student in category three. As might be expected, much of the home interaction (socialization) information is found in our "home living patterns," category four. All home behavior *not* directly related to school (e.g., doing housework, eating, and the like) is included here. The focus here is on all interaction at home that is not clearly intellectual or academic.

Category five, while also focusing on home interaction, is specifically concerned with the intellectual flavor of the home as it is today and as it was in years past. Any family members' deliberate and consistent attempts to teach (or learn) are noted here.

Eligibility Criteria

To aid in the analysis of my assumption that *family intactness is not a necessary or sufficient condition for high quality learning in the home*, families were chosen that fell into one of four distinct family groups:

1. Two-parent families with at least one high-achieving twelfth grade child;
2. one-parent families with at least one high-achieving twelfth grade child;
3. two-parent families with at least one low-achieving twelfth grade child;
4. one-parent families with at least one low-achieving twelfth grade child.

Merely by grouping the case studies into these categories, questions may immediately arise about the plausibility of a null hypothesis that the *number of parents will in vivo determine children's school success*. The four groups of families have each had somewhat different experiences. Families in two of the four groups include a high-achieving twelfth grader but differ in their intactness. The other two groups of families also differ in their intactness, but are the same in the sense that one family member is a low-achieving twelfth grader.

To qualify for selection, the family of each student met the following criteria: total family income is reported by the parent(s) to be at or below the official government-defined poverty level ($5,038 for a family of four in 1974); the family had at least one senior in high school anticipating graduation in June 1974; parent(s) had a generally low educational level during child's elementary years (this period was chosen because it is the time when parents are thought to be most instrumental in the child's development); family lived in a poor or near-poor urban area and the student attended a neighborhood school; family is Black and is willing to have its privacy invaded by a stranger probing into the home life for at least two consecutive days.

Each student's achievement level (high or low) was based on his composite score from at least three factors in a four-factor index: grades as reported by the student, reading and math achievement score, student's self-evaluation of ability, and teacher's perception of student's "promise."

Getting the Sample

The families in this study were selected from the files of a community educational service agency, referrals of teachers in the neighborhood schools, or as a result of a student's own request to participate. A number of families were contacted and asked to participate in this study but most of them declined. Even the offer of modest payment did not change the minds of these low-income parents. I soon discovered that my approach was scaring people away. Their usual mood was "What government agency does he work for?" Or "I wonder if the welfare people are trying to investigate me again." Or, as one woman told me after I had come to know her a little better, "I thought you was the police."

After much experimentation and after a number of refusals, I finally found a method for gaining acceptance into more homes. I telephoned families and always asked to speak to "the man of the house" first. I told the parent that I was doing a term paper for a college class and that I might use the information I collected to write an article describing the work of the educational service agency in the community. I told them how I had obtained their name and that they had been described as persons who were interested in their kids' education. I told them I wanted them to talk about some of the things that were wrong with the school, some of the ways they thought their child had been affected by the school, and "other community issues." I told them also I wanted to compare how the parents feel about those issues with how the student felt about them. Finally, I told them I would administer a questionnaire and conduct a tape-recorded interview "to study in class," but that I did not anticipate having to be in their home for more than a few hours.

This method was much more effective for me. I had found "the key to the family door."[4]

Getting the Data

Academic research on the specific ways Black youth are "educationally" prepared by their families is sketchy. The observed functioning characteristics and tape-recorded interviews with ten urban school youngsters and their families only begin to fill the knowledge gap in this area. The conclusions of this study are tentative and subject to further study with larger samples. The family systems reported here represent an initial effort to document variations and continuities in the family life-styles and psychological orientations of some low income Black families.

No established standard method for studying whole families exists at this time. Family therapy, field methods, projective methods, controlled experiment, or some combination of all these approaches are the most common procedures. This study uses field methods (i.e., interviews, questionnaires, and observations of family interaction) with normal (i.e., nonclinical) families, first, because of the wide latitude they provide in conducting exploratory research, and, second, because of the opportunity they provide for gathering data on the dominant patterns and processes in small groups.

The data for each family were collected over a six month period using taped semi-structured interviews, participant observation, and an attitudinal questionnaire. An underlying presumption was that to *begin with a battery of closed-ended, structured questions would be premature if the goal was to identify and describe the patterns of educational influence in actual Black families.*

The interviews were conducted with the aid of a specially developed outline that allowed for unencumbered inquiry into family unit functioning. The form and order of questions was not rigid. Questions were asked at the interviewer's discretion.

Background Information.—General history of parent(s); pattern of migration from South; reasons for leaving; work history of parents; attitude about present environment and life circumstances; planning of family; attitude about city upon first arriving; social experience of student as a child; early childhood functioning; early parental influences (moral training); racial and political attitudes; church participation; past and present dreams and ambitions of parents; problems encountered.

Home Living Patterns.—Parental concept of child rearing; decision—making process; parental expectations in terms of child's behavior, past and present; role responsibilities in the home; division of labor; housework; sibling relations; family congruence; interaction with kin, with friends, with neighbors; methods of parental control; parental handling of student's time and space; student's attitudes toward parents and other adults; family outdoor activities; recreation; daily rituals.

Educational Orientation.—School plans and goals of parents and student; career plans of parent and student; parental aspirations for child; parental expectations; learning rituals in the home, for example, reading, hobbies, games, and other activities; association with formal educational agencies, for example, schools; self-concept of student; student assessment of school performance; attitude on the purposes of schooling.

The questionnaires were developed especially for this study. There were two forms of this 98-item instrument, one for students, and another for the parent(s). Items were intended to measure family disposition toward education, family ego strength, level of ethnic particularism, family integration and congruence, family encouragement, attitudes towards females, and personality characteristics of family members.

The participant observation portion of the study was originally designed so that the researcher would actually live in these homes for two or three days consecutively. This goal had been drawn from the words of the anthropologist Jules Henry, who once argued that "direct observation of families in their native habitat, going about usual business" could furnish new insights into family influences on child behavior.[5] The rationale presented by Oscar Lewis guided our selection of a day as the time unit for the study. He states:

> The selection of a day as the unit of study . . . has many advantages
> for science as for literature and provides an excellent medium for
> combining the scientific and humanistic aspects of anthropology. The
> day universally orders family life; it is a small enough time unit to al-
> low for intensive and uninterrupted study by the method of direct ob-
> servation . . . It makes possible a quantitative analysis of almost any
> aspect of family life.[6]

I did not, however, restrict myself to a single day with each family unit. Yet, I did not sleep in any of the homes due to lack of space and general inconvenience to the families. When adults were in the home, I was there. I also spent considerable time following family members around on their normal routes, going with them to the store, to proms, to school sports activities, giving them rides to work, helping them buy food and prepare meals, eating and drinking with them, listening to their disputes, and so forth. The time actually spent in most of the homes exceeded the 48 hours (two day) initially expected.

During the entire period I was with family members, I was gathering process-oriented data for use alongside the information being ascertained from the interviews and questionnaires. Examples of the family processes I observed included the extent and kind of table talk, the presence or absence of laughter, basic interpersonal styles, rituals, and other family activities. During the participant observation phases (when I was looking, listening, and asking in order to understand the "logic" of the family units better), I attempted to observe and record basic trends of family interaction and the more specific structure of interactions between the achieving student and other family members. I was guided by the analytic categories as I looked for home dynamics that might prove to be important.

Interpreting the Data

The case studies were constructed by classifying data into categories according to the five conceptual categories. These classified data were subsequently coded into one of the specific sub-dimensions of the categories. When warranted by the data, new sub-dimensions were added to the categories. What emerged was a collection of statements and observations for each family that provided a description of (a) family themes and background variables, (b) early and current family activity patterns variables, (c) parent and child personality variables, and (d) variables concerning family members' educational orientations. The emergent analysis enabled me to describe in a systematic way a range of social processes within a particular family unit.

Hess and Handel describe this data analysis procedure as a "back-and-forth free movement" between data sources (questionnaires, interviews, observations), during which you compare what people have said about a particular issue, finally reaching an interpretation that is congruent with all the available data sources.[7] This approach is akin to the "grounded theory" or "constant comparison" method of generating theory advocated by Barney Glaser and Anselm Strauss.[8]

A general assumption guiding our data analysis was that whatever any family member says and does takes part of its meaning from what other family members say and do. Home achievement patterns, then, are generated out of the interactions between the students and other family members. From the interviews, questionnaires, and direct observations, I expected to uncover the specific dispositions and behavior-processes in high achievers' and low achievers' families.

Controls were set to deal with perennial methodological problems of reliability and validity. I attempted to ascertain the dependability of my observations by checking against material from the taped interviews and questionnaires. The Gordon Persons Conceptions System for Content Analysis served as a computerized data sifting and classifying device, and a quantitative check against many of my qualitative observations of personality characteristics.[9] The idea was to use my personal observations, the interview data, and the questionnaire items with the computer printouts of the family psychological profiles as checks against each other when analyzing a particular category of family behavior. This overall procedure proved very helpful in the conceptualization of family communication styles.

The larger question of validity is not as easy to answer. Have we really measured the factors in the family that influence educational success? These case studies may be viewed as representing only a "moment in a process" of the family unit's evolution.[10] Ultimately, this question can only be answered by conducting other investigations in this area. I expect that other studies that follow will measure the similarities and differences in the home behaviors of achieving children (and nonachieving children) over time in diverse cultural groups.

Characteristics of the Family Units

The case studies describe the social dynamics in ten Black families living in three low-income Chicago communities. In each family at least one person was a twelfth-grade student who expected to graduate from high school in June 1974. However, in five families the twelfth-grade students were markedly more successful in school achievement than in the other five. The case studies are portraits of different types of home lives found among academically differentiated age-grade cohorts.

Data were originally collected with a selected group of sixteen low income twelfth-grade students and their respective families. I decided that the target population would be high school seniors because they have virtually completed their K–12 public school careers, their families have been with them throughout elementary school and high school, and their public school academic records are as comprehensive as can be found.

In five of our sample families, two parents were in the home; the remaining five families were single-parent (mother only). In two of the two-parent families, the target student was rated educationally "successful." Three of the two-parent families had a senior offspring rated educationally "less successful." In two of the single-parent families, the target student was rated "less successful." The three other single-parent families boasted a student rated educationally "successful."

Family Type	Successful Students	Less Successful Students
One Parent	3	2
Two Parents	2	3

Major social background characteristics of our sample families are presented in Table 2.1. This table provides a demographic scenario of the family backgrounds. We see that our sample (N = 10) is closely divided with respect to the number of male and female students in each group. One of the successful students was first born and three were last born, while one of the less successful students was first born.

Most of the parents were under fifty years of age and, with one exception, all the mothers were born in the South. Every family had been established in Chicago for over eleven years. In general, the families of the less successful students were larger but the two groups were evenly matched with respect to employed and unemployed mothers. Educational levels of mothers of successful children appear to be slightly higher than those of the mothers of the less successful children. Three mothers (one in the less successful group) had graduated from high school at the time of the student's entry into grade school. Seven of the mothers had secondary schooling.

TABLE 2.1
Social Background Characteristics of Family Units

Group / Student	Occup. Father: Industrial shop	Occup. Father: Factory level	Occup. Mother: Employed	Occup. Mother: Housewife	Educ. Father: 12–13 yrs	Educ. Father: 9–11 yrs	Educ. Father: 8 yrs or less	Educ. Mother: 12–13 yrs	Educ. Mother: 9–11 yrs	Educ. Mother: 8 years	Age Father: 50–52	Age Father: 40–49	Age Father: 30–39	Age Mother: 50–52	Age Mother: 40–49	Age Mother: 30–39	Birthplace Mother: Elsewhere	Birthplace Mother: Chicago	Length in City: 11 and over	Length in City: 1–11 years	Sex of Student	Birth Sequence	Number of Offspring
High-Achieving Students																							
Group I — two-parent homes																							
Chivers	X			X		X		X						X				X	X		F	5	12
Treppit		X		X		X				X		X				X	X		X		F	1	4
Group II — one-parent homes																							
Hayes			X					X						X			X		X		M	Last	8
Johnson			X					X					X			X	X		X		F	Last	3
Farland				X					X				X			X	X		X		F	1	3
Low-Achieving Students																							
Group III — two-parent homes																							
Gaines	unemp.			X			X		X				X		X		X		X		F	3	10
Jackson	X			X		X			X				X		X			X	X		M	2	4
Wilson		X	X				X			X	X				X		X		X		M	4	
Group IV — one-parent homes																							
Jones				X				X							X		X		X		F	1	7
Harris			X					X								X	X				F	3	6

Students were classified as high achieving or low achieving on the basis of school performance profile ratings (i.e., academically successful versus less successful) and were also classified according to family structure. The student was rated based on a composite score derived from a four-factor index: student-reported grades, and class rank, student-reported reading and math achievement scores, teacher's perception of child's "promise," and student self-perception of ability. Let us now look at the case materials for five successful students.

3. The Family Life of High Achievers in Two-Parent Homes

In the first two families, the Chivers and Treppits, both parents are in the home and the student is performing successfully in the neighborhood school. The major behavioral and psychological patterns that set them apart from the two-parent low achievers are (1) parents' beliefs about their own responsibility in the child's academic pursuits, (2) parents' sense of control over their circumstances (the degree to which life had worn them down), (3) the type of routinized social activities engaged in at home by family members, (4) the expectations for the student, and (5) parents' supervision strategies. In addition to these distinctive traits, families in this group distinguished themselves from *all* other groups in two ways: the conjugal relationship tended to be more egalitarian in terms of greater maternal decision-making power and there tended to be a value consensus between the parents on issues relating to child rearing and the student's academic development. Fathers made greater efforts to be supportive (at least psychologically) of mothers in the home.

As with all ten families to be presented, the basic strength and coping resilience of these two families under adverse economic circumstances is apparent. There is no good way to measure the fundamental family spirit in these homes, but its presence may readily be sensed. A more detailed analysis will follow the high-achieving students' case histories and another analysis will follow the presentation of the case studies of the low-achieving students' families. Group differences will be discussed at these junctures.

The Chivers Family

The Family Theme and Background

Many low-income children's efforts in the pursuit of a formal education are directly related to the student's having experienced years of devastating economic hardships. Black, low-income parents often function for youth projectively as models for how not to end up. These parents, anxious for a better life for their children, may look to one of the most hopeful institutions for American Blacks—the educational establishment. Historically, religion and education have been pursued vigorously by poor urban

Blacks as problem-solving institutions. Opportunities for economic improvements, albeit unequal, are seen as available through "education" or "schooling."

It is not uncommon to find instances of poor Black parents mightily stressing the virtues of schooling to their offspring. They will assure you that their children have never had the frightful experiences of "our generation." They will remind you that schooling is a privilege, a pathway out of poverty and into the good life. Most often these Black parents, for a variety of social reasons, did not personally experience that "privilege." Consequently, they are very determined to see that their children have this school experience. Despite their desires, economic, psychological, and social needs frequently battle with these parental ideals and values. At stake is the educational future of a human being, and the possible opportunity to escape poverty through job mobility. The Chivers family is preparing for this opportunity.

Mr. and Mrs. Chivers make their home in an old brick house in a deteriorating ghetto community on Chicago's West Side. They live on the second floor in the "two flat" building. Inside there is a fairly large living room area (15 x 17 ft.) and an equally large dining room area. Though the furniture is not glamorous, it certainly is adequate for the household. An operable color television is the newest addition to the house. The couches, covered with cloth covers, have been used for so long that a person sinks far, far into them when sitting. Pictures of Marie (the target child in this family) dressed in a high school graduation robe sit on top of the television. There is a large, sturdy dining room table which is used primarily as a place to sit, talk, and do homework. Seldom is it used for eating since there is a kitchen table used for that purpose. There are three bedrooms serving nine people; with nine people this relatively large house seems small.

In addition to Mr. and Mrs. Chivers, there are seven young people who live here: Christy, 23; Marie, 16; Carla, 15; Janie, 13; Douglas, 3; Stacey, 1; and Michelle (Marie's child), 14 months.[1] At 52, Mr. and Mrs. Chivers consider themselves "nonactive" Catholics. Mrs. Chivers has always lived in Chicago. Mr. Chivers was born in Tennessee, but came to Chicago when he was 3. They consider Marie to be the eldest offspring in the home at the present time. Actually she is the eldest offspring who is not at present married.

Initially skeptical of my motives, the Chivers ultimately proved to be extremely cooperative. The following field note was made during my first visit.

> When I ring the doorbell, Mrs. Chivers opens the door at the top of the stairs with a beer can in her hand. We greet each other. She appears defensive, perhaps embarrassed, as if she shouldn't be seen

drinking in my presence. She says "Come on in" and quickly goes back into the kitchen as I seat myself in the living room. In a moment she returns without the beer can. She then asks me, "Ok, now will you tell me what this is all about, because you talked to my husband [by telephone] but I don't know what this is all about." I explain the project as "a study on Blacks and education." I tell her I want her, her husband, and their daughter to participate. She then tells me she is not about to answer anything personal, that if I want to know any of her personal business, I had best not even start the study because she is not going to answer anything personal. I say, "I don't want any information from you that you don't want to give to me. I'm not interested in your personal life. I am only interested in you and your daughter in terms of her education." After our discussion she is more willing to participate in the study. Mrs. Chivers tells me that Marie has recently received a phone call from a man who identified himself as being with the Board of Education. "He sounded like a white man," Marie states. "He said he was doing a study on how students feel about inner city versus suburban schools. But I got upset when he started asking me all these very personal sex questions." She continues, "He knew about my baby and he asked me if I knew anything at all about sex. Well, he knows I'm not a virgin so why should he ask that?!" Mrs. Chivers periodically listens as Marie and I chat together.

I attempted to establish rapport before I conducted the taped interviews. This was not difficult after Mrs. Chivers decided that my motives were honorable.

Although Mr. Chivers is the primary breadwinner, Mrs. Chivers is the one actually managing the flow of activities in the household. In the home she is a take-charge person, giving instructions and checking to see that they are accurately carried out. She also works part-time in a nursery school facility. Mrs. Chivers is a thin, light-skinned woman (possibly some Indian ancestry). Slight in stature, she might even be called youthfully petite were it not for the telling body signs of worry and hard work. She is extremely energetic and an aggressive talker with expressive hand motions. Even in her fifties, Mrs. Chivers is a very attractive lady of 5 feet 3 inches and 105 pounds. In contrast, Mr. Boyd Chivers cannot be described as good-looking at all. Indeed, he looks like what he is—a man who has done hard manual work for over thirty years. He is tall (6 feet), has a pockmarked face, and has only a few teeth left and very little hair. Mr. Chivers now wears a skull cap (usually associated with certain Islamic sects), torn and wrinkled work pants, worn-out shoes, a short-sleeved T-shirt and a thin, light green jacket.

Marie Chivers is a tall (5 feet 9 inches), shapely, light-skinned (like her mother) girl of 16. Her personality can be described as quiet and subtle.

Although soft-spoken on the surface, she is an intelligent, talkative, relatively mature young woman.

The Chivers childrens' activities are circumscribed by their parents' economic limitations. From youth, Marie has been made aware of the form and order of the household. Like most children, she learned quickly of the household protocol implemented by the parents. She clearly recognizes the primary role each of her parents plays in the home.

> You see, my father is what I'll call quiet and my mother is talkative. Like, when they would come home he would be tired. Sometimes he'd talk to us but as far as gettin' down to school work, that was Mama's thing. He still got a bit of the old-fashioned in him that way. Now, he'll play with the babies more than he played with us when we was little. When we was little we was scared. We was scared to say "lie," we'd get a whipping. But, now he's more easy.

While Boyd Chivers has softened his approach to the younger children, Mrs. Chivers has also adapted her child-rearing philosophy to a more liberal approach than she once held. Her relationship to Marie is a more protective one. Whereas Mrs. Chivers once proclaimed that any daughter of hers who became pregnant would have to "get out," she now impresses a different theme on the children. Marie states:

> My mother said as long as you're trying to make something out of yourself, she'll help you. She don't want you laying around and doing nothin'! She doesn't mind helping you as long as you trying to help yourself.

Some of the 12 Chivers children were gone from the home before Marie was even born. The children were born and raised in "sets," allowing for some semblance of economic survival. Of that experience in economic gymnastics, Mrs. Chivers relates:

> We're not living extravagant, but we get by. Say maybe Marie needs a new dress to be in a play or show—well, it's much easier to get these extra things if both of us work; now if just he works, he'd get it but that may mean "We'll pay Peter this time and let Paul wait," switching [payments] around a little bit.

For most Black people, economic hardships are nothing new. Past generations have had to struggle for minimal survival. Then, as today, the familial routes toward survival were varied. Sometimes these goal-pursuit strategies were handed down from earlier generations of Black parents. There is some evidence that Mrs. Chivers derives her predisposition for the two-parent family model from her own parents' orientation. Of her parents, Mrs. Chivers states:

> My mother and father were a different generation. When I was a kid, my mother and father didn't have too much schooling. They were

born and raised in the South. My mother never had to work a day in her life. My father, he was a smart man, but he was not an educated man. And he always helped us with our homework. I don't think my father went past the fourth grade, but my father could help us with our high school homework. And he always wanted us to get a good education.

Mrs. Chivers further reveals:

But they didn't push, you know what I mean. In fact, when my mother died, my father really didn't insist that I stay in high school; I have a high school diploma but I got it through GED [high school equivalency certificate] just a couple of years ago. . . . I never had time to go back to school raising children. But my father thought nothing wrong with me dropping out of school after my mother died to help him raise the rest of the kids although I had an older sister, but I was more willing to do more work. He could tell me to do anything without any hassle, therefore, he wanted me to be at home to help out with the cooking.

Mrs. Chivers felt a responsibility to succeed her deceased mother despite the fact that she was not next in line for the position. Her older brother and sister avoided the role of mother-substitute in this motherless family. This and other evidence from the interview data and from home observations suggest a predilection in Mrs. Chivers toward conjunctive roles of family organizer and solidifier. Perhaps even more interesting is Mrs. Chivers's perception of the role-modeling impact of her father:

I wasn't even aware of how I copied so much after my father until after he died and I was saying "My daddy did this" and somebody say "you always talk about your daddy." I wasn't even aware of it, you know, but I guess he really did influence me a lot, but I didn't even know it.

Could it be that there is a cause-effect-cause relationship in the Chivers' history which is multigenerational? The available evidence may be too brief to answer this question with complete confidence. We can, however, document that this feeling of responsibility to the family unit also exists in Marie's behavior. Taking responsibility for her younger sisters' school performance, Marie explains:

She's kind of hardheaded. I have to fuss at her or do something to make her study. I want her to do more than what I'm gonna do. I always want us to get ahead.

This "drive" may be considered a significant orientation from a 16-year-old girl speaking of her younger sister. Motivational styles do filter through the familial chain.

Early Child-Rearing and Familial Practices

Marie's childhood years were characterized by maternal assistance with educational tasks, family cohesiveness, a sense of responsibility, and supportive family rituals. These features tended to provide psychological strength for Marie. Her level of ambition appears to have been growing during these years. Marie recalls that she received a large amount of help with spelling and English when she was in her primary grades. Marie exhibited primary dependence on her mother during these years. (She would later indicate that her pregnancy was an attempt to gain a feeling of independence.)

Mrs. Chivers has functioned as the coordinator in this household, while Mr. Chivers acts as a silent partner. Mr. Chivers feels he has had a less direct hand in Marie's schooling. His influence on Marie's schooling is probably not totally lacking, however. He opines:

> The majority of my time is spent trying to make a living. She might have seen that—me trying to make a living all the time and how hard it was without an education, that could be some influence on the child.

Mrs. Chivers has only recently worked outside the home. She didn't really work seriously until her youngest child was in school. Primarily, Mrs. Chivers has been responsible for Marie's schooling guidance. Mr. Chivers further explains his role:

> We've always talked together about things that concern the children. We've always talked about it and I've always felt the same as she did.

My own interpretation of Mr. Chivers's statements and attitude was that he had resigned the child-rearing responsibilities to his wife, with rare exceptions. In this role, Mrs. Chivers has focused her attention on stressing self-respect and purposeful schooling in the children. She states:

> I always told my children that they don't go to school for a love affair, they go to school for an education. And it did not matter whether a teacher liked you or not. You didn't go there to be liked. You went there to get an education. And if you acted like a young lady or a gentleman you could get the respect of people whether they liked you or not.

From these early years Marie appears to have "caught" a spirit of familial cohesiveness encouraged by her mother. This family tie or bond revolved around music and song activities initiated by Mrs. Chivers years ago. Explaining the family singing rituals, the Chivers relate:

> Mrs. C: We got the singingest family in the world. They like to sing. Singing people are happy people, you know, if you sing, you can't cry.
> Mr. C: You sing to keep from crying.

Mrs. C: But I used to wash a lot of diapers when I had my older kids and at that time we were too poor to have a washing machine so I'd bend over the bathtub and in the apartment we lived in, my landlord lived downstairs and he'd hear me sing and he'd say, "Oh you're the happiest woman I know." And I say, "I have to sing to keep from crying. I sing every time I wash diapers." It was pretty good, you know. Learned a lot of songs like that anyway.

This ritual of singing was transmitted to Marie as a child from her older sister. Marie recalls:

I remember we was little and my sister had us in here and if we didn't hit the right note they would fuss at us and we would cry. We would be saying we gon' make some big money. We thought we was going to be stars, you know.

The significance of this discourse process becomes even more noteworthy since it is between sisters. Older sisters have taken on some of the responsibilities of the mother. In this instance, the older sisters bolster the impact of the mother on the younger girls. We see this family assistance pattern being transmitted still further in Marie's relationship with her younger sisters.

My little sisters is closer to me because I be home most of the time and I go to school with them and everything. My big sisters don't live here [but] if I have some kind of problem I'll go to my big sisters because I'm still close to them, but because of my younger sister's age, I don't go to them with my problems. My big brothers, they hardly come around, maybe once a month or something like that. Well, girls understand, they've been through it more so than boys.

Allegiances based on gender in the Chivers family may help explain differential patterns of growth between the boys and girls. With respect to the family unit, however, there appears to be a generic cohesiveness. Both Marie and her mother remember eating hot dogs and french fries together, playing together, riding bikes together, and engaging in similar "family" events. At the same time, individual differences between siblings appear to have been given healthy respect by Mrs. Chivers.

We try to teach the kids everyone is not good in everything. Where one is good in math and the other in reading or one may be good in history or the other may draw very well. Just like Janice and Marie can draw very well. Carla couldn't even draw a stick doll. She used to say I gave her a "bad" pencil, and the other two had to show her it wasn't the pencil; it was her ability, you know, but they can't be good in everything.

On the basis of her belief in individualization, Mrs. Chivers provided a great deal of psychological, emotional, and educational assistance to Marie during her preadolescent stage of eleven and twelve years old. Marie expressed feelings of despair and insecurity after being graduated from the elementary school to the junior high school. The new school environment coupled with a home environment which at that time had "enough problems" apparently caused Marie some early anxiety. Immediate attention to Marie's anxiety was provided by Mrs. Chivers through verbal encouragement. After less than a year, the supportive school climate provided a cushion to make the experience less traumatic:

> In sixth, seventh, and eighth grades, we had a system that was a "person-to-person" relationship, rather than teacher-to-student. We didn't look at each other as an adult or a child but as "person-to-person." They took three specific groups of kids and they taught us to work with computers and build up our IQ scores, reading scores, math scores, and at this time we were consider ed the highest sixth grade class in the school. I'd say that's what really started me off 'cause we was kind of lost at the school I came from before. They didn't teach you anything. As long as you came there it was OK.

The dual support system—school and home—provided Marie with much of the necessary impetus to tackle her schooling beyond these early years.

Largely by way of example, Marie's parents taught her the value of family unity and intrafamily support. Marie made this lucid observation:

> My parents don't get tore down when something goes down. They stick together. Like if we need something and know we can't get it, but we really need it—like when my mother's purse got stolen—we all stuck together. We really needed that. We tried to not be evil and we gave understanding to her and let her know that it was not her fault that her purse got stolen. I liked them cause they sticked together in times like that.

Marie has been able to derive greater inspiration from family activities because she is integrally functional in the family matrix. Her responsibilities include "watching" (babysitting and guiding) the younger siblings as well as caring for her own child.

Mental Health: General Attitudes, Values, and Personality

Consistent with the Gordon Persons Conceptions System, interview data suggest that Marie is proud and independent. Her parents possess a strong sense of race and self-pride. During those early problem years, Marie maintains, she was overcome with fear and a lack of confidence. It is clear that her parents, especially Mrs. Chivers, extended large doses of emotional support. Marie recalls:

> In sixth grade I felt I was kind of left out because it was a new school and everything. I didn't know anybody. So they started really pushing and encouraging me more to go. I might or might not have

went and they knew this, so they pushed me for some reason—I'm not sure—but for some reason I felt everybody was taller than me. I felt little. And I was scared. When I came there I felt I was looking up to everybody. (But naturally in sixth grade you would look up to seventh and eighth graders.) But I just felt scared; it was a altogether new environment and I just didn't know how to cope with it. So she helped me to get my head together. She said, "Oh, it's gon' be all right. Don't be afraid." So then I went and found that most of the people on this block went to school there, you know I got over it.

Mrs. Chivers believes that confidence is instilled by making children feel they are "somebody." She has attempted to engender feelings of pride in herself and in her children as human beings. She remarks:

I'm like Jesse Jackson [nationally known minister], they are somebody. They are people, you don't run a person down if they make a little mistake or they don't get a grade as high as what they think they should, you always just encourage them to try just a little bit harder and let them know they are people, that whatever they do, it wasn't the worst thing in the world. But if a momma or father is forever telling the kids: "You're no good" or "you're dumb" or "you could have done better" or something like that. I make them feel that if they don't do it, they're letting their ownself down. Not me. But they have to have a certain amount of pride to want things nice themselves, to want to know a little more than the next person because, you know yourself, you feel good if you think that you are a little smarter than somebody else.

Racial pride is not directly confronted in Mrs. Chivers's approach to life. Mr. Chivers, however, feels that Whites are foes to be contended with. He maintains that Whites are "not afraid of nothing. He's prejudice—he's the most prejudice thing in the world, I understand that." Mrs. Chivers tries to temper these attitudes in Marie. She teaches that:

It is a bad thing that people put people in categories. I don't like to judge people by color, because when they go to school, they're going to meet all kinds of people. And they're also taught by different kinds of people. If they have a chip on their shoulder on account of the color of a person's skin, they're in trouble right away.

Marie considers herself to be "Black conscious." She expresses concern about the fact that Blacks are being "pushed around and everything" but denies any political orientation. She is possessed of strong personal ambition and pride. Of her pride, Marie reveals:

I want to be noticed and to be noticed you got to be something, even if it's a garbage man. You got to be able to do something . . . I be trying to do something so that somebody might say, "Hey, that's that Chivers girl who did that, you know."

An independent young lady, Marie is not interested in marriage until "I can get myself together so that if he doesn't act right, I can, you know, do what I want to do." Ambitious and anxious for success, Marie observes that:

> I just feel like I have to do something all the time. It seems like I got so little time to do so much in so I try to do a lot back and let somebody work for me.

She further reveals:

> Everything I do has to count. It's got to amount to something. I clean up the house because I don't want to live in a raggedy junky house—things have to mean something to me before I can do 'em. If I do something, I say I could do better than this. And what's so killing is that if I want to get an A and I get a B, I feel bad.

Marie is now expanding her horizons. She claims a group of people two and three years her senior as her closest friends.

> I feel more at ease and I don't have to worry about somebody coming up to me and start something because we could talk it out; we don't have to come to no punches—they're more grown-up like.

Again, Marie's attitudes are close to her mother's who "just can't imagine not making it." In one observation I noted:

> Mrs. Chivers's influence on Marie's social outlook and beliefs appears significant. As she shows me around the house we stop to observe a collection of pictures. Mrs. Chivers says, "Yes, that's Marie's baby right there. That's Marie on her graduation. I told her to wear a natural [Afro hair style] because you can look back and the hair style tells you about the times." After looking at the picture for a few moments longer she said, "You can say, 'when I graduated we were wearing a natural,' so that's the only thing you could tell the times by. I thought she looked very nice in that." Mrs. Chivers looks as if she wants to preserve that graduation moment in her mind—possibly for tradition.

Mrs. Chivers, then, tends to encourage feelings of self-worth, while bolstering her family's sense of hope. She instills in the children the belief that things will get better. In her own words:

> So if you've got enough personal pride, you go as far as you're able to go—and then I tell them to go one step further. And that way, you might get what you want out of life. And then if you don't, at least be big enough to live with what you do have. I used to tell the kids when they were little, if you have to be a bum, then be a good bum. Whatever you are, be a good one. And then you're satisfied with yourself.

Marie has also shown development of her self-concept through her approach to her womanhood. She has become more comfortable with males. She, like many women, does not feel necessarily limited as a woman:

> I [once] felt limited, like I could only do so much. Now I don't feel like that. I feel I could do anything. Times change, and I've met new people. And you start gettin' older, the teachers start telling you different things. And you don't see it on TV. And you know that women are not supposed to be limited to just this. We have these "rap sessions" at school and different people—models, policemen—people from all walks of life. And we find out that this is not just a man's world. Everybody's in it.

By working things out in her own mind, Marie has developed an inner peace, a feeling of confidence about who and what she is. This self-understanding makes the road to greater heights a clearer path for her. The passage from adolescent to adult status, then, is a smoother process.

Marie Chivers's Gordon Persons Conceptions System profile indicates she perceives her social identity primarily in terms of her roles as a Black and as a female. Her significant role allegiances are most prominently student and friendship orientations. She also thinks of herself in her future occupational roles ("what I'm going to be") and her kinship relationships within the family setting. Unlike her mother, Marie envisions herself as living in a middle-class to upper-middle-class life-style. Mrs. Chivers speaks of the family primarily in terms of its low-income social class status. A small element of political conservatism is also registered for Marie, possibly suggesting a tendency toward social conformity.

Education and the acquisition of "security" head the list of Marie's major life goals. Short-term gratifications are satisfied through certain recreational (e.g., singing) and social activities (e.g., dance parties). Sex is not totally excluded. Drugs are not utilized as a means of gratification. Her transcendental concerns are most prominent in her intellectual and cultural character. A cooperative, approaching, loving, helping interpersonal style is mixed with a dependency on others in Marie's approach to the world. A psychic state of unhappiness or dissatisfaction suggests an explanation for her positive emphasis on ambition and hard work. There follows, not surprisingly, a feeling of immediacy, of urgency. Importantly, Marie holds a positive academic orientation in her life-style. Perhaps more significantly, there is a strong sense of competence, moral worth, and self-determination in Marie Chivers's profile. Her self-image is an extremely positive one. Her time orientation is geared toward future concerns although her life-cycle references are mostly in the here-and-how, emphasizing childhood and youth. She feels her best years are yet to come.

In-Home Living Patterns and Responsibilities

Mrs. Chivers feels it is incumbent to stress the need for responsible performance in household activities. Economic factors ("I couldn't afford having my children tearing down because I couldn't afford to pay for things") play a significant part in Mrs. Chivers's organizational approach to home maintenance.

> There are certain limitations you put on children. You don't put them out there to be tempted to do anything wrong. It's stupid for anybody to say, "OK, I trust my child so it can go anywhere it wants to go." You wouldn't send a kid, because you trusted him, into a dope den. If you have no guidelines for a child, then you're not raising the child. You have to set a certain amount of rules and then let the child live within those rules. They're going to stray from them a certain amount because they're not gods. They're not perfect. But they don't go so far as to make it bad, you know what I mean?

Mrs. Chivers normally supervises Marie's comings and goings. Mrs. Chivers is the undisputed boss on the issue of curfew. She simply but firmly insists on "reasonable" behavior within the home. Marie's time at home is spent on activities such as cleaning house, caring for her baby, studying, watching television, or singing. Mrs. Chivers exhibits a clear knowledge of how and where Marie spends her study time within the household.

> Most of the time they're right there in the dining room. Sometimes they go in their bedroom, and between looking at TV, they study and play records. But they [study]. Sometimes they just sit right down on the couch together and one of them will ask a question and the other one will answer, back and forth.

Additionally, Marie's mother guides which settings she visits in her out-of-home activities. The line between guidance and dominance is sometimes razor thin with respect to Mrs. Chivers's involvement in some parts of Marie's life. Mrs. Chivers comments on Marie's friends:

> To tell the truth, Marie is not the kind of person that has too many friends, maybe it's because by the time Marie got big enough to actually accumulate a lot of friends, I was working so it was necessary for her to come straight from school.

Pertaining to jobs, we see further evidence of maternal spatial control:

> The only job Marie has ever had in her life, she worked for me one summer in the day-care center reinforcing Sesame Street. And then she had one little job, she worked in a shoe store up on Madison Street so she didn't keep that very long.

On boyfriends, Mrs. Chivers reveals:

Marie only had one serious boyfriend and that's the father of this baby. He went to school with her. I don't encourage a close relationship between them. I don't mind if he comes to see her sometimes, but they are not married, and I don't believe in playing this daddy and momma game, see. When he grows up and gets a job, and she gets through school, and they want to get married, fine.

And on academic guidance in schooling beyond the 12th grade, Mrs. Chivers says, "If I havé to pay for her, she's going to stay here in the city." Mrs. Chivers cited economic reasons for her desire to keep Marie in Chicago. But further dialogue revealed that Mrs. Chivers was most concerned that Marie be in a position to take responsibility and care for her own child. Being in another city, Mrs. Chivers insisted, might make this impossible.

It is not difficult to see the pattern of systematic time-space control wielded by Mrs. Chivers. This control has been utilized to guide Marie in certain directions desirable to Mrs. Chivers. Most often Marie does not disagree with these emphases. Acting in a spirit of love and concern, Mrs. Chivers is mostly satisfied ("They're not a disappointment to me") with her children. There are no kin relationships (outside the basic family unit) which figured significantly in the achievements within this family. Cousins, aunts, and others were seen as basically responsible for their own situations. Only in dire emergencies are they consulted for help. This orientation was seen as an example of positive self-reliance.

Educational Orientations in the Home

Many processes in the Chivers's approach to Marie's schooling represent adaptations to the family's economic situation. Survival at the highest comfortable level, given limited monetary resources, is a continuous aim. Educational decisions are very often based more on economic practicality than on what is preferred or desired.

No matter how much I want her to have an education, I just can't take every penny I have and put it towards her education. I have another child who's coming out of high school, and I also have another child who will be graduating from high school in two years, and then we have to live, too. And unless you have a bank account, which I do not have, you just can't swing it, that's all.

To Mrs. Chivers, a high school education is indicative of success, since Marie is the first in the family to achieve it while still at home, and it provides some opportunity for Marie to support herself. She would like to see Marie acquire further schooling only if there is a chance to "learn and earn." Similarly, Mr. Chivers views schooling as an agent for attaining occupational goals. Occupational goals are pursued for their social and economic ends. There is a faith that schooling can change a person's economic condition. When asked about his years working in the factory, Mr. Chivers stated:

> Well, I'd rather . . . I'd rather be rich. Well I say that's my punish-ment for not having an education, by not going to school, it wasn't no harder than it is now, I don't think. The reason I got the job was that I needed money. So therefore, that was it. I didn't need the schooling.

Both Mr. and Mrs. Chivers are oriented toward the goal of "making it," being successful human beings in the society. The school perform-ance of their offspring is one area of concern in this quest. Mrs. Chivers fully accepts a role as educator and preparer of her children. Mrs. Chivers suggested that it is sometimes impossible to convince a moneyless person of the virtues of schooling over working for pay. The practical route is to pursue one's immediate survival needs. Schooling must wait until later. As one example:

> My oldest son, well he wanted to be a doctor, but, as I say, I have 12 children and he was trying to work and go to school at the same time. And he just couldn't swing it and I couldn't give him the help. So he doesn't live here and he has his own place and he works for the railroad—I think he's a key-punch operator now.

Marie feels less of a need to get a job immediately. She does not feel as great a responsibility to make a living right out of high school. Perhaps the social reality of young Black males is different from that of Black females. Whereas the females may be more oriented toward home and family activities, the males under those conditions may experience a greater urgency to "get out in the world." Marie has recognized the work efforts of her parents. With parental support, aspirations have developed and goals have been set to improve life. Marie wants to be a success and also make money—two goals not altogether separable. She recalls:

> Yeah, I saw how hard they had to work every day just to get one lit-tle thing. I saw that. They didn't go to high school [when they were young] so I thought if I could get out of high school and get some college, it would be easier for me.

And further:

> They always talked about how hard they worked and what a good education means, what really did it was when my mother went back [to school] to get her GED and got her diploma. If she could do it and take care of us, I know I could keep doing it, and I'm younger.

Marie gained an added sense of purpose toward schooling after her baby was born. Her felt responsibility to her baby was as great as her responsi-bility to herself. She has decided that a high school education is not enough.

> Well, after the baby came, I had something I had to take care of; and
> with just a high school diploma? That wasn't gonna do it asks for it,
> it's there. I felt I should do this.

Her immediate plans after graduation are to pursue a program in the field
of X-ray technology. There is evidence of remarkable self-direction in
Marie's approach to school. She realizes that, ultimately, whatever she
wants she will still have to go out and get. She is not predisposed to avoid
taking the initiative in pursuit of her schooling. According to Mrs.
Chivers, Marie has done a great deal toward furthering her own education.

> I thought at first she might be discouraged when she got pregnant,
> but Marie, she was the one herself that got the information about the
> Simpson School [a school for pregnant teenagers] and hands this in-
> formation to me and asks me to take her over there and register her.

Wishing to avoid marriage until after she has finished her formal education, Marie pushes for success, independent of others. She wants to maintain her self-confidence by seeing what she can accomplish without direct
help from others. She reflects:

> I guess without someone helping you, you would feel more success-
> ful. Instead of somebody tagging along behind you, telling you what
> to do.

Marie is determined to meet her educational and monetary goals. She
expresses an increasing confidence in her learning abilities and is not
afraid of competition.

Marie's parents provide support for her confidence by maintaining relatively high levels of expectation. Mrs. Chivers exhibits her concern about
Marie's school activities by becoming involved in school issues affecting
her daughter. Mrs. Chivers watches to see that Marie gets the grades she
deserves.

> I always insist that if my child makes excellent grades you give the
> child what is earned. If he makes G grades, you give him a G. I
> don't want you to grade them higher than they deserve. Neither do I
> want you to grade them lower than what they earn. They'll feel de-
> feated, you know.

Also, Marie has lived a somewhat different existence from that of her
older brothers and sisters. This suggests the probability of different family
adaptations at different life-cycle stages. Schooling appears to be a more
realistic option for Marie today than it might have been for offspring
during even harder times a few years ago.

Mrs. Chivers does not believe in presenting financial rewards for good
school performance. She cannot accept the notion of "paying people for
doing something for themselves." She will, however, attempt to protect

her children against irregularities at the schoolhouse. One recent problem with the school counselor prompted her to take a visit to the school.

> But this lady—her job is to see that a student's program is filled out right. Marie knew she had to have this "credit" for gym. She was reassuring Marie that everything was all right, but she really didn't have the gym credit. But I had to be sure myself, before too much time passed by. So I went up there to see her—I didn't go up to see her, I went up to see the principal, and he told me to go get this lady and this lady tells me that the principal doesn't have time to look at everybody's case. So I told that lady, "that may be the case but this is one that he's going to look at." But I was going to the Board of Education and everywhere I could think of to see that Marie could go ahead and graduate. I thought I had better just take off work and go up there.

Marie's mother, while supportive, does expect her to fulfill her duties and responsibilities. There is a feeling that shortcuts won't really help Marie in the long haul. Mrs. Chivers impresses that there is no substitute for putting in good, hard, honest effort.

> I've seen her and, you know, she may ask me sometimes "Is that the way you spell that?" Or some such thing, I tell her to get the dictionary because I'm not helping her do anything if I spell the word wrong. And sometimes I don't know how to spell it anyway. *[Laughter]*

Over time, Marie has come to appreciate the posture of her parents. She is comfortable about investing the time and energy in her school-related tasks. The realities of living—no, surviving—have made the task clear.

> My family's always telling me "try to get ahead cause it's hard out there." I can see what's happening to them, that it's hard, and that you really do need an education to get ahead.

High parental expectations and vigorous support serve to help clear the pathway to good school performance in this case. An action attitude ("Get up and do something for yourself") appears to foster focused action during Marie's behavioral responses.

Encouraging pep talks about education have heightened this youngster's pursuit of schooling. Regular family discussions on education and careers have indeed had a modelling effect on Marie's goal orientation. As Mrs. Chivers observes:

> We've always talked education in the home and maybe it's because my husband and I, we, don't have a lot of education. But we want better for our children than we had for ourselves. And if all your life you've talked it, it becomes a way of life.

Similarly, other education-oriented activities are performed which contribute to the process of learning. Customarily, these activities take place regularly over the life course. They have become rituals. One such educational ritual involves Mrs. Chivers and the younger children. Her approach to teaching children can be seen in the following observation taken from field notes:

> She is a supportive person. As she handles Marie's one-year-old baby, feeding it, she says, "Yes, that's right, say 'spoon' " and the baby attempts to say the word.

Marie adds further insight about her mother's approach.

> At one time she was working at a hospital and she would come home about 3:00 and we were coming home from school about that time. So she would let us go off and do our stuff and she'd be talking to us then—like she'd be standing in the kitchen cooking and be saying, "OK, one plus one is what?" If we say 3, she'd say, "No, you know it's not 3, it's 2," you know.

Learning is clearly taking place in these "practice" situations. Regular, almost daily, verbal inducement to explore their world also helps the Chivers' children.

> They're not afraid to speak their mind. And I don't mean by being sassy. They know that if there is something they want to get into, some club or organization, they don't have to feel like they're less of a person than someone else. She belongs to this Alpha Omega Club and Black History Club. They are told to try to get into everything. That there is no reason why they can't do anything that they want to do. And they feel like this. They must go on and apply for things.

Another ritual concerns doing homework after school. Mrs. Chivers no longer checks Marie's schoolwork every day. If Marie is graded poorly in some area, then Mrs. Chivers will more frequently check her performance. "But," Mrs. Chivers says, this check is seldom necessary because:

> She always has been one that studies; maybe has to study, I don't know. I don't say that she's a brilliant person, but I know she applies herself, and that may be the reason she gets good grades. She's a homework freak—both her and [her sister]. They get together every night there. They always study. You can't get that girl to stay home from school when she's sick. She doesn't like to miss school at all.

Sometimes the Chivers children will study together. They will break the monotony of the study session by singing "soul" songs together. This does not appear to impede their progress toward completion of the assignment. Rather, they appear to get refreshment and stimulation from this activity.

Reading is also a regular responsibility of the children. Mrs. Chivers discovered long ago that those children she had time to read to as an unemployed mother obtained better school reading scores than the ones who were in the primary grades during her periods of outside employment. Marie remembers reading regularly, even as a young child of seven.

> My mother let us read anything. She didn't care what it was—papers, books, newspapers, any kind of books as long as we was reading, cause like she told us, "it takes different kinds of reading to really learn really well." If we found it, we read it, you know.

Home practice in reading and math unquestionably aids Marie in her school endeavors. This practice may sometimes be formal or it may be disguised as a type of game. Whichever form is used, learning is usually the result. Whenever Marie did something in school, she would bring it home and show it to her parents. Home activities were then designed "on the spot" to buttress the concepts being taught at school. Mrs. Chivers has worked with Marie in a variety of ways to ensure learning. Much of this assistance appears to have been helpful.

The Treppits

The Family Theme and Background

On some occasions young, striving, migrant Black families from the South are seriously affected by the phenomenon of "urban overload." Although personal goals are sometimes attained, the accompanying tensions and stresses on urban poor families in pursuit of better living often force them to question the wisdom of their activities. As fathers struggle continually to provide their family's basic economic livelihood, external pressures frequently affect them physiologically and psychologically. "Success" under these conditions is a doubtful prospect. If a father has kept his family fed and clothed, while slowly watching his own health fail, can we consider it success? Perhaps nervous disorders such as hypertension can effectively make a "successful" life an unpleasant one. It is now known that Black men suffer in inordinate numbers from diseases that result from stress. In the Treppit family, the father's stress has come about as a result of participating 18 years in a northern big-city struggle for survival. The following data may aid in our understanding of this phenomenon as it affects the educational performance of our subject, James Earl Treppit.

Born in Jackson, Mississippi, Mr. Frank Earl Treppit is a 35-year-old father of four boys. They are James Earl, 17; John, 16; Paul, 14; and Edward, 13. Mrs. Gloria Treppit is 31 years old. They have been married for 18 years, aged 17 and 13 when they were married. Marriage had been a total commitment for them before they even reached adulthood.

Frank was taught very early that a man must always have a responsibility to his family. A man should never send his wife outside the home to work unless there is no other money source. Her work is with the children. His worth as a man, he was told, would depend on his ability to support his wife and his children. Without much education, Frank Earl, and Gloria, with 6—month-old James Earl, came to Chicago 17 years ago to raise a "normal" family (i.e., father as breadwinner, mother as housewife). Little did he know at that time, however, that poor Black southern families in the North had to overcome obstacles that would seriously challenge the fortitude of even the strongest human personality.

The Treppit family has lived for 17 years in the Far Southland Public Housing Projects. Away from the city's center, this area has a poor "quality of life" reputation because of high unemployment, high rates of crime, and relatively low levels of educational productivity. The area is in the southernmost part of Chicago proper. Known as "the Gardens," this area consists of residences that are all two-story structures interconnected so that they resemble a motel complex. The building complexes, called "blocks," give the appearance of a giant square of houses with a large dirt space in the center which may once have been a garden. At the outer areas of these massive slabs of concrete are "play areas" where the younger boys and girls jump rope and play baseball, and the teenagers congregate to talk and sometimes play basketball. There is a parking lot (usually glass-splattered) adjacent to each of these "block" complexes.

The Treppit home is furnished inexpensively, but adequately and neatly. The apartment has an upstairs and a downstairs. The downstairs area is furnished in a way which seems to conflict with the forbidding, dull blue walls in the apartment. The living room consists of a floor model hi-fi system, fairly used upholstered couch and matching chairs, a wooden cocktail table, and two lamps, each one on an end table. There is also a metal case with four shelves holding a few novels, six trophies, and framed color pictures of each of the boys. The kitchen, in addition to the normal appliances, has a washing machine and a table with five chairs. The upstairs consists of three bedrooms and a small bathroom. As one stands at the top of the stairs, the bathroom is seen immediately ahead. To the left are the three bedrooms, Mr. and Mrs. Treppit's room being closest to the bathroom. The two older boys share the bedroom next to their parents' room, while the two younger boys share the bedroom closest to the stairway. This house, like other public housing units observed, has somber steel and brick walls. Inside it is livable but not particularly comfortable or pleasant.

Mr. Treppit operates a welding machine in a factory. After four years, he considers his present job the "best" one he ever had financially. Mrs. Treppit has never held any regular long-term position. Like her husband, she sees her role as housewife and mother. Mr. and Mrs. Treppit are described in my field notes as follows:

Mr. Treppit is about 5 feet 7 inches tall, slight-medium in stature, with a medium brown face. Though he is 35 years old, he looks and acts like he's 25 to 28. His short Afro hairstyle and his exceptionally trim physique give him the appearance of a young bachelor, not a man married for 18 years. He is dressed in a simple but neat, open-collared, pin-striped shirt and dark pants and house slippers. His general demeanor is tense.

Mrs. Treppit, 31, is short (5 feet 2 inches) and overweight. A woman of very dark complexion with short, "pressed" hair, she sharply resembles the Black woman who plays the character of "Florida" on the TV programs *Good Times* and *Maude*. Her even white teeth contrast against her dark skin. She is wearing inexpensive pink slacks and a green turtleneck sweater. She is a very warm person who, though not particularly outgoing, smiles a lot and seems genuinely to enjoy people. She reiterates time and again her philosophy, "I believe in living and let live." James Earl is eighteen years old and the first born in the family. He is about 5 feet 8 inches tall, thin, firm build, medium-long (3–4 inches) Afro hairstyle, with handsomely sharp, blocky facial features. He maintains a grade point average which barely qualifies him for inclusion in the upper 20 percent of the senior graduating class. He attends an all Black high school in a low-income area.

Mr. and Mrs. Treppit came to Chicago from Jackson, Mississippi, in 1957 with a plan—to improve their lives and the life of their child. Initial enthusiasm slowly gave way to agonized regret as the dream was transformed into a nightmare. Mr. Treppit now feels like a prisoner of his environment, "stuck" as it were, unable to get away. He now openly longs for a taste of the country climate he knew as a child. He now maintains that country living, while not perfect, was infinitely more relaxing than Chicago has been.

Mr. Treppit was born seventh into a family of thirteen children. His entire family, except two sisters and his parents, have moved to Chicago. While in the South, young Frank Earl was raised in agriculture. His duties were to plow the fields and otherwise help the growth of the crops. Schooling was a secondary activity for his family. The primary concern was harvesting a good crop. Mr. Treppit remembers:

> I really didn't get the education I would have liked to because my parents weren't able to put me through school, you know. It was pretty hard when I was starting out in life. Like when I was really interested in going to school, I might have to stay out to plow or something. So when I got done plowing, they'd say, "You can go to school today." So, I couldn't get my mind settled on one thing, and I guess that's one of the reasons I didn't get no further than I did.

In the southern farming environment, children were expected to shoulder heavy responsibilities at early ages. This fact of life had consequences for boys and girls alike. Mrs. Treppit remembers that girls who became pregnant were summarily dropped from school. They were expected to sacrifice further schooling in the interest of their new family. She recalls:

> There just wasn't any opportunity. Once you messed up, you were just out of school. That's what happened to me. After I became pregnant, I couldn't go back to school . . . They didn't have a place for you to go. They considered you a plain dropout . . . You couldn't have no baby and start back to school again.

After moving to Chicago, Mrs. Treppit did temporarily attend night school, but additional pregnancies and new regional adjustments made it difficult for her to put any serious efforts into education. The responsibility of making a living has subsequently taken priority over any formal schooling. The only type of education the Treppits see as valuable must be practical. It must offer relatively immediate monetary rewards. Their primary concern is with paying the bills. Says Mr. Treppit:

> We got a family. It ain't big, but four kids and you try to do halfway right by them, it's sort of hard to work and attend school too. It's hard for me to concentrate on school. Can't learn anything. It's more or less wasting time I believe. I did try a trade as a mechanic. That lasted about six months and I just dropped out for the simple reason on my job we worked in shifts and at that time I had no seniority to pick a shift. So one week I'd go to work at midnight, the next week the second shift or the day shift. It was just sort of hard to continue and I just gave it up.

Mr. Treppit had to work on two different jobs (one full-time, one part-time) during earlier years in order to provide food and shelter. Continual job responsibilities requiring many hours of work have meant limited time for personal enrichment.

Mr. Treppit has had to provide for his own survival since he was fifteen years old. By having a family at seventeen, Mr. Treppit adopted a totally responsible approach to life. He feels he has never really had any opportunity to be carefree. Mrs. Treppit speaks of her husband:

> A lot of things he would have wanted to do he knew he could never do them. And he knew if he came home from work and he had messed up, he would find a family cryin', you see.

After a certain period of time the pressures of continuing to *provide*, when providing is dependent on the availability of work, may affect the physical health of a person. These pressures may be manifest in a variety of ways. If no outlet is taken from time to time to relieve these pressures, internal disorders and diseases of the body are likely to develop. Mr. Treppit has been experiencing serious stomach problems for the past several years now. He remembers that in the days when he had two jobs he was always wishing for more sleep. Soon his stomach began hurting constantly. He suffered a long while before finally submitting to hospitalization three years ago. The hospital test results, however, uncovered nothing. He was told his stomach problems were "just nerves." Mrs. Treppit did not know how to interpret this analysis. She began to blame herself.

> This was what made me start wondering. I was wondering if it was maybe us getting on his nerves, or was it me. He kinda liked [the kids] pretty well so I thought maybe it was me. I don't know. I was wondering if I was the one getting on his nerves or stopped him from something. I don't know how to put it but he's been complaining about it so much I often wondered.

Mrs. Treppit has since developed a slightly different notion to explain his ailment:

> He probably got his nervous stomach because we were married when we were pretty young—he was 17 and I was 13 when we got married; after we got married we went right away into responsibilities and we've been in 'em ever since. I was thinking about that the other night.

Mr. Treppit attributes his mysterious ailment to the Chicago "climate." He constantly despairs of his condition. It is extremely painful, gnawing, repetitious. He feels that the city is too confining but he must stay because he has nowhere else to go. When asked to describe his biggest dream, Mr. Treppit responded that it was to:

> Go back to Mississippi and "set up camp" as they call it and take it from there. I'd like to be out where if I wanted to holler loud, nobody could hear me—whatever I wanted to do, get away from it all. It's too congested here really, up North period, up here, the weather, even the water is different. I was noticing last year when I was down South it just takes a little bit of detergent to get all the lather you want but here when you're washing dishes in it, before you've finished you've got to add more soap. How or what it is I don't know. But I do know this, if I'm down South for a couple of weeks, I feel much better and the sunshine down there seems like its different. I can stand more heat down there, you know.

Mr. Treppit consciously avoids taking out his frustrations on his family. Mrs. Treppit and the children feel free to act as they normally would, without fear of reprisal.

The Treppit household is warm and welcoming. The family dog is named Bones. Neighbors frequently visit the Treppit household because there is always a relaxed feeling of being welcome.

> No grand overtures are made to make the neighbors feel at home outside of courtesies such as asking, "How are you doing?" and

hanging up the coat. He feels perfectly free to drop in, sit, and discuss personal concerns. The degree of openness is unusual in this home.

There is a very refreshing human atmosphere in the home which is brought about by Mrs. Treppit's ability to "hang loose" with other people and an exceptional brother-sister type of interaction between Mr. and Mrs. Treppit.

Early Child-Rearing and Familial Practices

Most of the family processes have been generated out of the socioeconomic context of the Treppit home. Home duties and responsibilities are carried out with the thought that Mr. Treppit must leave home to hunt for dollars ("I'm out there trying to see what I can catch to bring home"), while Mrs. Treppit's function is to maintain the household and nurture the children.

James Earl does not get to see his father at all during the week. By the time school is out, Mr. Treppit has already gone to work. When he returns from work, everyone is already asleep. On weekends, James Earl is involved in social activities and Mr. Treppit is resting and spending time with his wife. Interaction between father and son occurs only a few hours on Saturdays and Sundays. There has seldom been a period when Mr. Treppit was able to sit down and spend significant amounts of time with his children. When the children were younger, there were occasional vacations when the entire family had the opportunity to be together. These periods occurred most often during the summers when schools were not in session.

James Earl relied more heavily on his mother than his father for early guidance. He has never really known how to approach his father. Mr. Treppit always seemed quietly available while still commanding respect. But his silent behavior, different in form from Mrs. Treppit's, coupled with his limited presence, made the young James Earl worry about approaching his father. James Earl remembers having to overcome a seemingly unwarranted fear of interacting with his father.

I would have this fear. Not that he beat me or anything like that. I was just, I don't know why. He never did anything. Like now, he haven't whipped me or did anything in five or six years—since I was small. He don't do nothin' like that. And if he do get aggravated, he talk to us about it. I went to [my mother] mostly. I might be scared to tell my father something happened to me. I don't want him to think to come down on me. I want him to be proud of me and stuff and don't want to tell him no kind of problems. It might make him kind of mad or low-rate me in some kind of way so I wouldn't tell him. My mother seemed like she might understand better than my father 'cause she be with us more—more than my father.

Now that James Earl is getting a little older, his perspective has slowly changed. He consults with his father more often.

> I go to him with something on my mind. You might need your father. Your father might be able to help you when your mother can't so I go to both of them.

Young James Earl received a large amount of care and attention from his teenage mother. His parents provided his food and clothing. He learned to "be without" and did not expect anything more than the bare essentials. His mother would explain to him that the family was doing the best it could. He learned to ask for something only if he "really need it and really want it." His mother was always attempting to provide an atmosphere for him which avoided the stresses she has experienced. James Earl recalls:

> I don't think I had no kind of responsibility when I was young. I wasn't able to do too much. I was small. I be short and my mother let other people baby-sit us and stuff. But I never had too much responsibility because she never left us alone that much.

Mrs. Treppit made every attempt to supervise, guide, and punish her children appropriately. As a youngster, James Earl seldom proved to be a discipline problem—at home or in school. He spoke only when it was appropriate to do so. Mrs. Treppit cannot remember any school-related behavior problems:

> All through school all his teachers have always said that he obeys and everything.

Mrs. Treppit has followed her children's personal development closely over the years. She and her husband have agreed that the responsibility for the children must lie primarily on her shoulders. Mr. Treppit's primary responsibility is to provide the necessary economic resources to enhance this development. James Earl has repeatedly been told of his responsibility to respect the wishes of his parents. He knows what behavior is appropriate and inappropriate. Through continued maternal guidance, he has developed strong moral codes and generally acts to "do what's right."

Mental Health: General Attitudes, Values, and Personality

James Earl is now developing into an independent, free-thinking, self-reliant individual. As a youth, James Earl received a classic American conservative value orientation. He was taught to love God, to respect others, and to work hard in life. The constant pursuit of immediate material gratification, he was told, is foolish and dangerous. His father was especially vocal when the subject involved the development of values. Mr. Treppit suggested, for example, that a man's family needs should have a higher priority than his personal desires:

The average one of us likes the big fine cars and the nice clothes, something we haven't really been used to and you get a chance to do this thing and it just go to your head; and you think you're really up in life and you ain't done nothin' but lowered yourself in a sense. A lot of us don't even have food to eat, but if you got a big car, then you "into something" you know, and your kids are probably hungry. And the average one of us wants to get a big car as soon as they're able.

James Earl follows in his father's tradition by avoiding negative community influences such as gangs and drugs. Though he is not a churchgoer, James Earl carries a healthy respect for his fellow man. He is not disposed to racial bigotry. He would like to see others reach the same heights he plans to reach. He states:

I want some of my friends to be where I'm at so we can all do it together.

James Earl has not given his parents much cause for alarm. He has developed into a relatively well-adjusted young man. A sensitive person, he takes life seriously. He is often contemplative and analytical in much the same way as a company president responsible for millions of dollars might be. He exhibits no problem being cooperative. Even though he doesn't get everything he might want, his insight helps him cope. He does not blame his father for not providing more to the family. He says:

I understand his position so that's why I don't even think about it much. I see him laying there sick sometimes, his stomach be bothering him, so I don't even be bugged about it.

One of the most striking characteristics is James Earl's level of maturity. Having watched his father, James Earl knows what it is like to struggle for survival. Mr. Treppit describes him:

Well, he's very quiet and he's not really a hard head, not a bit hardheaded; I haven't had no problems with him too much. I would say, comparing him to some I see, I wouldn't have anything bad to say about him after that. He's a pretty good kid.

As a teenager, James Earl apparently possesses the insight and judgment necessary to carry on a smooth familial relationship.

James Earl has been careful, however, to maintain his own individuality. Self-reliance and independence are characteristics he is at present developing for himself. He knows he cannot allow himself to become a victim of his father's malady. He has his own life to live.

I don't like the way he gets sick but there's nothing I can do about it. If I had a chance to do something, I'd try and help. But I don't have no chance.

Family experiences have helped James Earl in the formation of his goals. He has learned perseverance from his parents. He has learned to be prepared to act alone, without assistance. Much of the time there will be no one to help in the attainment of goals. High school, for example, was initially difficult for him. (He barely qualified as a "successful" student for our study.) He considered giving up. He kept trying, though, and his grades improved.

> I thought about just that, giving up on things but I never did. When I first came to high school, making them low grades, I thought maybe it should be easy but it was hard, high school. I could have just given up but I went on and did it; it's all right now, but, then, I was glad the semester was over.

James Earl realizes that his parents have helped him as much as they can and that they were especially encouraging and supportive when he wanted to give up. The rest of the push has come from within himself. James Earl has begun to develop the independence which will be necessary to make his own journey toward success. The first step, he feels, is to pursue his own occupational choice, not the occupation that someone else may have in mind for him. When asked if he would like to work on the same job as his father, James Earl stated:

> For the time being maybe, but not permanently. I'd rather go back to what I want to do. That may not be what he wants to do, but . . .

James Earl has begun to pull away from the apron strings which the family relationship has provided. He no longer studies with the younger boys, as he once did. He now prefers to go to the store, school, and elsewhere, alone. Mrs. Treppit views him as " more or less a loner" now. He does not allow himself to be influenced by the other boys in the neighborhood. Mr. Treppit comments on his autonomous attitude toward school friends:

> He don't have too many friends; I like that. Well, I wouldn't say he don't have too many friends; he seem to be friendly with everybody, but he don't seem to have too many kids he really hang around with. I don't think he's easily persuaded or he'd probably have dropped out of school before this. Most of his old friends who he used to be with have dropped out of school and have real bad habits—smoking, drinking.

Ever cautious of James Earl's behavior, Mrs. Treppit is happy to see continual progress being made by her son. She knows that it is easy for low-income teenagers to slip into bad peer groups and become delinquent. Mrs. Treppit is keeping watch over James Earl because, as the oldest child, his outcome may have a profound influence on her other boys.

James Earl's Gordon Persons Conceptions System Profile indicates a strong identification with student, friendship, and occupational roles. Desirous of nice material objects, he is anxious to pursue intellectual avenues to obtain his goals. Somewhat uncomfortable with his present level of academic competence, James Earl is determined to work hard to make a better future.

In-Home Living Patterns

James Earl enjoys a high status among his peers because there is a mother and a working father (not stepfather) in the home. In the projects, two-parent homes are more the exception than the rule. Importantly, there exists a spirit of harmony and friendliness in the Treppit home, as turmoil and strife are kept at a minimum. Mrs. Treppit is largely responsible for this development. Mr. Treppit presents an amicable attitude as well. Neighbors feel free to visit and chat with Mrs. Treppit for short periods of time. Items are often borrowed and exchanged. The following field note captures this process:

> At about 12:00 noon a neighbor, Sam, knocks and walks in. Sam says, "I want to borrow that record again. I messed up the tape I used to tape-record it the first time." Mrs. Treppit is busy preparing her husband's bag lunch for work and simultaneously peeling potatoes for dinner. She says, "Oh, go ahead and get it; you know where it is." Sam searched for several minutes and after not finding it, looked toward Mrs. Treppit. She said, "Oh, James Earl, why don't you find that record he's looking for?" James Earl searched for a few minutes before discovering that the record was still on the turntable. He handed it to Sam, who thanked them and left, promising to return the record later in the evening.

Relations between neighbors are friendly, but controlled. Visitors are careful not to take a lot of liberties with Mrs. Treppit's time, since she is usually engaged in household chores. These chores include washing, cooking, and cleaning. Almost all interpersonal activities take place during the normal performance of household chores.

When he is not in school, James Earl spends most of his time in the home. He seldom receives any friends into the home. He does not have any friends he feels close enough with to invite into the home. He knows they will be scrutinized by his parents, who expect him to choose "nice" friends. His mother is very cognizant of his associates and his activities. She knows that:

> When he was young, he had 2 little boys he'd be with most of the time, but now he be with this little girl, that's just about it. He has another little friend, Robert Johnson, and they would be together sometimes; other than that he be right in the house looking at that TV or playing on the guitar or doing his homework, or listening to his tapes, whatever. He got some tapes. [He and his brother] sit

around here and tape on the guitar and listens to it. I don't know too much else he do.

Mr. Treppit is also watchful of James Earl's behavior. He knows that it is impossible to be around the home at all times, so he attempts to be especially observant of James Earl when he is in the home.

James Earl has begun visiting his girlfriend weekdays from 6:00 P.M. until the 11:00 P.M. parentally imposed curfew. This development has been a recent cause of concern for Mr. and Mrs. Treppit. James Earl feels he is now old enough to be allowed to experience a relationship with a member of the opposite sex. Since he wants to visit outside the home, Mrs. Treppit has decided to allow him to do it as long as he agrees to take his sixteen-year-old brother, Johnny, with him wherever he goes. In this way, Mrs. Treppit feels she still may exercise some control over James Earl's activities. Johnny is reliable in reporting all of his older brother's activities to his parents. His mother reasons:

What could he be doing that his brother couldn't know about? If he don't want his brother to know, it must be something wrong somehow.

Johnny is amused at his older brother's perturbed attitude toward him. Johnny knows that his parents will not allow James Earl to visit at all if James Earl refuses to take him. Johnny learns a lot from James Earl. Because of the unsolicited closeness *outside* the home, however, James Earl often complains and bickers about Johnny's behavior in the home. In one field note, we see an example of this.

Johnny, the second oldest son, observes his older brother frequently and probably learns quite a bit from watching James Earl handle himself. As we sit in the living room talking, Johnny is watching literally every move James Earl makes. James Earl twice admonishes Johnny to "stop lookin' right down my throat." Johnny says, "I'm not lookin' down your throat; I wouldn't want to look down your throat"; Johnny then laughs. James Earl frowns and turns away from him and he continues his observation.

James Earl does not like his younger brother's continued presence on visits to friends because Johnny will laugh at James Earl's style of interacting during visits to his girl's home. Under these circumstances, petting, necking, and other such activities are kept at a minimum.

Mrs. Treppit wants James Earl to stay in the home after he graduates in June. She hesitates to encourage him to leave home since she believes he basically functions quite well in the home environment. James Earl prefers to stay in the home for a few years after high school graduation. He explains:

At home I'm just more relaxed. That's something I'm trying to figure out. When I'm home I can remember things. Like reading, I'm just more comfortable. . . . That's why I stay at home a lot. It's more comfortable at home.

James Earl plans to attend a neighborhood junior college which will allow him to keep his place with his family. In this way, Mrs. Treppit can continue to provide nurturance and guidance to James Earl as he completes the final years before adulthood.

Time and schedule conflicts make in-home living adjustments imperative. The family seldom eats dinner together because Mr. Treppit is hardly ever in the house at dinnertime. Nevertheless, familial cohesiveness is stressed and maintained. To Mrs. Treppit, her family is her life:

> You see a lot of people working and they got a beautiful home and beautiful clothes and then you see their kids is all warped. Now I don't care how much money I could get, if I could get a million dollars I still wouldn't want that. I'd rather see my family more or less together than I would want any kind of money. If somebody could really offer me a million dollars, I still wouldn't accept it. I go all out for my children.

Mrs. Treppit has been a mother since she was 13 years old. Her family represents the only life she has really known. Her primary function in life is the successful maintenance of their welfare. She carries a love bond which is so strong that her happiness is directly related to how her family feels. She says:

> Once they're all up and well and nobody's sick, I feel good, as long as my family is all well. I think that pleases me more than anything else.

James Earl shares his mother's love for family cohesiveness. He feels closer to his family than he does with any other persons. He knows he has been truly fortunate to have two parents who have consistently attempted to provide a loving home environment. As the eldest, James Earl is expected to guide the younger boys whenever both parents are away from home. He is not allowed to punish them in any way. He must treat them with love. If they disobey him, he will report to his mother who will then either talk to them, spank them, or take away privileges. Again, most home-related activities are supervised and conducted by Mrs. Treppit. This has been her role for eighteen years. Mr. Treppit refuses to "put my wife to work" even though they could use the money. He says:

> We ain't really living as bad as I see them. I look at it like this: You never be able to do everything you want to do, as long as you doin' a halfway decent job.

Entrenched values regarding domestic roles make it extremely unlikely that Mrs. Treppit will ever work outside the home as long as Mr. Treppit and the children are there. For them, a working wife represents failure, not success. It is an action which will only be used as a last resort.

Educational Orientations in the Home

A salient feature of the Treppit household is the totally supportive posture of Mr. and Mrs. Treppit toward their children's educational welfare. The parental support of James Earl's educational endeavors is provided because of a belief that lucrative jobs may result. Attainment of the job is considered the most important goal to reach. The job is the key to a better life and success in schooling is viewed as a means of securing the job.

As the first family member to attain a high school education, James Earl enjoys an increasing status within the household. His goal is to improve his position over his father. He wants to assure a better life for himself than the one his father has experienced. He believes schooling is a necessary activity in the quest for an improved social and economic position; schooling is a necessary evil which must be endured. His desire for economic improvement is the primary force behind James Earl's schooling desires.

James Earl has not enjoyed a particularly strong socialization into academic activities. He has been encouraged by Mr. and Mrs. Treppit to study when he must. There has been little emphasis, however, on making school learning a way of life. To Mr. and Mrs. Treppit, neither of whom finished high school, James Earl doesn't need to study much more since he is "doing well." (James Earl is a C student.) Since James Earl has only intermittently vigorously pursued schooling activities, he knows he has not been maximally trained in the subject matter. He finds study, then, a chore. He states his ambivalence toward academic pursuits in this way:

> Really, I tell you. I don't like school. I like to go and learn things because you have to go.

But he feels he is capable of rising to the academic occasion whenever it becomes necessary:

> In college I'd probably study more, get the four years in right away, get good grades and then get out. I can remember most of what I study if I'm interested in it. I think I'm an average student.

James Earl has usually performed to the expectations of his teachers and parents. Although these expectations have been less than maximal, they still create challenges for James Earl to meet and overcome. James Earl realizes he has accomplished more in school than most of the people who are important to him. ("I think I'm the smartest in my family. I'm the smartest, and I do more studying than any of the others.") Despite the fact that James Earl has never been comfortable with his reading skills, schooling has not been a major calamity for him. In elementary school, where obedience and conformity were half the battle, James Earl did well. In fact, he found it quite easy to handle. His mother has always received positive reports on his "school progress."

Well, they claimed he was very good. He wasn't like top in the class, but behavior-wise all his teachers said he was one of their very best students.

He was never expected, though, to develop college-level study skills. He describes his high school experience as loose and uncivilized. Realizing the resultant limitations of his high school training, he hopes for a different college experience. He senses the expectations will be higher.

Really I think it's going to be more civilized than high school because you have more stricter rules. I don't know that much about college, but in my opinion it would be stricter there because you can't do most anything you want in college. You have to get down to serious business in college. You have to study in college too. That's going to be the hardest thing for me right there until I get that chance and make up for the lost time I had in [high] school.

James Earl's comments reflect a high degree of self-motivation and direction. He has learned not to expect much encouragement from his friends, most of whom are not education-oriented. College represents the unknown to James Earl. Because of his perception of the quality of his high school preparation, James Earl initially feared going to college. In some ways he still fears college, but he knows he must not allow his fear to stop his progress toward his goal. He plans to tackle it successfully. This extraordinary drive is indicative of his sincerity in his desire to attain adequate schooling. He says:

I didn't want to go at first because I thought I might have a whole lot of books to read and I didn't like to study that much. But I said I was gonna take my time and read them books and go on and get it out of the way. I don't know why I didn't want to go. I guess I didn't want to read a lot of books. I was kind of lazy then. But I know you're gonna have to do something if you want to get a job.

James Earl has received very little assistance from parents and teachers in planning his course of action in college. His parents have tried to offer some advice but they do not know enough about higher education to be thoroughly helpful. Through oversight or neglect, his teachers have provided very little guidance and direction.

Like other young Blacks, James Earl has decided that schooling is a requisite for "making it" in society. He believes a high school diploma is not enough to accomplish his goals. He first considered attending a trade school for automobile technology but later decided to go to a four-year college and obtain a degree in computer technology.

Mr. Treppit has been especially instrumental in helping James Earl to formulate his current goals. Mr. Treppit has stressed the relationship between schooling and survival. He states:

This is what I'm trying to explain to James Earl, I want him to [succeed]. The only way he can do this thing is to be even smarter than I was because things is getting tougher instead, you know every day things is getting out of reach. And there's no way I can get him these things. Now I told him he can get them on his own but he's gotta get this here [schooling] finished. So I told him all you can do to survive actually is to have an education these days.

Spiraling inflation in the economy has made the concern for survival even greater. Mr. Treppit knows that James Earl is extremely aware of his future prospects without a successful school experience. According to Mr. Treppit:

He sees that he will have to have money. He knows he will have to have money to do something he would like to do and to have, and he knows he will have to have an education to get it. I do believe that's why he knows he has to have some college.

Mr. Treppit feels he understands the realities of existence without schooling. He wants James Earl to understand these same realities even though he has simultaneously attempted to protect James Earl from some of the hardships. Mr. Treppit would like for James Earl's goals and aspirations to be truly his own. He does not want to force his son to accept any other person's notions. He wants James Earl to think through his own solution.

I'd like James Earl to do whatever would interest him. I make no decisions for him. I'd be interested in whatever he is, in order for him to get this job, whatever it is. He gotta be interested. I told him I would like for him to [go to school] but I don't want him to go because of me. I want him to be interested in it because you're not really going to be a success at anything unless you have your mind to it. So, it's up to him.

James Earl certainly appears to have his "mind to it." He believes his continued happiness depends on his ability to accomplish his goals. He believes strongly that nothing will stop him. He plans to give a total effort to his college studies. He says:

When I get to college, I know I'm really going to do good because I'm really going to study 'cause I think I'd like to take four years out of my life to do something I really want to do. I'd be good at it and happy for what I did. I'd rather take five years out of my life and be happy the rest of my life than take no years out and be sad all my life.

James Earl does not actually know what to expect from college, but he clearly knows the effort he will exert. He knows that his parents are expecting him to take schooling seriously. They know that his entire future may be at stake. Mr. Treppit does not want his son to face the same pressures *he* has had to contend with. More options are available, he feels, when a degree is attained. Personal experiences make Mr. Treppit even more vehement in his assertions.

> You can't just go out there and find what you want, tell the Man, "Well, yeah, I want this." This is what I've been trying to explain to James Earl. If you got this little piece of paper, then you can do these things. But in my case [I] more or less go along and take the bitter with the sweet, you know. Well, nobody I guess makes what they want to make.

We can see that Mr. Treppit attempts to soften his hurt by rationalizing his economic position. At the same time, however, it is brilliantly clear that Mr. Treppit wants his son to have a different life. He wants his son to be equipped with the skills he will have to have in order to do well as a Black man in society.

> Like me, now, I could take a trade; but as far as going to college. You probably don't get too old to go there, but I don't know, I believe it's easier when you're young than to wait until you get my age or older, you know.

Although he not-so-secretly longs to return to school, Mr. Treppit feels his strongest allegiance to be the immediate and continued welfare of his family. This means that he must continue to work long, hard hours at low pay.

An argument cannot reasonably be made that James Earl is academically inclined even though he is educationally successful. As stated earlier, he does fulfill the limited expectations of the teachers. This suggests that he possesses a certain level of discipline. He displays unusual patience with the guitar, which he plays daily. He is also the champion chess player in the school club. He is a positive thinker who believes in himself. Mrs. Treppit observed that her sons will often put intense effort into their activities. "They likes to try to *win*."

James Earl admits that schoolwork does not excite him at all. He has been slowly improving his study habits so that they are approaching the status of ritualistic behaviors. He makes it clear, however, that such activities as reading and studying are not desirable to him.

> The only thing I read is like stuff I need for school. When I read it and I think it's useful to me, I can remember things. I don't read anything just to be reading. I don't study that much at home either. Like when I have a special assignment to do I study for that. But I know in the future I have to do some studying even if I don't have no assignments. But I don't like to study, not at all. I'm in the top 25 percent of my senior class. I'm up there, I ain't back there, but I could be higher but for study.

There is a cognizance that improvement will be mandatory for successful college pursuits. Over the past year, he has been slowly disciplining himself to read more. He can see the positive effects of his actions.

> My reading habits right now aim to help me because my vocabulary is getting better 'cause I'm reading more than I used to read. It used to take a long time for me to read, but I read a little faster now.

One ritualistic educational behavior already in existence in the Treppit home involves homework assignments. Homework is perceived as a normal, expected activity to be accomplished. Unlike reading, whenever homework assignments are presented in school, James Earl automatically and willingly carries out the task required. He has been expected to do homework since he began first grade. Mrs. Treppit relates:

> You don't have to get after him to tell him about his homework. If he got homework to do and go out and start playing ball or wherever he's going, he'll come back. He don't forget. He's always been that way. Like I say, I don't have any trouble with him doing his homework. He automatically do it on his own, more or less.

We notice that Mrs. Treppit *expects* James Earl to do his homework. She knows that this activity is important for his school success. She does not place the same expectation on him with respect to reading. She, in effect, has allowed him to avoid reading. Her early difficulties with reading as a child have convinced her that he has done his best. She feels he should not be expected to do "too much."

> He reads what he has to read. It has to be something he kinda interested in. Some children just loves to read. He's not one of them type of kids.

We may observe a tacit acceptance of James Earl's reading habits. This acceptance was carried through James Earl's primary grades. Mrs. Treppit now acknowledges that he needs improvement in reading, but she does not know how to help James Earl effect this improvement. Because reading has been seen as a chore, homework assignments that require reading have frequently been viewed as exceptionally difficult undertakings. The existence of the homework ritual, however, has assured that reading skills would not be totally ignored in the home.

Another type of educational ritual which has been performed in the Treppit home is parent-son discussions emphasizing the rationale for schooling and education. Repeated conversations occur between James Earl and his parent(s) about the role of education in his life. This activity serves to increase James Earl's level of awareness of his own goals as well as the wisdom of his parents' wishes. James Earl has experienced these discussions since elementary school, but they have been practiced with greater regularity since he entered high school. These kinds of discussions ultimately persuaded him to pursue a higher education.

> My father and my parents talked more to me about going to college. I really didn't want to go, but he kept telling me about it and he kept telling me about it and then I went back to school and the teacher said, "yes, you can get a degree in that subject."

James Earl's father, through repeated dialogue, has emphasized again the importance of doing well in school. He mother has taken up where Mr. Treppit left off:

> I talks to him all the time about these things. I imagine he might get tired of hearing them all the time because he gets an earfull all the time. He might be sick of hearing it, but as I say, I "washes his face with it" all the time. He asks me questions, like maybe, "Why didn't you go to school?" He says probably that's why my husband be sick all the time, because he's disgusted because he don't have the money he'd probably like to have. He be seeing a lot of dudes, like he calls 'em, who have a pretty car and maybe he would want one. Yeah, he talks to me about it. He try to figure out why a lot of things happen. He say when he grows up there's a lot of things he want to do for his children, and he don't think it's smart to have too many children. He say he want two children, you know, and he don't want his wife to work.

Mrs. Treppit has found it easy to sit down and talk to her son about his concerns. Since schooling is central to his entire goal orientation, it is often discussed. Mrs. Treppit has noticed that James Earl has lately become more serious during these conversations. He realizes that he will soon embark upon his biggest journey in the educational arena and he has every intention of continuing to succeed.

4. The Family Life of High Achievers in One-Parent Homes

A 1981 census report placed the percentage of school-age children in Black single-parent families in the United States at 46 percent of the total Black child population. (In comparison, about 25 percent of the nation's children are living in single-parent homes.) This high percentage of Black children in female-headed families, and the frequent treatment of them as pathological, may prompt a special interest in the following three case studies. We will take a long look at the way some mothers are managing their homes successfully during the inflation-recession of the 1970s. The reader will be struck by the leadership behavior and the sheer will of these mothers to persevere in spite of the economic and societal resistance they encounter. How their children are affected by the parents' goals and themes becomes a most intriguing story.

We will see that one of the parents is in the midst of a serious struggle with her daughters to get them to avoid sexual intercourse if at all possible. This case history pinpoints what might be considered a general limitation of this study. I have purposely chosen to look at family life from the primary vantage point of its impact on children's *school* behavior. In the Farland home, however, the most crucial issue was not school behavior. Rather, the main issue for this mother at that particular stage (the daughter's adolescence) in the mother-daughter life cycle revolved around men and sexuality. What effect this major family issue might have had on the daughter's school performance is a matter of speculation and conjecture. I might note that I spoke with the daughter's teacher about two years after I had gathered data from this family. The teacher indicated that while the oldest daughter had graduated from high school on schedule and had gone on to take a clerk-typist level job, the second girl had delivered a baby and had, at least temporarily, dropped out of school.

In most respects, the psychological and behavioral patterns found in this group were identical to those found in the two-parent families in Chapter 3. The major difference between the two-parent and single-parent families was the creative use of other persons to reinforce parents' goals for their children. The approach of these single mothers to their circumstances is an example of sheer determination, persistence, and strength.

The Hayeses

The Family Theme

In low-income families a key factor in the educational success of a child may be a strong parental religious-spiritual orientation. A mother who directs her children toward moral values in society, while strenuously curtailing their contact with potentially negative or "bad" community influences, can usually obtain the children's respect. As this respect is attained, it is possible for the mother to effect a strong educational orientation in her child. It is particularly important that the child learn the appropriate values at an early age so that the child's value orientation may become a way of life.

Within the family unit we may have the most ideal studio for the development of the moral behavior we consider desirable for children. By creating the guidelines at early childhood stages, it is possible for parents to set the tone for future pre-adulthood activities. Mrs. Hayes, a quiet, strong-willed mother possessed of great fortitude, saw these possibilities and pursued them.

Mrs. Hayes and her son Anthony live in a public housing project apartment. Anthony's older brothers and sisters have moved on to live outside the home. At seventeen, Anthony is the last child of Mrs. Hayes, who is a matronly fifty years old. The Hayes's apartment is, structurally, a simple brick unit. Inside, the three-bedroom apartment is neatly furnished with old but sound furniture. There is an aura of old-fashioned hominess. Mrs. Hayes takes great pride in the fact that she has had the same furniture for the duration of her children's growing years. She has had her sofa for about fifteen years, for example, and her kitchen table is sixteen years old. With eight children formerly in the home, the furniture has been remarkably well maintained. The old consolette, the couch, and the end tables in the living room take up most of the space. There is little space in which to walk around in these traditionally small apartments. Mrs. Hayes has lived in this apartment since the building was constructed in 1962. The brick floors have been covered by the housing authority with black tile. The living room chairs are cloth-covered, and the windows are all covered with steel bars. These bars, mounted to prevent burglaries, qualify as a fire hazard because they not only prevent entry into the home but will most effectively prevent any emergency exit as well. Orange and white curtains cover the window bars. Inexpensive decorations attempt to give color to the surroundings. Flower decals, for example, are affixed to the cupboard doors in the kitchen.

The Hayes household can be described as quiet and homey but slightly somber. Eight children have been raised in this home. All eight children are very supportive of their mother. Howard is 30, Jeffrey 29, Kitten 28, Milton 27, Booker 23, Christopher 20, Doris 18, and Anthony is 17. Mrs.

Hayes has had three unsuccessful marriages. She recently went through divorce proceedings for the third time in her life. She maintains the husbands "weren't quite strong enough" to cooperate with her "like they should. I couldn't depend on the fathers." She has provided the necessities for her children by working hard most of her life. She is satisfied that some of the children's needs have been met:

> I was able to pay the bills and see to them going to school and keep them in clothing, and get them an education.

Mrs. Hayes has four children from her first marriage, one from the second, and three from the last marriage. Anthony has high respect for his mother. He has seen her struggle to make his survival possible. He believes that her work is potentially dangerous to her health. A very articulate young man, he says:

> I don't like it. I don't like it at all. She works at a factory making coats, and I worked there over the summer. Last summer I worked there, and she's not getting paid very much, and I want to see her take a rest for a time and retire. That's why I want, partially why I want, to get into a co-op school so she won't have to worry about paying for me.

Mrs. Hayes has worked continuously since her teens, when she first came to Chicago with her parents from Birmingham, Alabama. Like most, she came in search of opportunity. Her initial reaction to Chicago was positive. She married as a teenager without finishing high school, a decision she now regrets.

> My mother really wanted me to finish school. That's just one of the reasons why I try to encourage my children to get their education. At that time it didn't seem like it was necessary like it is today, especially with a girl.

To her way of thinking, Mrs. Hayes made a terrible blunder by not finishing school. Her parents were not poor. In fact, her background was middle class. Her father owned a small restaurant and her mother was a seamstress. There also appears to have been an intergenerational family pattern of striving toward success. These strivings, however, have not been without some perplexing results. Pressures to reach material goals placed a great strain on Mrs. Hayes's mother. Mrs. Hayes reveals:

> I guess all down through the family, my mother's side especially, there was quite a few educated people in her family. My mother was smart and that helps a lot. I'm sorry I didn't finish school. My mother had a nervous breakdown and me being the oldest, there was a lot of pressure on me. You see, there was my mother who had to be thought of. I had a lot of responsibility on me. My younger sister and my brother—there was three of us, two girls and one boy—and my

mother would leave mostly everything to me at that time. This was the only thing I could do that would really help her because my mother or my father wouldn't dream of me getting a job. She's been with me most of the time. I have to be concerned about her because she has that heart trouble

This testimony reveals that Mrs. Hayes has felt a strong sense of responsibility for her family of origin as well as for her family of procreation. Mrs. Hayes has maintained a close relationship with her mother. She wants to provide a home one day for the two of them. The housing projects have not been the panacea originally envisioned by Mrs. Hayes. In fact, she now despises them:

There has been a drastic change from when I first moved here. In the first place, I never—if it had been like this, I never would have moved to this area. The next reason I moved to this area is that my mother lives on 43d and Michigan, and at that time I needed someone nearby to keep an eye on the children while I worked, and they weren't in school then. However, this place was beautiful at that time and the management was a lot different. And they saw the parents cooperating with them. However, it changed so much I would never bring my kids up around here if I had it to do all over again.

Anthony is not content with his present environment either. He now spends a great deal of time at school. Neighborhood crime has made living here a burden. The housing projects were seen as a stepping stone to attain a nice, cozy little home in a less congested area of town. For this purpose she has saved her money for years. Rocky marriages have made it difficult for Mrs. Hayes to reach her goal, however, because her spouses had other plans for the money she saved. In one of the field notes we see some problems left from her last marriage:

Mrs. Hayes's strength as a person comes out often when she talks about her troubles with her husband. She would not discuss it on the tape tonight. After the taping, however, she talked about her divorce. She seemed concerned but not emotional as she discussed her plans after Anthony goes away to college in three months. "I'll be alone then," she says, "but I'll make it." She talked about how her ex-husband had tried to cheat her out of a house. "He won the house as part of the divorce package. We had accumulated a decent-sized savings account and he had gotten a building with tenants. But when the divorce came through, he wanted to keep it all. He sold the house to another family and tried to destroy my deed so that I wouldn't have legal claim. But legally the house is mine. I will get it eventually, but it has been rough on me going through the courts trying to straighten this thing out. Lawyers fees continuously build up." I told her not to worry, that she would be okay. She stopped and, as if finding new energy from somewhere, deeply breathed in and said, "But with the Lord's help, I sure will."

Mrs. Hayes wants to get the house matter corrected before her mother dies. She fears this will be soon. Mrs. Hayes has not been totally disheartened by the pitfalls in her life. She is determined to maintain a positive attitude toward others. She enjoys helping others; it is part of her warm personality. She credits her mother for this attentive orientation.

My mother brought me up around people, trying to help people. My father was always nice to people, but I think the training a child gets is mostly from the mother.

Mrs. Hayes has, in turn, prepared her own children to serve others. She considers this preparation the "Christian way."

At her job, Mrs. Hayes is viewed as a loyal and hardworking employee. Her boss, who is White, has often sought her "motherly" advice on personal family problems of his own. Indeed, she is his best employee. She is sometimes invited to the boss' home for dinner. He laments that his children are now "smoking dope" and "going wild." He has often openly expressed admiration of Mrs. Hayes for her success with her children. Mrs. Hayes's description of her relationship with her boss was reminiscent of the loyal servant who has been in the family for years. For Mrs. Hayes it is a good relationship. She is grateful to God for her blessings. She says:

But I've always been grateful you know. I've been thanking God all along. See, you pray to God to go with you and guide you and you'll be protected. So the good things I have had have been through my children and I am really grateful. I don't have everything I desire to have—maybe I even feel I've been cheated out of some of the things I should have had. But still, for what I do have I'm really grateful. I've never had any problems with my children. That's a blessing, it really is a blessing.

Anthony has observed his mother in acts of kindness and generosity. This altruistic orientation is now so common as to be almost taken for granted.

I've noticed that from times way back—from times way back. When I was very young, like people of this calibre, she'd invite them in to have breakfast. She'd always try to help them with their kids, like clothes we weren't wearing, she'd give them to them. Anything she could help out with. She'd often take them grocery shopping and oftentimes give them food if they didn't have anything to eat. She'd always talk to the boys around here. I know of several times, my mother would always go over and talk to them. I can remember one time the cops were standing there with a boy around the store. He was running off at the mouth and the cop pulled his gun on him and my mother jumped in front of the boy and told the officer, "Please don't shoot him." You know, that's one incident I really remember. I'll never forget.

Mrs. Hayes actively talks with the neighborhood rowdies about the ugliness of fighting and the beauty of loving. She admonishes these boys to respect their parents by "doing right." In one field note I observed:

Mrs. Hayes spends a lot of time on the phone talking to members of her church. She seems to derive her satisfaction from making others a little less lonely. She offered me breakfast this morning. She seems to be a very warm person. She is expressive with her hands, using gestures to convey concepts. As she talked about family together-ness, her hands were cupped as if to offer a precious gift or receive water from a stream. Later we listened to some of the things we talked about on tape on a previous visit. Her activity in the ghetto, attempting to reform some of the kids is interesting. I asked her if she was the neighborhood "crusading counselor." She simply laughed.

Anthony is a bright, articulate, and congenial person. He is a mature person in that he is able to discuss his own life in a thoughtful and often provocative manner. He is now one of the top ten seniors at his high school. The following description was made during my first visit to the Hayes's home:

Anthony is about 5 feet 8 inches tall and weighs about 135 pounds. He is big in the upper region of his body and small in the lower re-gion—a wrestler's physique. He wears glasses, has a light brown complexion, and sports a closely cropped head of hair which could be called a short "natural" Afro. His overall appearance is reminis-cent of what is probably the stereotypic high school math or science wizard, a committed, pleasant person, and mostly anxious to engage in intellectual discussions.

Additionally, Anthony impresses one as a very responsible young man. He is active in a variety of school-related activities. His Gordon Persons Conceptions System profile reveals some other interesting facets of his personality. Like most of the other successful students surveyed, Antho-ny identifies most closely with his gender (manhood) and his racial (Black) statuses. He views his most important roles as that of a student, a family member, and a friend. Conservatism dominates his political orien-tation. While his major life goal is security, Anthony derives much of his short-term gratification from sports and recreational activities. His pri-mary interests concern intellectual and cultural pursuits. Interacting with others in a cooperative manner, Anthony is a giving, active person with ambition. A socially aware person, he believes in integration and social harmony. Filled with self-assurance and self-determination, he thinks pri-marily of future concerns.

Early Child-Rearing and Familial Practices

Since Anthony's father was not around during his early years, Mrs. Hayes insisted that the older children "look out" for the younger ones.

Many of the out-of-home activities (e.g., movies, skating, and so on) involved Anthony and his older brothers. The older children accepted their responsibility in this helping role. The importance of familial unity was stressed by Mrs. Hayes. She remembers that:

> They were always happy when they'd go and when they come back and I enjoyed listening to them—where they went and what they did. And when they was growing up, we had hot toddies with honey and lemon and we had beer and they would taste that when they got of age, and as long as they're together you don't have to worry.

Because Mrs. Hayes took great care to explain the developing circumstances in her marital situation to young Anthony, he could not be disillusioned about his father's status in the home.

> My father is still my father. He comes around to visit us every once in awhile, but he just wasn't here sometimes when I needed him, so I counted on my brother for everything I needed.

Mrs. Hayes feels that it is important to prepare children for life by setting the correct tone even as the child is in the mother's womb. Spiritual food should be presented to the child even in these early stages of development. This cannot be done, she believes, without God's help.

> I prayed to God to help me plant good in that child even before it was born, because there's a lot a child can get before birth. And I was instructed in what to do and what not to do when I was carrying my child, 'cause whatever you do, whether the father or the mother, will somewhere be in the child. They gonna inherit some of that. It pays especially for young parents to do right so that everything will be right with the child even after birth. This is just nature, you know, that children will inherit some of those [physical and psychological patterns] from their parents.

Even with a diligent approach to prenatal care, she believes that reinforcement is necessary to insure desired child behavior. Mrs. Hayes has always insisted on respectful behavior from her children. Whether in the home or at school, the children would think twice before engaging in inappropriate behavior.

> Once I had an idea that one of my daughters was quite talkative [in her class]. So I bawled her out in front of the class and I told her the next time I was going to come and I was going to bring the strap. So, I didn't hear anymore from that.

The children in the Hayes's home were made aware, even at six and seven years old, that they were expected to be responsible persons. They were expected to be reliable and functional within the family unit. Mrs. Hayes demanded strong character in her children. Anthony recalls:

> We all had responsibilities even when I was in second or third grade. I had my own door key. My mother and father would go to work and

it was up to us to come home and do what we were supposed to do. And during lunch periods, I came home and ate my lunch and went back to school. When school was over, I came home and cleaned up and did whatever I had to do.

Mrs. Hayes feels that children are capable of operating as responsible persons. They must understand that they will have to endure the consequences of their actions.

Mrs. Hayes was careful to give verbal praise and otherwise reinforce acceptable behavior. She was not hesitant to give credit to her children for their accomplishments. Extreme care was taken during Anthony's early years to be liberal with her praise. Perhaps she felt that he needed these reassurances most at this time. Anthony remembers many of these occasions.

Well, she often—how do you say it—she often told me I was doing well; like when I started the math club in fourth grade. Or times when I was doing good in art—I had a great thing for art, I like to draw a lot—and little things I do with my hands. I used to go to craft and what have you and she often complimented me on these things.

The maxim "success breeds success" appears to describe Anthony's childhood years most accurately. At Christmastime, Anthony would examine his toys to see how they worked. He remembers he was always taking things apart, but he never built anything. He also remembers being rejected for a double promotion in the second grade. This experience jolted him.

The teacher was giving advanced double grades and during that time she didn't select me and I was sort of wondering why, so she explained to me my grades weren't all that good. I pouted a little bit, but after I got myself together, I started trying to do a little better and my math ability came out until, in third grade, I saw it was very good.

Mathematics is Anthony's best subject. He now handles sophisticated technical automobile blueprints requiring math expertise. While in the primary grades, Anthony had already begun to carve his niche. He was expected to study and do as well as he could.

When I was young I was at the head of the class. As far as math was concerned I understood just about everything she was saying. Since I was understanding, I had to explain things to others about what was happening. It just picked me up and that was why I chose it. People looked up to me.

In fourth grade, Anthony was given a larger responsibility. He headed the student math club in his class. The club's purpose was to think "up things we could help other students with, if they were slow." Mrs. Hayes liked the helping aspect of these activities. These early experiences have been repeated in high school.

AH: We have a math club today at Dunbar Vocational where students come to you on your free periods. If they need help you explain different things to help them with their classes.
RC: What's that called?
AH: That's the math-tutor club. We also have a slide rule club where we learn things on the slide rule and help the other students. We have our own badges and stuff.
RC: So ever since fourth grade, at various periods, you've been in positions where you served as a helper of others?
AH: Right. Very much so.

Anthony has been positively affected by these early experiences. A solid foundation appears to have been built through home and school activities. Through a sense of family togetherness developed over time, Anthony now exhibits an unassuming willingness to conform. He shares the basic norms and values of his mother.

Mental Health: Student Attitudes, Values, and Personality

One of the most salient features of the Hayes family is Anthony's marked maturity. He is able to function with an air of emotional control and self-awareness. His clear perception of his goals is especially noteworthy. He knows what he wants and will compete to get it. Anthony's school behavior reflects one aspect of this competitive orientation:

This Chinese guy, Sam Lee, he's a good friend of mine. We're competing to see whose rank is going to be the highest in the class. He's number 4, and I'm number 5. I like to compete for things like that. I see it as striving for something that we need. Something to make us go.

Anthony's relationship with his brothers, however, is stronger than that of his school buddies. He admires his twenty-year-old brother and wants to gauge his own success by usings his brother's accomplishments as a yardstick. Of his brother, Anthony says:

He did things so well, to me he was a perfectionist. He liked to have things done just right. He accomplished things by doing things that way. That's why I like to follow in his footsteps. But I want to go into the fields I see fit for me. I want to do things in the *manner* he did, not to do what he did. I had a competition with my brother, to be better than he was. It's still going on really. It's still going on.

Anthony wants to do as well as he can, thereby satisfying his mother and himself. Although competitive, he is cooperative in his relationships with others. Anthony never seems to misuse his independent stature. He is willing to help others. Mrs. Hayes is happy about this part of his personality.

Yes, he likes to work. He's very liberal. He speaks his mind. He doesn't hide anything. He's not tight. If his sister needs something, it's all right. If they call him and need something and he's got it, it's all right.

Anthony is a generous individual. His present values do not encompass the attainment of a large number of material items. Because he could not afford to buy a lot of clothes, a car, and so on, his present value system helps him avoid frustration.

I'm one of the luckiest guys in this neighborhood because my mother is giving me just about everything I need. It doesn't take that much to satisfy me because I don't need that much. I don't have to have that much in order to make it. You give me some shoes to walk and something to cover my back and school. I'm really involved in school now. That's all I need.

This attitude has been developed over time as an adaptive survival response. Like most other children, Anthony once wished for the things the other kids had. He considers these desires part of his "wild stage," a period he has since outgrown. As he describes it:

Well, I saw my friends doing things I wasn't allowed to do, or things they could do I didn't have enough money to do or something like that. I wanted some of these things, too. At the time I didn't realize my mother couldn't furnish some of the things they had, so I just had to overlook all of it. I always wanted the things other people had, but I knew I couldn't have them. So what could I do? I couldn't do anything.

Anthony had to come to grips with the financial circumstances in the Hayes household. Through the understanding of these circumstances, he was able to develop the patience to defer these desires.

Anthony's ability to function in this selfless manner is due at least in part to his self-awareness and his self-confidence. Anthony credits his brother Christopher for helping him appreciate his accomplishments and possessions. Anthony is comfortable with himself. Mrs. Hayes is awed by the scarcity of serious problems for him. In her judgment he seems to handle things very maturely.

I don't know any real problems that Anthony has had. There was an incident once when Anthony struck a boy who was abusing a girl down by my daughter's place. I don't know if the boy was molesting the girl or what, but anyway he struck the boy. That was when he was protecting a girl and she was one of my daughter's good neighbor friends. As far as anything else, if there was, it was minor. No real problem.

Self-confidence and desire exude from Anthony Hayes. He acknowledges his present accomplishments while striving for higher goals. His goals are strong and clear.

The main thing that influences me is my idea that I'm going to make it, get ahead. I want to be on top, and seeing that the rest of my family didn't make it, you know, I'm the last one. My brother started to go to college, but he got married and everything, and the one that's in college now, he's barely going, but I want to be the one who goes straight through, to make it all the way to the top.

Mrs. Hayes, a highly religious woman, has not been able to keep Anthony in the church. He still is, however, religiously oriented. Mrs. Hayes started Anthony in the church choir and other church activities, but he has not participated in a few years. He first started losing interest when part-time jobs made it difficult to find time.

And I just started steadily drifting off altogether. I still feel the same way. I feel people should get involved with their beliefs, but I don't feel I have to go to church to do it. My home is just as good as any place, so if I had to do any kind of religious acts, I feel I can do them here as well as anywhere else.

Anthony feels that his actions toward others, not his church attendance record, are more reflective of the quality of his moral and spiritual behavior. Anthony is proud of his membership in the school organization National Conference for Christians and Jews (NCCJ). He is involved in another multiracial group in which a person can "just talk out the problems you had in school and around your home and things like that." He feels simply that "we're no different from other people." While proud of his own ancestral heritage, he does not get terribly excited over racial issues. He likes to avoid hate-oriented encounters with members of other races. His approach to prejudice can be seen in his account of a recent incident.

I was right on 43d Street and there's nothing but Blacks in that neighborhood, and I got on the [subway] and I sat down right next to this White lady and she looked at me and said, "Why don't you go sit by your own kind." I looked at her and said, "What's wrong with you? I paid my money and I'm going to sit where I want to sit." So I sat down, and she stood up and looked at me and started calling me all kinds of niggers and this, that, and the other. Everybody was looking and saying, "Don't move, sit right there. If she don't like that, she can move." And we kept riding. She was still standing up at 35th Street and she moved to another place and sat down. This other Black lady said, "I like her nerve," and she got up and went back there and sat down next to her and the White lady got up again, and went to another seat. Another Black person got up and sat next to her and she stood up all the rest of the way downtown. I was shocked at first, but I started to laugh, thinking how ridiculous it was. When I got home I told my mother about it and she was saying, "You have to look over that, some people just ain't got it." I think it was hilarious.

Anthony's reaction to this incident is almost predictable in light of his mature approach to life. He has developed a successful coping strategy for comfort in his environment. He states:

> When things get downright serious and they might ruin me or ruin my ideas, I try to avoid them, get away from them if I can. I don't get nervous or mad about anything. It just takes a lot to upset me. I laugh at something before I get mad.

Anthony has developed a strong-willed approach to life. He is able to avoid being psychologically and emotionally upset by his environment. He is disciplined—capable of sticking with a task with which he is involved. An active person, Anthony is most relaxed after he has accomplished his chores.

> When I want peace and quiet, I usually go back in my room and go to bed, just lay down and go to sleep. Now that I started wrestling, I want to get more sleep. I sleep very well now that I'm busy all the time.

Anthony's mother feels that his exposure to a loving, secure home environment is the key to his success. She has encouraged her children to express themselves in family conversations. She feels she can learn a lot by listening to her children.

> He's very understanding, he's a thoughtful child; he doesn't talk too much. But sometimes he will. If anything comes up, he knows how to express himself and he will do that. Which I allowed all the kids to do this. I don't think it's fair for a parent to not allow his child to speak. I listen 'cause even now, I'll go say something and they'll say, "Mama, you shouldn't say it that way." They are my children true enough, but they can tell me a lot of things to help me.

We can see here a pattern of familial communication and interaction in which the parent is a dominant, but not dominating, figure. Although the primary roles may be clearly defined with respect to who has authority, vehicles are created which allow the child free expression. In this state it is often easier to work with the children. They feel a larger involvement in the family process and, in turn, take it much more seriously. They also receive essential practice in thinking and using the standard language.

In-Home Living Patterns

The attitudinal disposition of Anthony Hayes is family-oriented. He will readily admit that, except for the people he works with at school, he does not do a great deal of "hanging out." On weekends he stays home most often. Most of his out-of-school activities are family-related. Both Anthony and his mother feel that he is more influenced by his family than by his peers. Again, the influence of his older brother is strong. Anthony can cite many instances of having been inspired and otherwise influenced by his twenty-year-old brother. His choice of a career (architectural drafting) was a decision inspired by the brother, who would bring drawings home from school. Anthony initially wanted to share in the esteem his brother enjoyed in sports. Of his brother, Anthony states:

> When he was about 12 he started playing baseball and won two trophies, and the next year he won two more trophies. Then he went to high school, he was running track and cross country and played baseball in his senior year, and he came out with about six trophies and three major letters, and he was also in the band so he was one of those busy type persons also. At first he started criticizing me, asking me why I didn't play baseball or why I didn't go into sports or whatever and after he left and I got into it, he started complimenting me on the things I was doing. And really that's what started me. I was a little bit jealous, and did say, "Wow, if he can do it, I can do it too."

Anthony's brother offered the support and encouragement that the father could not provide. Anthony admired and respected his brother enough to try to follow in his footsteps. Mrs. Hayes encouraged this respect through her insistence that the oldest child in the home at any given time should get the same respect accorded to adults. The oldest person was an authority figure. At the same time, the older person was expected to help and respect the younger ones. By establishing the sibling roles in this manner, Mrs. Hayes managed to get parentlike assistance in guiding the children. The intended purposes were clearly served.

> [My brother] just took over, like he took the place of my father. He corrected me when I was wrong, chastized me in the right way. He just set goals for me, things when I was young. If I just didn't understand he'd explain to me. He helped me out in a lot of ways. I always looked up to him. Just about everything I'd do I looked up to him. My father doesn't live here, and he was a great inspiration to me.

Even Anthony's older sister was able to guide his behavior ("She was like my mother"). Each person was expected to care for the next. This process is being repeated now that Anthony has nieces and nephews. He takes the youngsters to movies, bowling alleys, and other outings on weekends. The children do understand that he is the authority figure and the person to be respected. Again, the delineation of roles is functional and clear.

On Saturdays Anthony is expected to help his mother with housecleaning. He has developed a thorough distaste for this activity, preferring to "rest and do other things." He feels his weekday ritual is rigorous enough. Since elementary school, he has had full school days, followed by a homework session, and then a relaxation period watching television until bedtime. Occasionally he would visit friends who lived close by—most often next door neighbors. In high school, Anthony's time has been even more circumscribed by school activities. He normally awakens about 6:00 A.M. to leave home by 7:00 A.M. He does not return until 7:00 P.M. on three nights and not until 10:00 P.M. on two nights. He is usually ready to retire for the evening after he eats his late dinner.

Very little time is spent "doing nothing" in the home. Mrs. Hayes exhibits immense control over Anthony's home activities. She says:

> I never allowed too much visiting. I never let them visit too much and I never had time to let anybody else's children come here too much. It's not that I think I'm better than anybody but we always had the situation where everybody had something to do when they got home—the dishes, the cleaning, whatever. And then they'd do their homework, and then they had to sit down there and watch the television.

There is marked parental curtailment of the children's spatial parameters outside the home. Mrs. Hayes decides on Anthony's out-of-home activities. Because most are school related, she approves. Even while in the home, activities are outlined and most time must be spent doing something Mrs. Hayes considers purposeful. There is clearly a major maternal influence in the shaping of Anthony's time and space directions. By controlling where he goes and when he goes, Mrs. Hayes can influence what he does, with whom he does it, and when he does it. This fact can be seen time and again in the Hayes home.

Mrs. Hayes has made it a point to watch over her children's outside activities. She has often arranged to be with her children when they are playing outdoor games. She says:

> One time I was on the bowling team and sometimes I would take them with me. And a lot of evenings when I would come in, I would go wherever they were playing baseball. And then the father was good about that too. A lot of evenings if he knew where they were playing, he'd go.

Mrs. Hayes is critical of young mothers who do not follow their children's out-of-home activities. Parental supervision, she feels, should not end when the child leaves home. Of these parents she says:

> They just stay home and stay in their apartments and don't worry about it. So therefore if their children are out, they don't know what they're doing or what they're getting themselves involved in.

Because she recognizes the potential for a young child to become involved with street gangs and other mischievous persons, Mrs. Hayes feels justified in screening Anthony's friends. She explains:

I'll tell you, I never allow my kids to go too much with their friends. Wherever they go, I got to know where they are. I never allow too much visiting, not too much parties, even birthday parties or anything like that. I was always afraid that there might be something happening, since there is so much going on in the streets. So I just didn't allow it. So this is why most recreation [my kids] have is with each other.

Mrs. Hayes has been highly protective of Anthony. She has attempted to curb his associations with the boys in the projects. Social visits involving boys in the neighborhood are rare. Most of Anthony's associates are school chums who live in other neighborhoods. (Anthony attends a well-established vocational school which is also outside the immediate neighborhood.) Mrs. Hayes described one situation in which Anthony had developed a friendship with a young man living in the same apartment building.

He had one boy coming in here a few times and the boy would go back there [to the bedroom] and talk with him which I never cared too much for him going back there because there would be others coming in. But now the boy was always respectable. Around me, he was always nice. I liked him, he was quiet. He got a nice, quiet mother. But he ended up going into the army and he don't want to come back here and live. So that's about the only friend that Anthony had come in from the building.

This watchful process has been long and consistent. Anthony exhibits a strong moral sense of what is right and wrong, and accepts his mother's constraints. He explains that:

My mother doesn't give me everything I want. She gives me what I need, what she thinks is right she gives me, nothing out of the way.

Although Anthony now feels a bit more comfortable about accepting visits from his neighborhood peers, he still avoids inviting people to his home. He understands that his mother is still nervous about the notion. Even on dates, he will avoid bringing a girl to his neighborhood. Most of his dates live in homes in the south suburbs. He says:

I usually visit them, because I wouldn't want them to come up in this building because I wouldn't want them to get hurt or anything so I usually visit them, and some of their parents would refuse to let their daughters do it anyway.

However, there are hints that Anthony is beginning to venture into his outside environment more than in the past. As a basically outgoing, fun-loving person, he now feels somewhat stifled. He realizes that within a few months he will have to be away from his mother on his own. Anthony is attempting to prepare himself for this occasion. He has tried to explain this to his mother, who has not been totally receptive.

> One of the [problems] we have now is the fact I don't do housework like I used to. Mainly I be tired most of the time when I come in, and on weekends I want to get some fun and go visit some of my friends. So that's one of the disputes we've been having now.

Anthony admits that his mother has allowed him more freedom of mobility in the past two years. He attributes her relaxed posture to a perceived reduction in murders in the area and to his chronological development.

It is not surprising that Mrs. Hayes has been instrumental in the selection of Anthony's past part-time jobs. Mrs. Hayes has made sure that he was involved in work environments that were well supervised.

> The only jobs he's had was restaurants. He never had no paper route because that was such a rough job. Sometimes they jumped those kids and take papers and different things. So he never had a paper route. Now he worked out there where I worked during the summer. And he worked at this pizza place also—Nicky's. He worked at Nicky's restaurant in the evenings after school. He worked at McDonald's for a little while, and last summer he worked at a store selling nuts. But that's the last job he had.

Mrs. Hayes has attempted to keep her children occupied with "wholesome" activities, both inside and outside the home. While a slight resistance to this maternal control may be detected, Mrs. Hayes does not appear to have encountered any major conflicts. Educationally, Anthony is now a success and appears to be psychologicaly well adjusted. Mrs. Hayes explained her reasoning in expecting her children to be continually active.

> With the track and baseball and after-school studies, they were very busy so that when they got home, they were darn near tired. They didn't have any time for anything much else.

Mrs. Hayes has had satisfying results from her toe-the-line approach. Her children have not become victims of the environment to the extent most have.

Educational Orientation in the Home

Mathematics has been the subject which has been the focal point of Anthony's school success. Most of the praise and reinforcement he has received was based on his math accomplishments. Further, his eighth grade reading score was over twelve months behind the national norm. He improved this score in his high school freshman year, after being tentatively admitted to the selective technical school based on extremely high math scores. Now school is the most important facet of Anthony's life. Almost all of his aspirations grow out of school-oriented activities. He does not place a high value on material objects. New clothing, cars, and so on are not crucial goals at this time in his life. Anthony's mother is supportive of and encourages his value system. She is pleased with his emphasis on schooling. She has, indeed, encouraged this direction toward educational attainment. Mrs. Hayes is happy about her son's strong goal orientation. She describes Anthony's "drive."

> Now since he got in high school, his goal is education. This seem like it's mostly on his mind—his education. That's mostly what he's involved in. He's not interested in clothing or cars or anything. He's not like a lot of youngsters, cause he feels like he's going to get it. And he will; I wouldn't take anything for him. His understanding, the way he accepts things is like a much older person. He has a better understanding than a lot of older people. And he know when he's doing the best he can. He don't expect to push and reach the top too fast. He's taking his time and he's going gradually and I'm proud of him. He's looking ahead to the future. He was telling me about the house he was going to build one day. He's going to build that house. He's got high hopes.

Anthony has developed a strong sense of direction. He engages in purposeful behavior to meet the goals he establishes. He is on a mission ("If I don't, who will?"). His primary goal is to be the first from his family to graduate from college. He feels his chances of having an adequate financial existence would then be heightened since he theoretically would be able to enter the opportunity structure at higher levels. He says:

> I want to go to school so I can. I'll tell you one of the goals is to get my master's in mathematics and architectural drafting. That's why I want to go to school. If you're going to make it in society you got to be up there with everybody else.

After high school, Anthony plans to enter General Motors Institute in Detroit. He will be trained to design and develop automobiles. As an architectural engineer, Anthony expects to utilize his mechanical drawing skills. He will pursue the bachelor of science degree at this highly specialized technical college. He plans to live with his brother and sister-in-law while in Detroit.

Mrs. Hayes is happy that she raised happy, successful children. She sees schooling as a necessary vehicle to success in today's industrial society. Part of her role as a parent, she feels, is to encourage an academic orientation with boys and girls. Children must be educationally prepared for adulthood, since they will be adults a much longer time than they were children.

> And the cost of living is so much higher for most poor people, it takes two paychecks to make it. And so I try to encourage the girls

to go to school, too. It's not a sure thing how the marriage will go; it's not a sure thing.

The parents, she feels, have an additional responsibility to guide the child by attempting to offer assistance with school problems whenever possible. She has discovered that often her children only needed a little help to get started. "Then they would work it out for themselves." Mrs. Hayes perceives that her role is to help Anthony help himself. With this approach Anthony may maintain his independence. One excerpt from an interview highlights this fact.

AH: Oh yes, my mother loves to see us achieve things. Not for her to say, "My son is doing this or that." She just loves to see us make it, knowing that we are getting somewhere.
RC: Did she ever tell you that?
AH: Oh yes, she told me that quite a few times. Like right now even though she's sort of mad about me wrestling, [reducing] my weight and all, she's still glad to see me do what I am, participating, because she knows I'm doing well.

Mrs. Hayes is "looking forward" to Anthony's departure to college. She wants and expects her children to do well. When one of Anthony's grades recently dropped from an A to a C during wrestling season, Mrs. Hayes told him to consider quitting the team. Anthony decided to try to continue to wrestle and still raise the grade. He worked harder at his academic task and did raise the grade. Mrs. Hayes was pleased that her academic expectation had been met.

Anthony tries to please his mother because he wants her to be happy and respects her wisdom in handling life's trials and tribulations. He has faith that her requirements will be beneficial for him. The purpose Mrs. Hayes has for Anthony is clear—to become a healthy, sane, moral, upright, and intelligent person capable of making a living.

Mrs. Hayes has shown involvement in Anthony's schooling through periodic visits to the teachers. She will visit during formal open houses as well as on regular school days. She does not feel that the teacher should carry total responsibility for her children's education.

No, I don't leave it all to the teacher. I was always interested in what they were doing and how things were going in school. I used to take sometimes a whole day and at different times go around to different one's classes and see their teachers. I did this all down through grade school, high school and what have you.

Parental contact with teachers is viewed as mandatory behavior. Mrs. Hayes believes that a lot can be done for the child by periodically "hanging around" the schoolhouse.

Anthony is actively involved in a maze of school activities which enhance his educational orientation. Some of his out-of-class activities involve being president of the school's National Honor Society, president of the Lettermen's Club, a member of the Spanish Club, attending a college algebra course at the University of Chicago, and a host of other projects.

At home Anthony has engaged in certain educational rituals since he was in the third grade. Perhaps the most important ritual for Anthony was the homework ritual. He has been expected to do a school exercise every week night. His mother would check to make sure he had done this work. Anthony remembers his elementary school evenings:

> I came home and did my homework, and after that was when I went out and played because my mother always believed in doing what you had to do first, first.

Mrs. Hayes remembers Anthony's grade school days:

> The first thing they did when they came home from school, the bed was made up. That's the first thing they did was make up their beds from that morning. And then they did their homework. And only then if they had dishes to do, or whatever, they would do that. They had to do this before they could watch television or play or anything. So when I'd come in a lot of times I'd check over their homework. Booker, who was the oldest one, would help with anything that needed to be done.

Another educational ritual involved regular talks between Mrs. Hayes and Anthony to assess the importance of schooling. At these times Anthony was able to gain a better understanding of the purposes behind his mother's expectations. With this understanding he was better able to sit and perform the tasks. This early understanding might account for his present day high valuation of schooling.

The Hayes family represents an example of how love and reinforcement can be used to effect a positive attitude toward schooling. Mrs. Hayes's experience with her older children afforded her the capacity to "put it all together" in her parenting of Anthony. Her basically conservative approach to child-rearing can also be seen as an important factor in Anthony's development.

The Johnsons

The Family Theme and Background

The search for opportunity has carried many young, poor, recently-married southern Black couples to the northern cities. These families usually consist of people willing to work hard and regularly in exchange for fair wages. Once in the North, however, these families may endure poor work experiences and marital difficulties which precipitate the disintegration of their dreams and ambitions. Having experienced a certain amount of success during happier days, a dream-shattering divorce or separation virtually forces each marriage partner to find an alternative life-style in which he or she can best function. For the female partner this may require plotting an independent course for the survival of her attenuated family. In these mother-dominated homes, economic, educational, and personal improvements are often pursued with a quiet, steady determination.

At twenty-six, Mrs. Fannie Mae Johnson moved to the west side of Chicago in 1961 with her husband and children. The children, all girls, were aged 11, 7, and 5 years. A few years later, Mrs. Johnson moved into a south side public housing facility with the girls. Sheila Johnson, the youngest offspring and subject of our inquiry, was thirteen years old at that time. She was entering high school. After the divorce in 1965, the family had occupied another apartment in the same south-side area, prior to their current residence. Poverty conditions typified each of these environments.

Only three months ago, Mrs. Johnson moved again. This time she chose a far south-side apartment with more space. Sheila decided not to transfer from her current school, since she will be graduating in four months. Mrs. Johnson considers her new apartment to be better than the high-rise facility. The oldest girl, 23-year-old Patsy, has been gone from the family since she entered college six years ago. She now teaches in one of the city public schools.

The apartment feels more spacious (five rooms) than the other homes visited. There is a sense of quiet and calm in the sparsely furnished apartment. Mrs. Johnson and her two youngest daughters reside here alone. There is no loud music, yelling, or other distracting noise. The feeling generated is of a "thinking" environment. Except for the television, magazines and newspapers are the only forms of entertainment in evidence.

Mrs. Johnson, now thirty-eight, is a no–nonsense, intelligent woman. While functioning as head of the household, Mrs. Johnson works in a low-paying clerical position assisting nurses. Wise even beyond her years, Mrs. Johnson is able to articulate her thoughts with a rare precision and verve. She is a very dark skinned woman with short black hair and perfect white teeth. Her hands appear strong and firm—almost rough. She stands about 5 feet 5 inches and weighs 125 pounds with a gait which reflects a prideful image. There is awareness in her eyes. Her long, sloping forehead leads to a large nose and pursed lips. Self-confident and casual, she customarily enjoys an after-dinner cigarette—sometimes with a beer.

Magnolia Sheila Johnson is a 17-year-old high school senior. She prefers to be called Sheila; Magnolia is too "country sounding." She stands about 5 feet 7 inches tall, thin, with a chocolate-dark complexion, wide nose and large lips. She wears various Afro hairstyles. A basically pleas ant, talkative person, Sheila also possesses a remarkably piercing gaze. When she looks, one may perceive that she is reading his mind. She makes a careful effort to choose her words so that she is completely understood. She is now in the upper 5 percent academic group of high school seniors at her school and she occupies a spot in the school honor society.

Sheila's mother was born into poverty in Mississippi to sharecropper parents in 1936. Sheila's father was born into a similar situation. Mrs. Fannie Mae Johnson was a mere 15 years old in 1951 when she left the South with her new husband. Soon after their arrival, they both managed to secure jobs—he in construction work, she as a maintenance person. As a young girl, Fannie Mae's parents raised her in a loving, yet no-nonsense fashion. As the youngest girl in a family of sixteen, Mrs. Johnson remembers her parents as old, conservative, and intelligent. She still marvels at the ability of her parents to raise so many children successfully. She attributes this feat to the time her parents spent with the children and the firm hand by which they dictated house policy. Farming offered the family seasonal employment which allowed everyone to work together and be close to one another many more hours of the day. Mrs. Johnson observes:

> Well, my parents had more time to apply to us than I did for the simple reason the southern living is quite different from the northern living. The southern living is you working during the nice warm days. During the winter months is mostly the time school is going on and [they] don't have to do anything but sit in the house and eat and sleep.

Mrs. Johnson speaks fondly of her experiences as a young girl in the South. She remembers that her mother wielded profound influence on her as she was growing up. She remembers her mother as a teacher of Life who engaged the children in regular discussions to help them become mentally alert.

> When I was young, in school, my mother related to me as good as any mother could relate to her daughter. She wasn't a degreed woman, but I would take all the degrees in the world and put a match to them because they didn't know as much about life and living as my mother did without a degree. We had family conferences with my mother and father. It was a systematic thing but it wasn't on a weekly basis. It was once in a while we'd sit around the table and talk.

Mrs. Johnson derived a strong sense of love, warmth, and stability from her family interactions. She believes that she was prepared to handle life through her early southern experiences.

Early Child-Rearing and Familial Practices

Mrs. Johnson bases her child-rearing orientation on the one she experienced as a child. She feels there is a certain virtue inherent in being firm with children. Parental firmness, she believes, helps the child remember her or his role as a child. He (or she) was not an adult and would not be treated as such. Mrs. Johnson feels that, while firm, she has been more lenient with Sheila than her mother had been with her. She remembers that in her family the roles were clearly defined.

> But really, old people were firmer with their children than I was with mine, because you never knew if your opinion counted or not, because very seldom were you asked your opinion. You were to sit and listen, and if you were asked something and you gave an answer, you wouldn't know if they took your advice or not, because they would never tell you.

Mrs. Johnson thinks of herself as being more accepting of her own daughter's ideas. Still, she believes in creating firm roles and expectations as early as possible.

> My philosophy is, you have got to start at the beginning. You can't wait till they get half grown to let them know who is who and what is what.

Mrs. Johnson, we should remember, has been the parent primarily involved with the task of training her girls. Mr. Johnson, when he was in the home, felt that the woman of the house was naturally better suited for child training. He only participated in the guidance of his girls when a "problem" arose. The normal, everyday processes of child rearing were left to Mrs. Johnson. He'd say, "'They're girls,' and mostly leave it up to me." Although Mrs. Johnson did not totally agree with her husband's pronouncements, she accepted his reluctance to take equal responsibility for the day-to-day training of the children.

Mrs. Johnson received additional child rearing assistance from her mother. When the children were young, their grandmother often baby-sat while Mrs. Johnson worked during the day. This practice ended when Sheila became of school age. Mrs. Johnson's older daughters, Robin and Neecy, proved to be instrumental in the early training process. Already having gone through the early primary grades, Robin was most capable of assisting her younger sister in many curriculum-related matters. Sheila states:

> Anything I had trouble with, I came and asked her about it, and she would explain it to me. I would run home to my sister and ask her about it, "Well, Robin, why?" And she would sit down and tell me.

It became extremely important that Robin, the older child, take time with Sheila since Sheila's teachers exhibited "impatience" with her. Sheila demanded, sometimes unsuccessfully, large shares of attention from her teachers. The teachers had other children who needed attention. Similarly, her working mother could not do it all. The older sister–baby sister liaison tended to help close the gap between school requirements and child productivity.

Mrs. Johnson believes that school-age children are old enough to be held responsible for most behavior. It is within their power, she believes, to make correct choices. At school age they have, or should have, already learned the difference between right and wrong. They therefore, she says, can be legitimately held accountable for their behavior. Mrs. Johnson describes her early techniques for child training.

> At first I taught her how to wash ash trays and not to break them and how to care about things. Everybody had their own share to do; nobody was dependent on the other, unless someone wasn't feeling well, naturally you have to pitch in and help. But if everybody was feeling OK, and nobody sick, everybody had to do their own work.

Sheila learned to work with her family as a team member. These early parental expectations, miniscule as they may seem, served as initial goals for Sheila to reach. She had a job; her goal was to do her job well. Later, academic responsibilities would be added to these house cleaning responsibilities.

By watching her older sisters, Sheila quickly learned the excitement derived from reading. Because of her tremendous fondness for books, Sheila did not find her early school days difficult. She came to school with a well-developed interest in reading. Sheila says:

> I was interested in reading. I was always after my mother saying, "I want a new book. I want a new book. I seen so-and-so with a new book." I always loved to read. I never did what you call "study." I always liked to read, and I guess that gave me the ability to understand.

Durings these early years, Sheila was fortunate enough to receive attention from a variety of individuals—all of whom contributed in some way to her eventual success in school. Still, Mrs. Johnson guided the levels and direction of this attention. As the mother and provider, she has been the most consistent influence on Sheila. Sheila now expects maternal support and encouragement.

> My mother always praised us. If we came home with all A's or all B's, it was always, "that's nice" or "that's good," and she was always ready to tell us if we did bad, like "you know you can do better, what's wrong," or, "are you having trouble," or some thing, you know. [Even now] that's nothing, really.

For any child to consider this type of parental activity as "nothing" suggests it has been almost as routine as eating or sleeping. It is clear that Sheila's academic-oriented personality has been developed over her seventeen years. Early familial practices such as large amounts of time and attention paid to Sheila in a goal-oriented household have clearly been instrumental in her academic development. Sheila's grandmother (herself a mother of sixteen children), who often cared for her in the preschool years, helped nurture a child capable of overcoming certain deficiencies of the neighborhood school.

Mental Health: General Attitudes, Values, and Personality

Sheila's psychological orientation can perhaps be best understood within the context of her family. Mrs. Johnson believes strongly that women should marry and procreate. This attitude represents a psychological tradition carried from generation to generation in her family. Mrs. Johnson also believes women should be educated so that they could be self-sustaining in the event of a "bad" marriage. Having herself worked on many relatively wretched, low-paying jobs, Mrs. Johnson recognizes the benefits to be accrued from obtaining an education. Upon her divorce, Mrs. Johnson learned first-hand that a divorced, Black female high school dropout could not normally expect to provide adequately for her family. Mrs. Johnson considers her present financial struggle a result of an early "mistake"—dropping out of high school to get married. Consistent with her attitudes, Mrs. Johnson has attempted to prepare her daughters so that they will never have to undergo the same experience she has undergone. Her goals are to see Sheila get an education and raise a family.

Sheila has been most influenced by her own mother. While claiming status as an independent individual, Sheila still acknowledges a heavy debt to her mother. She explains:

> I want to be myself, my own individual. I want to make myself; I don't want to model myself after anybody—but my mother.

Sheila has learned to derive her feelings of belongingness and self worth from her mother. It has been largely through her mother that Sheila has come to believe in herself. She further expounds:

> I feel like this, I want my mother to be proud of me. Maybe she's proud of me now for the things I've done and accomplished, but I want to do something to make her sort of happy, because she's made me happy in my years—made me mad sometimes—but she's always made me happy. And when I was mad at her, it was her I always went to to make me happy again because she was just always there.

Sheila, as the "baby of the family," has been given less household responsibility and more parental attention than her older sisters. Mrs. Johnson believes Sheila was more "protected" than the older girls. In an attempt to prevent Sheila's "taking it for granted," Mrs. Johnson and the older sisters sometimes "tease" Sheila about her "privileged" status. This teasing prompts Sheila to do her "share." She says:

They used to like teasing me a lot and I couldn't stand it. Always telling me I was lazy and spoiled and stuff and I wasn't ever going to be nothing and just everything and I was going to be a "bunch of sense" laying around on mother all my life.

Sheila and her mother appear to have had a satisfactory period of what Eric Erickson has called "trust versus basic mistrust."[1] Sheila feels confident that her mother will provide her with protection whenever it is morally "right."

Boys are slowly becoming a part of Sheila's life. Her mother is teaching her the art of interacting with men. Mrs. Johnson encourages Sheila to be ostensibly submissive while still maintaining her sense of identity and individuality. Sheila's interaction with her boyfriend (and prom date) indicates her awareness of sex-role behavior. Normally outspoken and witty, Sheila still speaks her mind but is careful to avoid talking to the boy in any ego-deflating manner. Her demeanor is amicable and friendly, even slightly submissive. Sheila is adamantly opposed to making occupational choices which are derived from sex-role stereotypes. Mrs. Johnson has attempted to instill a strong sense of womanhood while still indicating to Sheila her importance as a person. Indeed, Mrs. Johnson reveals that she has taught Sheila that womanhood is good in its own right. Who should Sheila rely on? Mrs. Johnson says, "No man. Themselves and God." Men, she feels, are not the saviors of women. Therefore, girls should not, she believes, be taught that men are saviors. Sheila feels women should aspire to higher goals. Sheila describes her feelings:

I have never really liked the idea of being a secretary because I always thought of that as very stereotyped for young ladies; mostly every young lady you know. I wouldn't mind being a business administrator. Right now everybody up in school is taking typing.

We see traits of independence, self-reliance and high aspirations in Sheila's comments.

Racial tensions have not yet become a reality for Sheila. A product of the postrevolutionary 1970s, Sheila considers discussions of race, slavery, and the like, as fruitless exercises.

Most of the time I don't participate in things like that because I think in order for you to have or talk about a problem that's racial, you have to be out there to deal with one. So by your sitting back talking about "slavery this and slavery that" and "blah blah this," and going on and on, I mean like that happened a long time ago and if that's what's going to hinder your mind, you might as well go back and take yourself back with it.

Sheila's Gordon Persons Conceptions System profile indicates she strongly identifies as a female and as a student. Possessing a generally conservative social outlook, she set the acquisition of security as her major life goal. A normal teenager, Sheila likes excitement and recreation. She attends church irregularly but exhibits goodwill toward others. Sheila is further categorized as unhappy with her present situation in life but confident that the future will be better for her. A strong sense of self can also be detected and she can still work with others.

In-Home Living Patterns

The Johnson household is quiet, orderly, and maternally controlled. While the girls are allowed access to the household space, all activities have parental limitations and expectations with respect to the time and space dimensions. Family living patterns function so that all the family members are independent with each other. Duties and responsibilities are assigned by Mrs. Johnson and shared by all household members, who rely on each other for a smooth flow of activities. Cooking and cleaning chores are shared by all. In some ways, attempts are made at egalitarianism but a high degree of maternal structure permeates the household.

There is no one in the Johnson home during the weekdays. Mrs. Johnson works until 4:30 P.M. and does not return home before 5:15 P.M. On some days, her college classes keep her in school a bit longer. Normally Sheila will be the first one home at 3:00 P.M. She then engages in a daily ritual.

> I come home at 3:00 and catch the 3:00 story [on television]. Then at 3:30 it depends on how much homework I have, if it's a lot, I'll start on it and if it's not, I might watch television, the 3:30 movie, or fix me something to eat and take a nap, get up and do the homework. Later I eat dinner and wash the dishes, study and by at least 10:30 I'm back in bed.

Sheila's 19-year-old sister, who works and goes to school, does not return home until about 6:00 P.M. The oldest sister is now a school teacher and no longer lives at home, opting instead for her own apartment. Dinner is the only meal the family can eat together. Mrs. Johnson usually cooks on weekends; all weekend meals are eaten together even though everyone is involved in independent activities. Shopping, watching movies, reading, washing, and visiting are examples of these weekend activities.

Mrs. Johnson expects Sheila and Lucy to be capable of handling all aspects of house maintenance. Since Lucy now works *and* goes to school (junior college), Sheila is expected to do a lot of the housework. She has the most "free" time. Mrs. Johnson explains:

> [Sheila does] the work sometimes, housekeeping, cooking, and she had to learn these things. She doesn't work when she's out of school on the 45–15 plan [45 days in school, 15 days vacation year around] and I do work. It's no more than right she help share the work, because she lives here too, and if she has nothing to do and I have to

work, there's nothing wrong with her cleaning up and fixing dinner or washing or ironing, the works, and she knows how to do it all.

Sheila has been performing chores around the house for years. She is accustomed to this responsibility. She understands that her mother is working everyday to provide for her welfare. Roles are well defined. The interactional processes between Sheila and her mother are smooth and casual. There is seldom any bickering; instead family members attempt to enjoy one another. It is understood by all that Mrs. Johnson is the "parent." In one field observation we see an instance of this process.

Mrs. Johnson and Sheila have a type of buddy-buddy relationship in which Mrs. Johnson views herself as "the parent in a parent-child relationship." At times Mrs. Johnson leans on Sheila as a friend might. As I sit in the living room, I can see the two laughing at the dining room table. Sheila continues, pointing to Mrs. Johnson's stomach which is slightly paunchy. Sheila says, "I know you tell people you don't eat my cooking, but they know that's not true. You're wearing the evidence." They laugh again as Mrs. Johnson says, "OK, you see if you get any lunch money tomorrow." Mrs. Johnson looks into the living room at me and says, "She keeps me on the alert about my figure. Otherwise, I really *would* gain weight." Laughing, I said, "You two seem to have a lot of fun together." Lighting a cigarette she said, "Yes, we do; but she knows I'm her mother and I run this ship."

Mrs. Johnson and Sheila are able to talk openly about most subjects. Mrs. Johnson accepts friendly cajoling from Sheila. We see that Mrs. Johnson still subtly reminds Sheila who is the head of the household. By being the person responsible for providing Sheila's "lunch money," Mrs. Johnson is indicating the support pattern in the home. Sheila relies on her mother for food, clothing, and shelter. Still, the mutual respect and acceptance of family roles makes playful communication possible.

Sheila maintains a strong love and admiration for her mother. She has seen her mother struggle for years to attain a minimum level of existence; she also sees the present-day effort her mother puts forth to obtain money. It does not upset Sheila at all that her mother expects her to operate within well-defined parameters. Indeed, Sheila attributes her own successes to her mother's basically watchful, guiding, but flexible child-rearing approach.

Yes, I've had the freedom of choosing. Now I have more freedom choosing what I want and don't want than I did in the past. But I want to model myself after my mother as being a good woman, a good provider for my family if I ever have one, being strong and being able to get through—which describes a lot of things she's been through. Her strength held us together all these years.

Sheila is impressed by the intelligence her mother has continually exhibited in the day-to-day efforts at survival.

In spite of low income, Mrs. Johnson has been slowly improving her meager financial picture. In a community where some are starving, Mrs. Johnson and her girls are eating regularly. This fact in itself is commendable. Mrs. Johnson is grateful to her mother for "pointing me in the right direction."

> Most of the credit I give to my mother because she was firm and fair and straight with me. I think some of it rubbed off on me, and I was firm with my kids. Maybe in some areas not firm enough and in some a little too firm, you know, and I grew up learning to mind my own business, and I taught them the same thing. I grew up learning to pick my friends, and I've never liked a crowd or cared for a crowd and I teach them the same thing. Don't deal with a person by what someone else says; deal with them as a human being. You don't have to visit nobody every day in order to be a friend, and you don't have to be loud to be seen, and if you live and give respect, you'll get it. Maybe not from everybody but from most people you'll get respect.

We can see the value transmission between generations. Mrs. Johnson is strongly supportive of the child-rearing techniques which have aided in her personal development as well as the development of her children. Discipline and structure, within boundaries, are thought to be important as long as the child is in the home. Mrs. Johnson explains:

> FMJ: I don't think a mother's firmness is ever eliminated; regardless of how old the child is, she's always giving advice—what you should or should not do. But naturally, it is eliminated once you is grown and self-dependent in your own apartment or married.
> RC: Do you consider yourself a strict parent?
> FMJ: My children say I am, but I don't consider myself strict.
> RC: And what's the difference as you see it?
> FMJ: The difference as I see it is, strict, you don't have any privileges or pleasure. Firm is pleasure but there's a limitation.
> RC: Has this always been your guiding light as you raised your children?
> FMJ: Yes.

Mrs. Johnson has found that it is necessary to keep her own life under control in order to guide and protect the lives of her children. For years she has had to exercise discipline, self-control, and perseverance. She views the children's welfare as a perennial parental responsibility. Sheila perceives her mother's willingness to stay home and tend to her children's needs as indicative of parental interest.

She was interested. She's always taken part in what we did since we were small. She's always been there if we wanted something, and if we couldn't have it or if she didn't have the money right then and there, she'd always explain why. And she'd say, "Baby, you really don't need it, it's just something you want, and I'm looking out for your needs." And she was always there to take care of the needs that we had.

Mrs. Johnson's firm posture is acceptable to Sheila because it is laced with mother's love. This love appears to grow out of the strong respect Sheila and her mother have for one another. Sheila recognizes that Mrs. Johnson is primarily interested in seeing her children live the best life possible.

Mrs. Johnson exercises considerable control over three crucial areas in Sheila's life: her time, space, and friendships. This control is viewed by Mrs. Johnson as a protective measure against detrimental societal influences. As a young girl, Sheila was allowed to attend recreational activities, games, and social events only when accompanied by a relative. Usually these relatives were Sheila's older sisters, two nephews whom Mrs. Johnson considers "trustworthy," and Mrs. Johnson herself. Sheila was never allowed to walk to school alone. Her two older sisters accompanied her to school through eighth grade. Mrs. Johnson would tell Sheila to accept their guidance because "I know what's best for you."

Mrs. Johnson is keenly aware of Sheila's use of time and space. She has stressed to Sheila the importance of using time wisely. There is a perpetual knowledge of Sheila's level of performance within her time and space dimensions. Mrs. Johnson explains how this process was brought about.

There was a time for pleasure—we all had time for pleasure, my whole family. There was a time for TV watching and there was a time for playing which was included in the pleasure; and there was a time you had to study, and you couldn't just look at the book, you had to study, because you had to prove to me you studied, because if I asked you something and I see you was supposed to be studying this subject, you're supposed to be able to tell me something about it because, first of all, I was going to read it before I asked, and I had to know a little bit before I asked. And this is the way we did it. And I was either there when they needed me or as near as the telephone.

Mrs. Johnson did not allow the girls to "hang out" with others. Most activities took place within the home. Home visits with friends were limited and were restricted to "appropriate" times. The girls were held accountable for their behavior. In this way, Mrs. Johnson was almost able to predict the outcome of her children's behavior.

Mrs. Johnson's own predisposition toward education meant in effect that a strong educational orientation would be encouraged in Sheila. Mrs. Johnson's "firm" control over Sheila's time and space appears to have guaranteed the results.

Educational Orientation in the Home

Mrs. Johnson believes children should be expected to perform school tasks respectfully and intelligently. Punishment should be the result of unreasonable or inappropriate child activity. The southern schools were better than any other, in her opinion, primarily because "they did not hesitate" to use corporal punishment.

> The teachers had the authority to chastize a child with a spanking or a paddling when they were wrong. And you was sent home with a note by your teacher to your parent and you got another whipping when you got home. And they didn't pass you [because of your age]. They only passed you when you could prove you could do the next grade's work.

Mrs. Johnson feels she learned a survival strategy from her southern experience. Her own mother was most instrumental in this process. Mrs. Johnson now commands respect from others.

During my initial visit to the Johnson home, a television movie *Halls of Anger* totally captured Sheila's interest. The movie depicted the experiences of a Black teacher in a ghetto school. Sheila's intense interest in this movie was to be one of the first clues of the strong value she held for school and education. By every indication, education is placed at a high premium in the household. According to Mrs. Johnson:

> Know-how is not gonna mean too much. I experience this everyday on my job. There's been people working, and I will not call the job's name I'm working for, but there's people been working on this job where I'm working for eight years, some has been working hard, in the same capacity without a masters, without a bachelors, but holding a certain position. There's a lady come in, only been working two years with a piece of paper. Right away she's made a supervisor. With that piece of paper, she can show, this is where the money comes in.

Mrs. Johnson understands the importance of being credentialed by school degrees in American society. She believes that education is the only viable tool by which a person can survive comfortably. Sheila admits having received a thorough home education concerning the realities of the marketplace.

Attempting to put her beliefs into practice, Mrs. Johnson is pursuing a path toward her own self-betterment. She attends school part-time and expects one day to receive her undergraduate degree. She relates that she considers school to be a serious business.

> Sometimes I get up early enough in the morning to study before I leave for work or on the bus on the way to work. I've gotten up at 4:00 in the morning and studied before I even decided to get dressed or fix [breakfast].

And further:

I've always wanted to be a nurse, and I have this job working in that field, and I had the opportunity to go. My job sends me, something I wasn't able to do when the kids were small, on my own, because of financial problems.

Mrs. Johnson has struggled for almost two decades trying to increase her educational background. She also completed her remaining high school requirements as a part-time student.

High educational expectations increasingly typify Mrs. Johnson's attitude toward her children. She wants to see her children come closer to the American dream than she has been able to do. She argues:

I always wanted them to do better than I did because they had a better opportunity to do better than I did, and it goes right back to some of the firmness and the rules that you have set in your household.

Mrs. Johnson has extremely strong feelings about her children's educational performance. This attitude is a result of her view that education is the key to success. She would like her children to reach the highest educational level possible. She now places her entire faith in her children. Mrs. Johnson expects Sheila to reach all of her goals for higher education.

And if my mind leads me right, she'll not only get her bachelors but her master's. She will do it if she don't have to work. You don't know my baby darling. She'll go to school until she's 90 as long as she has got somebody to support her and don't work.

Sheila plans to stay in school as long as possible; she knows it is important to her mother. Mrs. Johnson intends to continue doing all she can to make her dream a reality.

Mrs. Johnson has regularly visited the teachers of her children. She has made them aware of her desire to see her children receive a "real education." The children have been taught to take school seriously. Mrs. Johnson has consistently checked their school progress.

I was always one to go to school and check on all of them very unexpectedly, on the children and on the teacher. Some of the things from kindergarten up until right now . . . I've had my debut in schools in Chicago in every school they attended. I can assure you they know me. And I've never had any problem with Sheila. Like I say, I've gone to PTA meetings and went to school for her and a lot of times I'd get off work early and I'd just go by the school sometimes and check on the kids and the teachers, because they're people just like me. I've made mistakes and teachers can be wrong too. They are respected by the people, but they can be wrong.

Mrs. Johnson is not intimidated by the school personnel. She views them as public servants who are employed by the community to do a job. Her intensive contact with the school has tended to buttress her efforts with the children at home. She expects the teachers to teach; and she expects the learners to learn.

At home Sheila is self-directed, but she utilizes all the resources she has available to aid her in completing academic assignments. She performs her academic requirements routinely and without fanfare. Since everyone in the home is attending school, they often discuss school assignments with each other. Sheila speaks:

> If I come across a problem [in school] and the teacher explains it and I still don't understand it, I'll research it further my self or I'll ask somebody like my mother or my sister if they know anything about it, but if they don't, I try to seek the answer on my own.

Sheila is able to utilize the knowledge within her own home with maximum efficiency.

Even Sheila's leisure time activities are designed to improve her intellectual performance. Educationally related activities such as word-choice games are regularly played. In one field note, it was observed that:

> Sheila and her mother spend a large amount of time playing a game with paper and pencil. The game's object is to unscramble blocks of letters which spell words found in a word list at the top of each puzzle page. There are about 20 different puzzles to master in each booklet. Since there are 20 words to be found among the scrambled letters in each puzzle, there is a total of 400 words in the entire booklet. Mrs. Johnson describes this activity as "meaningful" because "I improve my vocabulary skills this way." Sheila views this word-game activity as a fun, challenging exercise. Mrs. Johnson is at the dining room table after dinner working with one of the word puzzle exercises. Having some difficulty finding one of the correct words, she says (almost to herself) "Shoot, I know the word is here somewhere!" Sheila laughs and quickly goes to look over her mother's shoulder at the puzzle sheet. "I see the word," she states, "keep looking, you'll find it."

We can readily detect a process of mutual alliance, support, and encouragement in these vocabulary-improvement pursuits. The very fact that a word puzzle is seen as a respectable activity suggests there is an interest in intellectual improvement. The fact that Mrs. Johnson and her daughter regularly spend idle time seeking an academic challenge and self-improvement indicates a strong educational orientation. With these activities they are attempting to keep their minds working and growing.

Other educational rituals performed in the home include homework and study activities, as well as educational "talks." Mrs. Johnson describes these educational rituals as "mandatory." During the days when Sheila was a preschooler, she insisted on participating in the family homework and study sessions. Her older sisters accepted her involvement and taught her with regularity.

> I was always pressuring them to teach me this, teach me that, and they'd be doing different things; and my mother bought me books, and I'd tell them, "C'mon, let's read this or read that." So when I was in kindergarten, it was really sort of boring because all they did was the alphabet and count to ten and tell me the colors and I knew all that, and I wanted to do something else.

Mrs. Johnson taught each of the girls their name, address, telephone number, and alphabet before age four. Early educational practice (through regular academic involvement) provided Sheila with a good preparation for initial school success. Mrs. Johnson insisted that the girls be accountable for their homework. In fourth grade they were all expected to learn their multiplication tables. Remembering these days, she states:

> They would always come home from school and do their homework and by the time I got home I would check their homework, and if they were finished with it, they could go outside and play when I came home.

We may observe the independence of the girls in pursuing their responsibilities during the mother's absence from the home. By supervising in absentia, Mrs. Johnson was able to control their time and space activities effectively. She feels that time spent studying cannot be idled away.

Mrs. Johnson, Robin, and Neecy have attempted to provide continual psychological support for Sheila. Any problem or concern is routinely discussed, options are weighed, and decisions are finalized. By providing Sheila with this feedback, Mrs. Johnson hopes to ease the day-to-day pressures which Sheila may experience. Sheila feels privileged that she has been able to verbalize her thoughts to her mother and sisters. She feels wanted, even needed.

> I always had a family, somebody I could always run to. My mother was always there. Anytime, somebody was always there. There was always somebody there I could sort of run to. That's the way I always dealt with it. I always, always had somebody to run to.

The psychological sense of security and safety Sheila has experienced has allowed her to function relatively free of many social and psychological pressures which grow out of the ghetto living experience. Mrs. Johnson has been largely responsible for the educational nurturance found in the home. This nurturance has helped Sheila to grow and develop educationally at a rate unparalleled in her family.

The Farlands

The Family Theme and Background

Negative interactions between parents serve to develop and perpetuate psychological orientations of family members. The coping strategies a family develops may be directly affected by a parent's past affiliation with a "no-good" spouse. A Black woman who has been deserted has oftentimes risen to the occasion and socialized her children positively. Her attitudes and actions with her children reflect her determination to be successful in the face of the "stumbling block" her former spouse presented. The life experiences of the mother with males (whether spouse, kin, or friends) produce attitudes toward men which are then transmitted to her closest and most precious resource—her children. This attitude may very well be reflected in every psychosocial facet of the family pattern, especially in the parental quest for the educational success of the child. One such family is the Farland family.

Mrs. Beatrice Farland is head of a household consisting of herself and three adolescent girls, Gail, 18, Debbie, 17, and Freddie, 15. Gail, the oldest, is the research subject in the family. Mrs. Farland has been separated from her husband for over ten years. She has not bothered to apply for a divorce after her "mistake" because she "just didn't want to go through the trouble." She does not appear willing to become totally unattached from him. Her children, she believes, would not be happy with another man in the home. She states:

> Sometimes Gail would say, "Mama, if Daddy would do right, would you take him back?" I could read between the lines when she'd be asking this. She'd be saying, "We don't want another man here."
> So, I made up my mind I would never get a divorce unless I was tempted to get married. But I knew I wouldn't get married because I promised myself as a child I would never have a stepfather for my kids, and as long as I was married, I knew I could never marry again, so I never filed for a divorce and Gail never bothered about accepting a man.

Due to past experiences, Mrs. Farland's attitude toward men has become entrenched. For years now, she has survived as a single parent. Sexual and emotional companionship has been extremely sporadic. Although it has been difficult, Mrs. Farland does not regret these years with her children.

A welfare recipient for eight years, Mrs. Farland has managed in her ten years in "the projects" to get a few comforts into her home. The Farland home is a public housing apartment in the most notorious "project" complex on Chicago's South Side. Immediately upon entering, one gets the feeling of smallness or closeness. There are three bedrooms, all of which are small and cramped. A plain plastic-covered couch, a floor model stereo, and a brown and red hassock all catch the eye immediately as one enters the living room. There are a number of doilies, family pictures, accessories, and other knickknacks complementing the furniture and walls. These accessories may have been bought and displayed in an attempt at middle-class identification, or at least comfort, in an obviously lower income environment. At $4,000 a year, Mrs. Farland describes herself as "middle" income. She expresses her greatest pride, however, in the affective characteristics surrounding the home.

> I wouldn't trade the love in my home for all the modern furniture and appliances in the world; that's like having a pretty woman with a bad attitude.

The impression I eventually developed of Mrs. Farland was not at all like the one I had at first. The following notation was made after telephone contact was first established.

> I talked to Mrs. Farland on the telephone. We talked for about an hour. From the tone of her voice I imagine her to be a slightly built lady. She seemed almost shy in her interactions.

This initial impression was quite inaccurate, however. Mrs. Farland is a very dark-skinned, 36-year-old Black woman, about 5 feet 6 inches tall, and heavy (about 150 pounds). One notation made shortly after our initial meeting follows:

> Mrs. Farland is a pleasant, hefty, dark-skinned woman who wears black framed 1960s style secretarial glasses and acts as if she is just as comfortable in pants as in a dress. She is an aggressive, business—minded person. Mrs. Farland reminds me of a spunky person with sufficient savvy to "make do," regardless of the situation she finds herself in. She speaks soberly, often using unique phrases such as "Believe me you . . ." or "I live for the day . . ." These phrases usually preface sentences delivered in a tone one might use to say "Life is hell."

Mrs. Farland is not at all ashamed of telling about the circumstances that have complicated her life. She speaks in a matter-of-fact, unassuming tone.

Gail Farland is a short (5 feet), dark-skinned girl with a very large bosom and large eyes. She is always respectful to adults. Her demeanor can be described as personable and quiet. One initial observation made suggests that Gail is "low-key" in her mother's presence.

> She is listed among the top 10 students of her graduating class. She appears almost retarded in her thought processes, judging by her slow verbal delivery. Perhaps it is her "lazy" speech pattern. She appears quiet, conforming, and conscientious. In her mother's presence, she is cooperative, almost "dull." Conversely, Mrs. Farland is very talkative. When I asked Gail about this she indicated to me

that, like her mother, she also talks a lot but mostly when she is in school. Her teachers concur.

Gail's Gordon Persons Conceptions System data reveal other general aspects of her personality. Based on the questionnaire and interview data, we see that Gail is most highly focused on her ethnic group membership and her roles in the family, as a student, and in relationship to her peers and friends. She is characterized as being less strongly identified with political-party allegiances and marital status concerns. Gail's political orientation appears conservative (extreme right). While her major life goal is the attainment of "security," she derives her short term gratifications mostly from sports and recreation, with a minimum emphasis on sex. Although she is not antireligious, she stresses an "unreligious" attitude. Her image of her body is basically a neutral one. Perhaps because of Mrs. Farland's many illnesses over the years, we see a slight concern with illness in Gail's profile. Her interpersonal style is cooperative and approaching as opposed, say, to an uncooperative and evasive mode of interaction. Interestingly, the ubiquitous psychic states of happiness and contentment were closely rivaled by an element of unhappiness. This might be some indication of a bittersweet experience brought on by the broken home and by ghetto living and other environmental factors.

Gail's social situation suggests that she has a perception of herself as being low in prestige and status. There are extremely few references to Gail as being socially aware and possessed of a feeling of immediacy. Importantly, there are strong systemic senses of competence and self-determination seen. Gail possesses a relatively high sense of moral worth and derives many symbolic rewards from responses to her self-determination and approval and reinforcement of her competence. It is significant that Gail's time orientations tend inordinately to center on future concerns. The present and past do not appear to carry the same significance as the future for this adolescent.

Gail has been trained to perform many supportive roles in the household. By her own admission, she has been heavily influenced by her mother. She states:

> I have a lot of responsibilities, you could almost say I was the second mama. I practically raised my cousins, especially the last baby, and my sisters too. But now that my sisters are that age, they're getting to the point where they don't want to listen to me because of my being so short. But if I say it loud enough, they'll listen.

Gail takes her roles seriously and always tries to do her best at performing required functions.

Mrs. Farland does not have a good relationship with her husband's kin. A native of Laurel, Mississippi, Mrs. Farland came to Chicago with her husband and children when she was 23 years old. Mr. Farland had secured a job, which he lost three months later. The only people Mrs. Farland knew in Chicago at that time were relatives of her husband. Some of these relatives provided temporary shelter for her and the children after Mr. Farland "deserted" the family. A newcomer to the city, without money and totally ignorant of big-city life, Mrs. Farland was forced to search the alleys for survival. She states:

> And I lived on 61st Street at the time and I walked down the back alleys and picked up bottles and carried them to the store to get the deposits so I could feed my children because we didn't have any food and they [her in-laws] were right there.

Mrs. Farland began "hustling" in every legitimate way she could. She began selling snowballs and penny candy as a corner street vendor. Due to a sporadic on-again, off-again relationship with her spouse, eight years ago she was forced to apply for welfare assistance in order to keep her living quarters. She explains:

> When [the kids] were young, 10 or 11, and I was doing two full time jobs and I would leave them in the morning and come home at night, and I worked two jobs almost 13 months and got sick, and from there I began to do a lot of things like maybe going to rummage sales for clothing, cooked dinners, made candy apples; completely made a warehouse out of my house, because I wanted my children to have most of the things they needed and some of the things they wanted. It wasn't easy at all. Their father was to give them $115.00 a week and we couldn't even get $15 out of him. We almost lost the apartment here. After we had to turn him in [report his desertion], I refused to ask him for support. That was before, and after, things got so bad I almost lost my house; I had to ask for help. Now I didn't ask for the help [welfare] because I really needed it; I asked because this was the only way to let [the housing authorities] know he wasn't living here.

The housing authorities apparently attempted to discourage legally separated and divorced spouses from living with their ex-partners. Threatened with eviction, Mrs. Farland did what she considered necessary at the time.

Mrs. Farland came from a poor southern family which she describes as "strict." She considers herself as having had to be accountable to *somebody* all her life—first her mother, then her husband, then his relatives, and now her children. But she wants to continue in this vein.

> I want to get married again. I guess it's because I started out early. My mother was as tight as the peeling on a sweet potato, ornery; then I got married and he had his days; and when we separated, I had another mother here—Gail.

Mrs. Farland has sacrificed for most of her life so that her family could be healthy. Providing for others is now a life-style in which she is comfortable.

Early Child-Rearing and Familial Practices

When Mrs. Farland was a teenager, she was married and living in poverty in the South. The search for opportunity brought her husband to Chicago to take a job in a factory. She and the baby followed soon after. The factory job, however, did not last long.

> My husband came up first and we stayed in the South. He got a job with Linco Bleach. We came here on Labor Day, September 5. They laid him off around Thanksgiving [of that same year].

The unexpected job dismissal was disastrous for the Farlands. From that point the marriage bond became less cohesive. A traumatic separation eventually followed. Mrs. Farland, feeling helpless and alone, made a determined decision to "make it" despite the odds. She described the manner she used to make certain her young daughters understood their school obligation.

> After my husband and I separated, I sat them around the table, I said, "From now on, anyone else bring me a note home with some bad remarks, I'm going to bring my extension cord down to the school and I'm going to whip you in school. You're going to twist your dress above your head and the area that's showing is where I'm going to whip you at."

An important element here is that a crisis situation appears to have spurred a determined drive toward academic and social success. Mrs. Farland knew then that the future would be far from smooth.

Receiving very little help and a lot of criticism from her husband's relatives (with whom she was living), young Mrs. Farland painfully learned the art of self-reliance. Considered naïve and "country" by her in-laws Mrs. Farland found it difficult to get support in her survival efforts. She describes one incident typical of this period:

> This was back like when I picked up bottles [from alleys] and took them to the store to get food for my children. It was unfortunate when a can of corn I bought for the kids had a worm in it. That shows how bad my luck was. When I went back to the store, I explained to the man what happened, a White man. I'm sure [my in-laws] got angry with me about that and wanted to put me out. I had "threw away a fortune" by taking this corn back with the worm in it. But my kids were hungry, and I didn't care about seeing [a lawyer] then, I wanted some food for my kids and when I explained it to [the store manager] he told me to get a shopping cart and get them

some food, and he went in his pocket and gave me car fare to bring the groceries home. I had to go through a lot of explaining about those groceries. One of my husband's sisters came in the store while I was there, and I told her what happened and she flew off the handle right then and there in the store, "go tell him I want the corn back," and I said, "I don't want the corn back, my kids are hungry." I was hurt because she walked out of the store, but when I went back, the blessing paid off. I never thought about something where I could have gotten rich, and gotten a big sum of money. I was glad the White man's heart was like it was, because those times, like I say, I was down anyway, and I only had my children; all I had then and all I have now is my children, and that's what kept me out of the nuthouse. Many times I wouldn't know day from night, that's just how sick and nervous I was. It was a miracle for sure, and I got so sick, all I could lean on was my children, and we had some tough times, but we made it, and right now we aren't suffering too much.

Mrs. Farland felt a strong responsibility for the immediate survival of her children. Feeling desperate and alone in her plight, Mrs. Farland felt completely justified in making those decisions by herself that would enable her and her children to survive. This course of action included socialization into "correct" values and attitudes.

Mrs. Farland attempted to acquaint her children with survival strategies for coping with their environment. Guided by her southern conservatism to cope with northern realities, Mrs. Farland used newspaper and television stories to warn her children about the dangers young girls should try to avoid. She illustrates:

I'd bring home some of the news and sit down and read it to them and say "look what happened to this li'l girl." I remember this one case where a man had taken a stick and messed a girl up, and they thought it was a hurting thing. It was "small," "wrong" to hurt a girl like this. And I said, "This same thing could happen to you if you open this front door and let the wrong person in." I said, "You can go to the door and say 'who is it' and it might sound like your Uncle Joe and be somebody else. He might disguise his voice. So don't bother about even answering the door. You all go to the back and watch television till I come."

Mrs. Farland read stories to the children and encouraged them to listen to the news in an effort to protect their physical safety. Knowing she would have to be away from the home for extended periods of time, Mrs. Farland attempted to equip the children with knowlege pertinent to their well-being.

I didn't want them to be afraid. Before we got those bars that go up to the window I used to take the shade and pull it all the way down and put a row of pop bottles all the way across it. That was my little game. If somebody hit that screen, pushed that shade, knocked that window out, them bottles would go down. "Nine times out of ten," I used to tell the kids, "They'll run away if they hear those bottles falling." I didn't want them to be afraid.

The techniques utilized in the home point out the adaptations made for survival in the inner city environment. Mrs. Farland's concern for her children was a primary motivating factor in her behavior. To Mrs. Farland, caution was necessary, fear was not necessary.

The norms and values internalized by Gail helped develop her sense of morals and responsibility to others. Ritualistic emphasis was given to the girls' moral conduct. Mrs. Farland encouraged group dialogue in an effort to employ psychological reasoning with her children. "Manners" toward adults in authority was particularly emphasized. Inconsiderate behavior toward others was considered personally embarrassing by Mrs. Farland and she refused to allow the children to embarrass her,

because I told them I would "take the extension cord and beat you right where you're embarrassing me at. You're not embarrassing yourself, you're embarrassing your home training and me, so if anybody else want to hit the teacher, you better get on the other side so you make sure the teacher know who hit him," because I never did approve of disobedient children and this is what kept me really going. Because when I get down to those things I really mean, I've always sat my kids around the table and around the table is where we always get our answers and this is the way I feel it should be. I let them know what I expect out of them and then they know what to expect out of me because I tell them. I tell them things about me they might feel afraid to ask me, even when we have a round-the-table discussion. I know the thing they would like to ask me and they still don't ask me, so I tell them I'm not right all the time.

Attempting equanimity while insisting on order has been a challenge for Mrs. Farland. She believes that Gail internalized "proper" morals by having been allowed to discuss and debate.

Gail was initiated early into household tasks and related responsibilities. She was taught to cook, clean, and manage the home, including rearing the young siblings. From Mrs. Farland, Gail learned money management and budgeting. On more than one occasion the children were allowed to baby-sit themselves with Gail as the guardian. Mrs. Farland remembers that Gail handled the responsibilities well:

They stayed in here. I'd come home at night, my house shoes would be sitting by the door, my bath water would be in there. The last one to bed would turn it on hot. By the time I got home it would be almost nice enough to get in. This makes you feel pretty good. You get home and they'd have the house clean. In other words, they were better when they were small than they are now. *[Laughter]*

We see indications of familial congruence and cooperation during these early years. A bond of love between mother and children ensured a mutual concern for family welfare.

There is further evidence of the early direction the children received under Mrs. Farland. About Gail especially, Mrs. Farland has observed:

> Anything I can do she feels she can do it as well. I'm proud of her. This is why I knew I needed to lead a respectable life, because she was easy to pick up patterns behind me, and I didn't want her to pick up the wrong thing, and this is why I led the life I did. Really, it's because of my children.

The fact that Gail is the eldest child may suggest that the role-modeling influence of her mother has had an inordinate effect on her personality. As the oldest child, Gail was the prime candidate to aid and assist Mrs. Farland in her attempts at survival in the poverty-stricken ghetto.

> She [Gail] learned to cook at the age of 8; I broke my leg. She made her first cornbread when she was 8 years old and she's been cooking ever since. Anything I can cook, she can cook just as well. Anyway I can clean the house, she can clean it just as well. I go sewing, she goes sewing.

Gail derives ego satisfaction from the maternal praise she receives. For her, this praise is a powerful form of encouragement. Practices begun in early childhood are now routine, receiving nourishment through regular maternal verbal reinforcement.

School provided another relatively positive environment for Gail. Academically and socially, Gail performed well and was liked by all her teachers. This early foundation provided the initial stairway for her eventual successes.

Mental Health: General Values, Attitudes, and Personality

Gail is basically a quiet, cooperative, likeable, adolescent girl. One of her strongest traits is her concern for others. She tries to help others whenever possible, while avoiding confrontation and conflict. She states:

> I'll be friends with my enemy. Why should I hate 'em? If I can get out of fighting or fussing, I'll just walk away from it.

And further:

> I like to see people smile, because I met a lot of elderly people in November and December last year [at a senior citizens' home], and one lady I know I made her happy. So it makes me happy to know I can care for someone. As long as I'm helping I feel good.

Gail would rather interact with small groups of people. Crowds are avoided whenever possible. In recent years, Gail appears to have become more introspective. She prefers the peace and comfort of her home over a noisy disco dance party.

Although quiet and accommodating at home, Gail will quickly demonstrate her drive by not allowing others to take undue advantage of her. In school particularly, she will monitor her grades carefully to make sure she has been fairly evaluated.

Gail carries a positive concept of herself and believes she is capable of changing her environment. Wishing to be treated with respect by others, Gail acts mature and respectful when outside the home. At the present time, Gail is more interested in interacting with boys than with other girls, who she feels, too often do little more than "gossip" and criticize one another at every opportunity. Males do not present the same problems, she feels, since they can be influenced by the behavior of the female. She explains:

> First, I carry myself in such a way that they don't embarrass me. I feel that if I get out of hand and act all wild and stuff, you know how some young ladies act, then they'll treat me according to the way I act. If I don't care about myself, I don't think they'd care about me. See, I just carry myself in the way I want people to treat me. Even an old bum may pass one girl and "call her out of her name" but I figure if I carry myself right, he may see me and say, "How are you doin', Gail?"

Gail's responsible approach to interaction with males is clearly a result of extensive moral training in years past. Spurred by her mother's conservatism vis-à-vis adolescent sexual behavior, Gail insists upon respect from the young men she has as friends.

Racial and political issues are not strongly emphasized by Gail. While discrimination and equality are realities of which she is aware, she does not consciously consider them crucial to her present circumstances. Having lived and interacted with Blacks for most of her life, seldom has she encountered personal instances of bigotry.

In-Home Living Patterns

Intrafamilial interaction in the Farland home is characterized by a high level of value congruence. Citing "love and communication" as predominant traits in the home, Mrs. Farland expresses satisfaction with "our organization." Conservative and parentally controlled, the Farland home is functional for all its members. In its hierarchical arrangement, Mrs. Farland is the boss, and Gail serves in the role of substitute boss—a position she earned through diligent past management. Gail's siblings are increasingly unhappy about the "old-fashioned" life-style they are expected to lead at home. Role-modeling effects have been greater for Gail than for her sisters. Gail states:

But my sisters—we love each other as sisters—but her idea is to run and run and run and she tell me I'm old-fashioned; she rather stick with my other sister because their minds is some place else. But my mind is like Mamma taught, and what they think is right, I tell them is wrong and not what Mamma taught, and they say, "You're old-fashioned" but other than that we're all right.

Except for the fact that the younger girls disagree with Mrs. Farland's instructions to stay away from boys, the family members generally function smoothly together. Mrs. Farland has taught the girls to cook, clean, save, protect, and otherwise effect their own survival in and outside the home.

In teaching the girls a strategy for survival, Mrs. Farland has wielded considerable control over the girls' time and space generally and over their home academic activities, peer relations, and sexual activities particularly. Wanting to protect the girls from negative social forces, Mrs. Farland has a hand in virtually every aspect of the familial matrix. All of Gail's behavior is ultimately monitored by Mrs. Farland, who feels that her child-rearing approach is necessary in these circumstances. Given the totally adverse social and economic conditions that the Farlands have lived with for years, Mrs. Farland's determination is noteworthy. Close-knit family ties, strong discipline and order, and a strong desire to keep themselves emotionally balanced are but a few features of the Farland home.

A welfare recipient, Mrs. Farland's adult history is essentially one of continual struggle to find ways to bring in "a few nickels and dimes" for the survival of her family. Although Mrs. Farland once sought the support of her neighbors through the use of babysitting services, she quickly found these kinds of arrangements very uncomfortable.

There was a lady lived in [apartment] 406 and I asked her if she'd keep my children for me, and she said she would. So when I got back home that day [my daughter] told me she didn't want to stay down there no more. They told me how that woman beat her kids, and made them sit in one place. I just couldn't take it. [After that] we had one of those round-the-table discussions.

At this point, Mrs. Farland's fiercely independent approach, coupled with her intrafamilial dependence, necessitated a talk with all the family members. These ritualistic talks appear to be a special feature in the Farland household. Issues are discussed and the opinions of everyone are encouraged. Mrs. Farland emphasized the need to respect the worth of all family members' opinions. She says:

I was always the type of person who wanted to pay everybody for anything they did for my children. If they [baby-sat] if I could just give someone a package of cigarettes, I did. I wanted to say "Thank

you" for doing this because I didn't want nobody to meet my kids
when they got grown and say, "Child, I had to do so and so for
you." We got enough problems already from their father.

She proceeds:

> So we had this babysitter for one day and when they got through
> telling me that night [that] they didn't want to go back, I explained to
> them what the law could do to you if anything happened to them,
> and how dangerous it was leaving them in the house. And even
> though they was as young as they was, they seemed to understand.
> They understood too that they at least didn't want this [particular]
> babysitter. So I guess this was what made them start out doing as I
> asked.

With the happiness of her children a central concern, Mrs. Farland always
listened to their expressed wants and needs. Perhaps Mrs. Farland knew
beforehand that the children would only be allowed limited latitude in her
neighbor's home. Through strategic placement, Mrs. Farland had shown
the children that other homes can also be strict.

Mrs. Farland's expectations of the girls while in the home are multiple.
Does this mean that ultimately we might expect to find high expectations
toward school? Not necessarily. But there could be. In the Farland home
major emphasis is accorded two concerns: how one "correctly" interacts
with a male, and how one performs in school. Much of Gail's cautious
attitude about men seems to have been learned from her mother. She now
feels that her mother's advice about noninvolvement is the best policy.

> I used to always say, "Mamma, I ain't gonna never have no boy-
> friends. Don't nobody come see me" and she'd say, "That's alright,
> you just keep right on." And now this year I have had more young
> men talking to me than I ever had. Now I'm doing pretty good.

Gail's initial lament is even more strongly embraced by the younger girls.
Mrs. Farland has discouraged most males from intimately involving themselves in serious family issues. A series of childhood experiences with an
incest-prone stepfather has figured heavily in Mrs. Farland's decision
never to expose her children to another man living in the home. She
explains this maternal protectiveness in this way:

> I had a stepfather and something grew in me about the stepfather
> [that] I didn't like, so that turned me against stepfathers. My stepfa-
> ther lived with my mother, came there when I was a child and as
> soon as my body began to mature his eyes were on me. So from a
> child on, I never wanted this to happen to my children. My stepfa-
> ther didn't actually [have to] want for anything. He was a good fa-
> ther. But one day this "something" came out of him and this was
> what his desires was—his wife's daughter.

She continues:

> I know all mens aren't ugly because I believe if all mens were this
> rotten the world would have been destroyed again. We wouldn't
> have no foundation if all mens were like this, but from my point of
> view I don't know who they are so I'm not going to take that
> chance.

The girls have consistently engaged in patterned behavior to try to insure
that no man will again occupy the home. This ritual involves sabotage of
the dyadic involvement between Mrs. Farland and every male friend she
has ever invited to the home. Gail especially would attempt to "jam the
machinery" when she suspected that her mother might be weakening for
a man. Mrs. Farland says that when any male friend visits the home:

> [She pretends] to have to come and get some water or some milk or
> "May I have a doughtnut?" something so that nothing would go
> wrong in here, that she would feel [might] interfere between me and
> her father.

Mrs. Farland strongly believes that her daughters do not *need* sex. Using
herself as an example, she says:

> I've been exposed to sex; I've [birthed] them. I had went 17 months
> laying in the bed beside my husband, 17 months and he didn't touch
> my body. I stayed without a man for 13 months after me and my
> husband separated, and God forbid now. Five or six months of stuff
> like this is nothing. It ain't driving me crazy. And I know they don't
> have to have it.

Mrs. Farland's attitude here has been accepted by Gail more than it has
by her other offspring. Gail's disposition toward accepting the values of
her mother has insured a schism with her siblings. Any attempt to get
"with it" by Gail is laughed at by her sisters, since it is considered
atypical for her natural character. Outside the home, the girls associate
with different sets of peers.

Primarily because of Gail's birth-order place and her allegiance to her
mother's proposed values, Gail has served for years as the surrogate
parent in Mrs. Farland's absence. Though Gail feels that her influence
over her siblings is now weakening, she still appears to have power in the
household. Mrs. Farland states:

> The other two girls stand much taller than her, she's like a midget,
> but if I'm not around, they know they take orders from her.

This power or authority appears to be a concomitant of delegated responsibility. That is, Mrs. Farland has given Gail both responsibility and authority in home affairs—a significant combination for Gail's psychological
well-being and family processes. A feeling of confidence and self-assur-

ance has resulted. Though Gail's authority role is sometimes challenged when the mother is not home, order is always reasonably maintained just as if the mother were at home.

Mrs. Farland has wielded a significant degree of control over the behavior of her daughters. She expects obedience "because I don't like anything to do with problems." She insists on approving all outside activities such as part-time employment, extracurricular events, and the like. Friends and associates are also monitored and approved. Sex habits are strenuously controlled. Mrs. Farland explains why:

> To me, this is the way I feel about it. The hurting thing is my daughter would give up her life for another child to come up and live when we had to suffer so hard without doing anything before she got the babies. You can't take any trips, you don't get to go out to see the world, anything like this. Now you have a new responsibility and you never have enjoyed growing up anyway.

We see that Mrs. Farland hopes to provide her daughters with an adult life, unmarred by the responsibility of an illegitimate child. A newborn child would, in her opinion, insure her daughters a life not much different from the present one.

Mrs. Farland is supremely confident of her control over her children's activity patterns. One clear indication of this fact is the assertiveness she exhibited in making a bet with a man in a tavern.

> I have complete confidence that my girls aren't gonna do anything to hurt me. If I don't know nothing else, I know this. I once won $20 in a bar when I bet this man that I knew where my kids were all the time. He was trying to say that Negroes can't keep up with their children, that they just let 'em run the streets cuttin' up. He was talking to some other people so I didn't butt in but then he turned around and asked me to agree with him. I said, "Mister, I've got three girls and you don't know what you're talking about." He bet me that I didn't know exactly where my kids were! So I called my home. Gail answered the phone. It was close to 12:00—this was on New Year's Eve night, the second New Year's Eve night I ever spent out of my house in my life—and I had been out since 8:00. I said, "Gail, there's a man here who is going to ask you some questions. I want you to answer whatever he asks you, OK?" You see, she would have hung up the phone if he had just come right out and asked her without my approval. I gave the man the phone and he asked her name, where they were in the house and had they been out of the house that evening. Well, they were where I knew they would be—in the bed. So I won me $20 and a fifth of V.O. After that man paid me, he was still trying to argue, saying that I was just the exception, and that he was still right by saying most colored people with teenagers don't know where they are at half the time. I can challenge anybody any night, and Gail's 18 years old.

We see that Mrs. Farland exercises spatial control as well as time control in the home. Certain child activities appear to take place in particular home areas, and Mrs. Farland almost always knows about where these activities are occurring.

The organizational aspects of the home and its relationship to the child's existence within the family structure might be said to *lead* children in an achievement direction—almost in spite of family circumstances, as it were. Mrs. Farland discovered that she could exert even more control over her children's outside activities if she could "get along" with them at home.

> I learned to get along with my children. I can sit down and play a game with them [but] then whip them for some dishes they didn't wash. I had to give [the 15 year old] a couple of licks the other night. She went to bed. She was angry with me and we had just got through playing cards. I play with you, we have fun together, and when I say, "Do what I say do," I want you to do that.

Mrs. Farland is devoted to the welfare of her children. She has made a personal commitment to provide for them until they leave home to venture out on their own. While in the home, however, the girls fully understand their obligation to the rules of the house.

Educational Orientations in the Home

At the time of this research investigation, the Farland household had succeeded in producing two high school graduation candidates in a city where 74 percent of the Black adult population has not completed four years of high school.[2] Mrs. Farland feels a sense of accomplishment in her guidance of her daughter's educational direction. Gail is ranked as one of the top ten seniors in the school. Her overall grades are above B level. The academic orientation of the Farlands is generally high. Mrs. Farland feels that Gail's desire for academic success is a direct result of some early hardships she witnessed in the family. In other words, Gail is interested in assuring her own future survival. She still remembers the days when her mother "hustled" candy apples, worked two jobs, and did various and sundry work for survival.

Perhaps ironically, Gail has developed few goals for higher education. Without knowledge of financial assistance opportunities and with no help from school counselors, Gail is undecided about her plans after graduation. Economic realities make it not at all certain that she will pursue a college career. Though she would like to attend, Gail's biggest reservation about attending college next year is that she would be embarrassed to be forced to return home from college due to lack of funds. Economics is seen here as a powerful deterrent to undertaking a college career. Her

tendency is to contemplate a job after high school. Mrs. Farland does not
encourage this tendency, but sees no other practical route. She believes:

> The best time to go to school is while [you] have it on your mind.
> You have a tendency to waver after you get out there and it gets
> good to you. That's why I never wanted my children to work be-
> cause money seems to have a way of changing thoughts in your
> mind.

Even with this attitude, Mrs. Farland still agrees with Gail that a college
education is at this time an impractical notion for her. Apparently it
becomes increasingly difficult to deny yourself a certain minimal standard
of living when there is an opportunity to earn money. Gail explains:

> Right now, I just wanna work. I'm not just ready to go to work in
> June, and in September go off to college. Like my friend, she went
> off to college and she had to sell her clothes to come back home.
> When I leave I want to have something so I don't have to come
> back; when I come back from college I want to have my diploma
> with me.

It is important that Gail's attitudes toward higher education are held
despite the relatively positive experiences the neighborhood schools have
offered her. As she describes it:

> I liked both grammar school and high school. All my teachers were
> nice to me. I was always almost at the top and even now I go back
> over to my grammar school classes and [teachers] still know me.

Mrs. Farland has strong expectations for Gail's successful completion
of high school. She insists that the girls be functional and cooperative as
long as they are in the home. There can be no discussion on this point.
She states:

> This is about as plain as I can give it. When those children graduate
> from high school, they can take their minds and do as they please.
> But if they're still living with me there are certain things they are still
> going to have to do in my house.

The desire to see the girls at least graduate from high school is an extension of Mrs. Farland's attitude toward the role she perceives for herself in
the academic development of her children. She feels it her *responsibility*
to serve as a supportive agent of the school in her children's formal
education. To illustrate further, let's let Mrs. Farland describe her own
behavior when one of her daughters showed disenchantment with school.

> Debbie came home one day when she was about in the eighth grade,
> crying, asking me if she could stop school. I was on the phone talk-
> ing to someone and right to this day they never did call me back to
> say, "Why did you hang up on me?" and I don't know who it was

'cause I put that phone down and, oh boy, I talked to that girl. I told her she was to go to school until she was 17 or 16, whatever it was. She said she'd be out of school then, and I told her that was how long she was going. So from that day to this one, no matter how cold, she goes. It was cold that day she didn't want to go to school but if she was going to work, she'd have to go; it's going to be cold either way. When she came home that day she was ready and if I had said she didn't have to go back, she would never have gone to school another day in her life.

Although Mrs. Farland is not at present engaged in any personal school pursuits, she is very determined to see her girls graduate from high school. Seeing the girls graduate from high school and avoid illegitimate pregnancies are top priority items in Mrs. Farland's values.

In addition to periodic school visits, Mrs. Farland has taken the initiative at home in helping the girls develop skills useful in achieving good school performance. By engaging the girls in informal learning patterns, Mrs. Farland has attempted to aid in their educational development. She speaks of the learning activities she used in Gail's early school years.

I played games with them, cards with them. I used dominoes to teach the difference between a 6 and a 4. She managed to just look at a 6, and she knew it was a 6. She'd look at a 4 and wouldn't have to count, she knew the difference. It helped her catch on to her numbers.

These activities were performed with ritualistic frequency. Mrs. Farland states further:

It was just something I always did with my kids even for training them for the pot; the next step was teaching them the alphabets. These were the things I always tried to teach them, and it was just a habit. I was at home all day long and we did something, like games. It wasn't so much as "teaching."

These family "games," performed during Gail's early years might be viewed as educational rituals contributing to (*a*) the self-discipline of the child, (*b*) the academic mastery of certain skills helpful in the school setting, and (*c*) general familial congruence. The fact that these games were not viewed as "teaching" activities suggests that Mrs. Farland was most immediately interested in the psychological benefits accruing from them. The allied goal (in addition to the schooling uses) appears to be the development of family cohesion and stability. This notion receives further support upon examination of other data obtained through field observation:

Mrs. Farland and I were sitting at the kitchen table drinking rum and coke. I asked Mrs. Farland to demonstrate one of their "rap sessions." She explains again that at least twice a month she sits the family around the kitchen table. She encourages each person to speak about anything or anyone in the household. Comments during this session may praise or criticize without fear of reprisal. She explains that reprisals administered just once might inhibit further interaction. Mrs. Farland and the three girls are all gathered around the kitchen table. The seating arrangement shows a circular formation. I suggest a starting point: something that has occurred since I have been here. Debbie starts by saying [pouting]: "Mamma, you and Gail been doin' all the talkin' since he's been here. What about me." Mrs. Farland says, "We haven't forgotten about you." Gail states that she feels her mother has been doing most of the talking since my first visit the previous day. Mrs. Farland did not register a complaint but listened to the girls' comments and discussed them. It looks similar to an encounter group interaction. While not becoming disrespectful, the children appear willing to say whatever was truly on their minds.

Mrs. Farland is a talkative person. Concerned that the girls have an opportunity to express themselves, she has attempted to create vehicles for her children to express themselves during the parent-child interaction.

Another learning activity used by Mrs. Farland that further affected family cohesion involved group teaching lessons with all the girls. Mrs. Farland explains:

> Gail and Debbie started in school together. Everything I read I taught my kids. There was a time when my kids were close together [in age] so whatever I told one I always told to all of them, so there never been a problem. My kids was 1, 2, and 3. Now they are 16, 17, and 18 years old. That's how close they are together. So whatever I had to tell Gail, I put them all at the table. We all wrote at the same time, they all learned at the same time. They had Debbie doing algebra before Debbie was ready for algebra, because when they would do their homework she would get out a piece of paper and try to do the same thing.

These activities have taken place as a part of the homework and study rituals in the Farland home. The girls are expected to do homework nightly; it is periodically checked by Mrs. Farland. Whenever she is asked, Mrs. Farland tries to assist her daughters by sharing information or telling them where the information can be found.

By acting in a supportive manner, Mrs. Farland has managed to maintain good communication with her daughters. The adolescent years have been more difficult. The younger girls more than ever are questioning the "old-fashioned" rules and regulations they must follow. Mrs. Farland hopes to "hang on" until the girls graduate from high school. When they graduate, parental dictates will be eased.

5. An Analysis of Dispositions and Life-Styles in High Achievers' Homes

In the previous cases, no matter whether the family unit consisted of one or two parents, specific psychosocial orientations and home activity patterns were seen clearly time and again in the high achievers' homes. These recurring processes and patterns, as a group, represent parents' styles of helping their children adjust to the student role by "sponsoring" or grooming them for that role. The interpersonal communication patterns in these homes tended to be marked by frequent parent-child dialogue, strong parental encouragement in academic pursuits, clear and consistent limits set for the young, warm and nurturing interactions, and consistent monitoring of how they used their time. Sociologist Bernard Farber calls this type of parent-child communication a "sponsored independence" style.[1]

Parents in these homes have taken the responsibility for guiding, nursing, and protecting their children during the pursuit of competent adult behavior. The specific characteristics of the parents' individual child-rearing style was determined, in large part, by their own upbringing as well as their perception of the degree of community support and/or danger to themselves or their progeny. The interpersonal processes of the communication style used by these parents can generally be described thus: parents consistently use their legal, psychological, and physical power to define "appropriate" behavior rather authoritatively for family members and then to allocate resources and delegate responsibilities to others in the household. These processes take place within a parent-child bond which is, itself, marked by clear standards for "appropriate" and "inappropriate" behaviors during specific events, established rules and norms for achievement, parental monitoring of organized and routinized learning activities, the search for knowledge from highly interactive social encounters, and adult provision of corrective feedback and sanctions to reinforce children's behavior. The parents who have sustained this type of home relationship have also been successful in producing bright, capable and well-adjusted children. The children, in turn, feel a deep and comforting loyalty to (a) their parents' expectations and wishes, and (b) their own betterment through involvement in achievement-related activities.

My strategy for analyzing the case studies will be to identify, present, and discuss the predominant domestic patterns that explain how families groom their children in high-quality (or competent) role behavior in classrooms. The discussion will cover seven categories of variables: (1) parents' historical experiences in home and school, (2) parent and child personality structures, (3) parents' themes, expectations, and norms, (4) family unit authority structures and power relations, (5) parents' management strategies, (6) home activity structures and processes, and (7) parents' correspondence patterns with schools.

Historical Experiences in Home and School

Parent's Experiences in Their Families of Origin

The case studies of high-achieving students indicate the existence of an intergenerational transmission of behavior patterns. Parents described their early home relationships with their own parents as being characterized by clearly defined role boundaries and asymmetrical status relationships. At the same time these parents felt that there had been much communication, cooperation, and mutual support. As a result of residential movement, limited educational and economic opportunity, and other family disruptions, the parents themselves had not achieved up to their own levels of competence. They had, however, implemented certain organizational and psychological patterns with their own children. Exactly *how* parents invoked these patterns with the high-achieving students will be discussed in more detail when our focus turns to the parents' social interaction patterns in their family of procreation. I will simply note here those social patterns that typified the parent's upbringing in their own families of origin.

In addition to the clearly defined role boundaries and status relationships in the parent's family of origin, at least three other psychosocial patterns are apparent. First, parents felt that their own parents had been diligent and direct in their supervision. Their parents had insisted that they understand and accept a shared responsibility for child rearing and family labor tasks. Second, these mothers had come to understand during their own childhood that the economic survival needs of the family would come first, and that all the family's physical and spiritual resources must be used to meet these needs. The mother's parents had never attained a high level of schooling themselves, and they were not especially insistent that their daughters pursue advanced degrees. Rather, their energies seemed to be focused more on organizing the family for economic self-sufficiency and personal survival. Still, these elders seemed to possess, and to pass on, a keen appreciation of the need for children to obtain an "education" and to strive for educational success *and* economic self-sufficiency. One of the means that had been used for "passing on" this sensibility was by ritualistically helping their young children with schoolwork. Third, these mothers recalled a household climate that had been dominated by routine caucuses by the elders and other family members. These events served as opportunities to discuss the family's crisis issues, assess the family's circumstances, and plan their future actions.

The children from these families, now the parents of our sample achievers, grew up holding a firm wish that they could have gone further in school. Having accepted that they have been victims of economic and educational underprivilege, these parents are working to create a sense of family progress and personal progress through the school successes of their own children. Parents have come to feel that if their own children are to have any chance at all of escaping still another generation of poverty, the children must become literate, articulate, and skilled in a craft.

Students' Early Experiences in Schools

Another part of the history of our high achievers concerns their social experiences during elementary and junior high school. All of these students could recall having at least one particularly warm, supportive classroom environment. They specifically pointed to impressions that had been left with them by teachers who had, in some way, given them special notice and had taken time to *work* with them. They also remembered their teachers as having provided them with opportunities to play responsible, leadership roles in the classroom. These high-quality classroom experiences were apparently still helping the students feel good about their abilities. Furthermore, parents had encouraged these students to maintain regular visits to libraries, to enroll in enrichment programs, and to engage in other academically oriented institutional experiences outside the school.

Parents' Early Socialization Behavior toward Child

As very young children, these students were taught pragmatic morals. They learned the difference between "right" and "wrong" (that is, acceptable and unacceptable behavior). They also learned under what circumstances certain social behavior was appropriate and how to judge when that same behavior was inappropriate. Parents managed to inculcate a positive educational attitude in these young children by buttressing their moral teachings with displays of love during home activities, expectations for responsible independence, and *trust* toward the child. By first stating their expectations, then labeling activities as "good" or "bad," and then working with the children through manageable, incremental responsibilities and tasks that parents considered important, the parents helped these children perceive that they too had a positive effect on the drama in the home and were genuinely making a contribution to their own improvement and to the well-being of the family. Parents reinforced these early dispositions and perceptions by offering liberal praise and providing multiple opportunities for attention to the child.

Parents were careful simultaneously to encourage and to maintain some cohesion-building family rituals that involved group singing, conversation, and reading aloud within an affect-authority relationship characterized by firm but warm supervision and support. During family discussions, the children would hear different viewpoints and interpretations on the same issue. It was out of these verbal activities that the students learned to make broad, universalistic interpretations of social issues as well as to understand the context-specific meanings of issues.

Parents were frequently assisted by expert caregivers (for example, relatives and other committed parents) and by older siblings in engaging the students in such diverse activities as role-playing games, show-and-tell games, rhyming and spelling games, riddling, problem-solving discussions, discussion of classic literary works, storytelling and fables, creative arts activities, writing exercises, language development emphasizing verbal articulation of the middle-class argot, math exercises, study of newspaper articles and magazines, analysis of charts and graphs, and other discourse events that overtly and latently taught language skills and social skills that enable the children to negotiate the classroom setting successfully.

The most basic function of these early home activities was to teach the children the following student-related skills: (1) classificatory skills for organizing thoughts and concepts, (2) problem-solving and decision making skills, (3) ability to ask and answer higher-order questions, (4) display of etiquette and social graces, (5) skills in consumerism, (6) skills in self-appraisal and self-improvement, (7) talent in articulating personal beliefs, (8) strategies for processing new information for long-term memory (and reasons for doing so), (9) efficacy in effective interpersonal communication in small groups, (10) skills in listening carefully to others, (11) skills in observing and analyzing the verbal and social behavior of others, (12) insights about interpreting other person's motivations, and (13) flexibility in playing superordinate, subordinate, and egalitarian roles.

A significant amount of television-watching was monitored at home and was supplemented by parental discussions and explanations. Parents believed that television programs influenced the way a person thinks. Parents felt that sports programs, educational programs, commercials, cartoon shows, talk shows, television movies, and television comedy and drama series displayed views of the world that were sometimes "real" and "correct" but often "fantasy." With a parent's assistance, the student learned to distinguish the illusory images on television from the "real" behavior of "normal" people.

Parents maintained consistently high expectations for the students' task performance by stressing the value of taking time and doing well in daily activities. At the same time parents made it clear that when failure occurred, it was understandable and not a reflection on the intrinsic "goodness" or "badness" of the child.

Parent and Child Personality Structures: A Social-Psychological Interpretation

Parent's Personality Structure

When I speak of "personality structure," I am referring to (1) the set of identities and perspectives held by an individual about each of the roles played in everyday life and (2) the individual's predispositions for behavior (behavior orientations) that are based on these perceptions.

The service structures in the community performed a particularly insidious function in shaping parents' motivation, sense of personal control, and other dispositions by allowing selective and unequal access to institutional opportunities and dangers. These organizational effects have been acutely felt by emotionally distressed low-income adult family members since the time they themselves were children, by subjecting them to an overwhelming array of worrisome and stressful school, work, and community experiences. The psychological confusion and emotional frustration that result from school and workplace biases and inequalities tend to wear many parents down slowly by sapping their energy, motivation, and drive. Poorly organized classrooms and stifling work settings make available fewer resources and support than are needed to produce quality learning in children. In short order, these circumstances tend to tear down the parents' coping strength. To some degree, all parents have been victims of these institutional strictures. Families from low-status communities are merely disturbed by them more frequently, more completely, and with more devastating results.

Parents' past and current experiences in the home and their past and current position in the marketplace are the primary determiners of their current psychological orientations (or disorientations). Whatever decisions parents make about what to do with their children in the home environment are influenced by the parents' own mental health and emotional well-being at the time the decisions are made.

Two social patterns contributed to the strong psychological character of these parents. First, their families had managed to avoid becoming victims of persistent, devastating traumas of a life-draining sort. In their terms, they were "just trying to make it" and were "getting by." Second, they had found mutual support groups (or individuals) within the family that soothed and comforted one another by being available for one another's day-to-day emotional and child-care (and sometimes financial) needs. Importantly, these parents were responsible for having initially sought and received the support of certain kin and friends and for later having maintained these internal family support relationships (e.g., adults helping children, older siblings helping younger sibilings). Because they had successfully held onto their own basic psychological symmetry, these parents were able to meet the challenges of establishing legitimate home role relationships, limiting or learning from household conflict, and otherwise managing the affairs of the home.

The high-achieving students' parents were further distinguished by their hopeful, forthright sensibilities about themselves and their children. Specifically, they possessed a belief in their own ability to see to it somehow that their children's needs would be provided for, a strong sense of goal direction and a hope and belief that things would get better, a penchant for managing their time and material resources prudently, a strong sense of self-reliance and independence, deep self-pride and personal integrity, a sense of the salience of the needs of their children, a belief that familism or solidarity with other adult kin and friends is essential, and a demeanor of organized, rational seriousness about their life conditions. Although life in society had handed these parents a series of psychological and emotional bumps and bruises, they had basically managed with the support and encouragement of kin and friends to maintain a sense of emotional calm and rationality.

Student Personality Structures

The high-achieving students in this study displayed similar personality patterns in terms of their generally high self-regard, their well-adjusted gender role identity and cross-sex relations, their sense of ethnicity or race, and their student role behavior. Parents have been instrumental in shaping the personality by actively catering to the child's need for emotional support, approval, reassurance, and other psychological resources. They have made continuous attempts to create a happy and emotionally supportive environment by engaging family members in home activities that produce laughter and gaiety. The child's need for approval is further satisfied through parents' and siblings' verbal and nonverbal (symbolic) evaluations. Nicknames and other personal identity descriptors generally connote complimentary or affectionate evaluations of the child. The total collection of these family evaluations forms a complex image or meaning in the minds of family members which the child perceives, internalizes, and ultimately identifies with as part of a general conception of self. Parents speak supportively of the child as capable, competent, and basically healthy in mind, body, and spirit. Most often, these students hold positive conceptions of their academic ability and high personal aspirations for success.

The high-achieving students have a strong nervous system, untainted by heavy alcohol and drugs, which helps them hold together in a stress-filled, strain-producing modern urban society. These students have the ability to make themselves appear "attractive" in the eyes of others. An authentic, "positive" energy (persona) is expressed in their moods and physical nuances. They maintain a basic enthusiasm and honest emotion about life and living. The students have a strong constitution and demonstrate unusual "character" and strength when confronted with tough situations. In severe adversity, they may accommodate to it with a quiet courage but will still retain a *desire* and resolve to strive beyond the temporary obstacles.

Parents and significant others are available during most major crisis periods over the life course. This reliable support network reduces anxiety and assists the resolution of inner conflicts and emotional struggles. This reliability occurs despite an unpredictable, often dangerous, and antagonistic extrafamilial environment. The period of adolescence brings about increased inner turmoil as students shift from the child role toward the adult role. Fear of failure, fear of success, self-doubt, uncertainty, and pent-up emotions are fairly normal character traits during this period. "Will I succeed? Will I fail? Should I repress my sex drive? Should I have sex before marriage? How often? What career do I want to pursue?" These are important quandaries for students as they learn to manage their lives. They learn (largely from parents) when and how to "act out" and when to avoid acting out. They are essentially adjusting to normal sexual, emotional, and psychological needs and urges. They most often display an inner control in the face of turmoil, which fosters healthy coping with life as it is developing.

The adolescent achievers basically comply with family norms and standards but retain the right to have "a mind of one's own." Parents show an acute awareness of students' feelings and moods. The assumption is that their children will be better people (possess higher talents and capacities) when they feel good about themselves. In many instances they readily point to the positive self-conceptions held by a child's "heroes" and other "role models" to "prove" their belief.

When students fail in a task or goal pursuit, parents offer reassurance and consolation. They try to teach the students to place failure in the appropriate context so that self-blame is avoided. Parents reaffirm the students' self-regard and sense of adequacy (ability) by verbally stressing their self-worth and importance to the family ("Don't ever let anybody tell you they're better than you, always remember that") and repeatedly telling them they are deeply cared for. These students learn how to talk to themselves and tell themselves "you're all right." With this orientation the students are able to bounce back from failures and inadequacies. They avoid using others as scapegoats for personal shortcomings. Rather, they quietly try to teach themselves with practice and work.

These students' strong, positive self-conceptions and high aspiration levels have clearly evolved from family interaction processes which had transmitted particular messages about their importance to the family and about the "appropriate" attitudes and values to have about themselves. It is through these group processes that the students developed an inner belief that they are capable of acting on (and ordering) their world. The students' basic psychological symmetry keeps despair, futility, and frustration at a manageable level.

The central personality pattern shown by these students includes a sense of independence and autonomy and a willingness to take responsibility. Superstitions, phobias, fears, and other psychic obstructions are not allowed to interfere with goal attainment—even though some fears are well founded. Though they sometimes placed their trust in extrahuman symbols (e.g., religion, astrology, etc.), these students never relied solely on "faith" to solve problems. Their independent, initiatory attitude was reflected in their verbal intentions to "get myself together" and to "improve my life." These youngsters tended to avoid extreme dependence on others; they believed that overreliance on others would ultimately breed a sense of inadequacy and defeatism.

Both males and females perceived their gender roles as salient identifiers of self. That is, the females and males were comfortable taking on the responsibilities associated with teacher and parent conceptions of what young women or young men should be doing. Both sexes seemed to participate in housecleaning, cooking, general family conversations, and the like, but many of their recreational preferences (boys with basketball and football, girls with gymnastics or volleyball) were sex-segregated.

In some cases, the parents' own experience with members of the opposite sex guided their approach to preparing their children for courtship. This role grooming process was particularly interesting and important for the females, who had to confront the possibly negative effects of a pregnancy on their aspirations. The process of learning gender roles is important to describe because of its direct effect in shaping educational aspirations. Opposite-sex persons were sometimes viewed by parents and children in negative ways (e.g., as exploiters and opportunists). These views had been passed on to children principally through messages parents communicated to their sons and daughters in their discussions, children's observation of adult male-female relationships, and, children's personal experiences with inadequate male figures. What mothers communicated to their daughters in their special relationships was a major determiner of female behavior toward males. How mothers portrayed "the male character" to their daughters was linked to their own interpersonal experiences with (and insecurities about) males. The mothers who strongly emphasized female self-reliance had frequently experienced unsuccessful personal relationships with Black males in which "I did all I could, but he was no count. He didn't help me." This lack of cooperation in personal relationships leads women to feel exasperation and stress, lack of trust, and a sense of being "alone in the world." Young girls are sometimes taught to try to "avoid relying on a man for anything" in favor of learning to "do for yourself." They were encouraged to become educationally, economically, psychologically, and (as much as possible) emotionally independent in relationships with "shaky nigger men," male philanderers, and wife beaters. As one mother put it, "You can't do with them, and you can't do without them."

From dialogues with mothers and daughters, I also learned that adolescent and adult males, for their part, sometimes viewed females as "no good." Fathers often told sons to "respect" females but would warn, "You can't let a woman *run* you, you have to wear the pants or she won't respect you." The women spoke of how commonplace it was for young males and females to experience a trust-mistrust ambivalence toward their mates. Females seemed to prefer a mate who made them feel comfortable in multiple roles and who could function comfortably in instrumental roles ("I want a strong workingman") and expressive roles ("who cares about my needs and my kids' needs").

These students are aware of the family social position in the local and national stratification system. Having come to terms with their own family social status and conditions of life, the students develop a strong sense of purpose about their self-improvement in school and work settings.

In school, work, and other community settings these students are likely to take a rational position in rejecting notions of an inferior Black morality, intellect, and ability. Frequently, they become perturbed or restless about current social problems. Nevertheless, they are usually at ease in multicultural environments and have usually had some sustained contacts with higher-status Black youth. The few interpersonal contacts they have had with culturally different persons have generally been positive and cordial. They tend to be easy to talk with and are usually quite inquisitive in social encounters. They insist on being treated with respect by resisting the social stigma of Blackness in favor of a more positive view of Black people. Even as they come to know and feel the effects of being a Black minority in a White majority society, they are clear about their Black identity. While high achievers strongly favor such ideals as equality and justice, they usually try to avoid direct racial and social conflict. They particularly prefer to avoid hostile confrontations with verbally abusive or oversolicitous Blacks and Whites. Furthermore, they see it as a waste of time and energy to harbor ill will against anonymous Whites merely because of the existence of such roadblocks as racism and discrimination. There is a more quiet resolve first to improve *themselves*. These students' active self-orientation is characterized by planning one's life.

In the classroom, the students are even-tempered, they handle situations of conflict and criticism with maturity, and generally they adapt well to the school environment. Parents have often shown these children how to avoid becoming upset when peers or adults try to "pick at" or goad them. The students initiate work interactions and perform other classroom functions with a verve that contributes to their own attitudes toward school activities. The students' internal locus of control is firmly established and contributes to their willingness to assume personal responsibility for school outcomes. These students are not over-awed or frightened by the accomplishments of other age-grade peers; instead they are satisfied that their own personal goals are legitimate and attainable.

The Family Intellectual Ethos: Dominant Learning Themes in the Parents' Consciousness

Nowhere is the family enthusiasm for learning more clearly indicated than in parents' perceptions about (a) the appropriate moral codes and standards for family members, (b) the dominant rules and norms in the household, (c) the proper disposition toward acquiring knowledge, including the basic educational goals and anticipated responsibilities for family members. The quality of children's excitement about and preparation for classroom lessons appears to be strongly related to these parental attitudes and values. Of course, these are the very household attitudes and standards that motivate family members to engage in particular styles of educational enhancement at home. (These styles are discussed under Family Activity Structures, below.)

Moral Codes and Standards in the Household

The particular set of standards and morals within a given home should be seen as the result of a family dialectic between rational and ethical family behavior. The particular moral habits taught by parents are based on both sacred theology ("This is God's message") and secular theology ("Mothers have that right"). Behavior is seen as right and proper, first because it is good in the eyes of the Lord, and second, because it is good in the eyes of the parents. Students who accept their parents' definition of morality have initially acted out of respect for the primacy of parents' standards. Very young children tend to feel obliged to conform to the rules laid down by adults and other siblings. Jean Piaget points out that "the group could not impose itself upon the individual without surrounding itself with a halo of sanctity and without arousing in the individual the feeling of moral obligation."[2]

Sacred and secular moral orientations are well developed in high-achieving students. As discussed in the section on parents' early socialization strategies, one of the very first lessons taught to young children in these homes was the lesson of right and wrong, good and bad. These lessons were always taught with reference to how they applied to expected codes of conduct in specific situations. The pursuit of schooling is interpreted by these students as a morally "good" activity. Parents believe that being an achieving student increases one's chances of enjoying a "good" life. They also believe achievement is obtained through regular practice and work. Parents have consistently spoken to the child about doing "the right thing" in challenging social encounters outside the home. "God don't like ugly" is a common parental saying that sends this message. Parents also teach that a "good" child is productive in school and work roles, is responsible, principled, thankful for the "blessings" of life, and concerned about the family. Parents discuss "do's and don'ts" with the child as an axiological dialectic. Students learn the " good" in avoiding people whose motives seem to be toward "trickinology" or "gaming." They derive personal fulfillment when they believe they are doing "the right thing."

Family Norms, Rules, and Expectations

Child compliance with parents' requests is the result of parental exercise of "legitimate power"—power or influence the parent obtains through the child's acceptance that the parent is a legitimate authority figure who should be obeyed. These parents use their influence to outline clearly the family rules, norms, and expectations that govern the child's home and school behavior. In fact, the standards that are set are the underlying bases for the household social order. Parental expectations for the child's learning take the form of achievement demands which are discussed, understood, and generally accepted by the child as part of a personal set of "justice norms" and moral or axiological standards.[3] When role expectations are precisely outlined and reinforced by the parents and other family members, the possibility of family misunderstandings and deviant behavior are minimized. Stated differently, children who (a) understand what is expected of them and (b) understand the personal advantages of doing what is expected of them find it easier to comply with parental wishes. They feel a greater sense of ownership of the norms and a sense of duty to the dominant household rules and standards. They perceive the home climate as a place where feelings are shared and responsibilities are performed with love.

Some of the family rules and regulations are established to control the frequency of the child's exposure to the outside environment (such as contacts with neighbors, peers, gangs, dangerous streets, community centers, and so on). The student internalizes norms concerning "proper" social graces, etiquette, and "common sense" actions during social intercourse when outside the home. These skills include knowing how to give excuses, showing "good" manners, and knowing how to make judgments about when (and how) to "fight back" in competitive social situations.

Parents' Dispositions toward Knowledge Acquisition

Parents of high achievers hold strong positive feelings about the necessity of schooling for their children. The consciousness of these parents concerning education is dominated by four fundamental dispositions. The first major disposition is the mother's apparent willingness and desire to put her children's growth and development needs before her own. Such mothers see it as appropriate to de-emphasize their personal wants as a means of seeing their children's personal development opportunities become increased. They believe that they are making a *contribution* to "a better life" for their children. In each of the families at least one parent has continually behaved in a responsible, dedicated, self-sacrificing fashion and, by examples, has given the developing child a positive model to embrace. The parents have usually made substantial physical, financial, and social "sacrifices" expressly so that the student can see positive role models and be motivated toward the "better life." This disposition is held by the youngest (age 33) and oldest (age 52) mothers of the high achievers. Most of these parents were very young when they first began making these sacrifices. This pattern is especially significant given the prevalent assumption that today's young urban parents are invariably less adequate as caretakers than were young parents of previous generations.[4] In spite of the stresses and pulls of modern society, these parents are often willing to give priority to the full range of their children's needs. They decided that their contribution to a better life would be a strong commitment to raising healthy children for a new generation—a commitment always requiring extraordinary personal sacrifice by the parent.

The second major disposition is the parents' perception of their own responsibility for helping children gain a general fund of knowledge, and particularly for assisting in developing the special literacy skills needed for classroom tasks. These parents do not believe the school should provide *all* or even most of the academic training and support for the child. All of these parents strongly believe that education training in the home is (a) a normal function of the parent role, (b) a necessary dimension of child rearing, and (c) an essential practice for guaranteeing children's success on grade cards and achievement tests. Parents define their *purpose* as actively working—alongside school efforts when possible—to strengthen their children's talents. Parents see themselves as *wiser* (if not "smarter") than the children and therefore feel justified in insisting upon this pedagogic role.

This view of their pedagogic role has been cultivated largely by their basic dissatisfaction with the family's past and current social status and their wariness about "blindly giving up [the] children to the schools for such a long time." These parents cite personal experiences that led them to believe the local school will not provide the children with a quality education as long as it is working in isolation from the home. They see parental noninvolvement, uncommittedness, and permissiveness as lead ing to children's social and academic failure. They are likely to say that "The world don't owe you anything; you owe something to yourself" or, sometimes, "I'm responsible for my own fate. If I don't do what *I'm* supposed to do, I don't have nobody to blame but myself. Right?"

There are clear structural consequences of this view with respect to actual parent-child educational behavior. Specifically, the mothers are more likely to monitor (and be emotionally encouraging to) their children's involvement in school assignments and other literacy-producing activities on a routine basis. Fathers, if present, sometimes participate but usually function as workers in physically demanding and time-consuming jobs. These parents are frequently involved with the children in many activities that require communication through reading, writing, and speaking. The mothers have developed a mother-child relationship that allows for this kind of interaction within prescribed parentally dominant role boundaries.

An intergenerational pattern of school pursuit was apparent in several families. Parents, as young children, were expected by their parents (and themselves desired) to attend school regularly. In some cases, the parents themselves have recently enrolled in school programs or other self-improvement endeavors. High-achieving students are aware of these parental pursuits and consequently come to understand the level of commitment that is needed for success in academic endeavors. They also learn to appreciate the psychic and social consequences that accrue from increased knowledge acquisition.

The third major disposition is the parents' perception that children are personally responsible for pursuing knowledge routinely. Parents of high achievers firmly believe that the children must attend classes, be careful listeners and evaluators, and actively participate in order to learn. Absences and tardiness are discouraged and, in fact, they occur infrequently. Even when classroom experiences are not positive, parents and older siblings advance a view that "things ain't so bad that they just can't be overcome." One bit of parental folk wisdom is "You can't learn it if you ain't in school to get it." Another way parents deliver this message is to say "You have to go to school if you want to get ahead, child." Many of these parents cannot bring themselves to condone school absences for "small" reasons because they recall their own childhood—when education was "a luxury" many people fought hard (and sometimes died) to obtain.

The students' school behavior is shaped by a clear, long-standing family code about the personal and professional worth of learning and a fundamental sense of duty about complying with classroom norms and family norms. Parents have taught the child that attending classes, involving oneself in normal classroom activities, and "getting along" with teachers and classmates are morally and socially "right" behavior; playing hooky or being disruptive or not working in class is "wrong" behavior. In the classroom, these students are expected to express overt acceptance (or at least accommodation) and respect for the teacher-imposed learning standards, ideas, and school codes of conduct for lessons. They generally find it reasonable and rewarding to comply with these adult expectations.

A fourth dominant disposition is the parents' expectation that the student will participate in some form of secondary training. While they do not *demand* that the child continue schooling beyond twelfth grade, these parents readily use themselves as reference points, repeatedly emphasizing that young people (particularly their own children) should "try to do better than I did" in educational and occupational attainment. During everyday conversational discourses, parents are prone to say, "Don't go through what I went through," or "You have to pay the cost to be the boss," or "If you don't get off your butt and go after it, you ain't never gonna have anything." Largely owing to parents' teaching activities and attitudes toward schooling, high achievers have developed a school success and self-improvement orientation.

These students frequently hold high aspirations and expectations for college training or postsecondary specialized technical training. Attainment of a high school diploma is considered important but inadequate for reaching their general life goals and specific job-related goals. In their view, the major function of educational achievement is to aid in securing a personally satisfying job in the labor market. Because these students are aware of the educational requirements and skills needed to qualify for the jobs (and pay) they desire, actions are initiated to search out information on college opportunities. The student reads about and visits colleges and universities, attends tutorials, requests booklets and brochures, takes entrance examinations such as the American College Test (ACT) and the Scholastic Aptitude Test (SAT), searches for academic advice, applies to schools, and takes other pertinent actions.

Decisions are made which require risk-taking behavior—the risk of failing or being wrong. The axiom "Nothing ventured, nothing gained" characterizes their risk-taking orientation. They know how to ask questions, and they seem to know when to take risks. Parents often serve as models and advisors who encourage responsible risk-taking behavior. Sometimes the student may even act out of impatience with parents who are perceived as lacking in knowledge about opportunities beyond high school.

The parents are usually psychologically and emotionally supportive of students' college aspirations. Seldom are these parents (who did not go to college themselves) able to provide adequate financial support or even specific strategies to the student, but they impress upon the student that help is available. Parents are continually on the lookout for academic development programs and part-time work opportunities for their children. Opportunities discovered through dialogue with neighbors, in newspapers, magazines, and other media are passed on to the student. Parents also encourage the student to see school and community educational counselors.

Family Authority Structures

Parent-Child Structures

Interpersonal relationships between parents and children and between siblings are guided by the rule-role norms, that is, ethics and codes of conduct that call for distinctly different role prescriptions and boundaries for parents and children. The procedure is quite straightforward. First, parents declare a clear status hierarchy among family members with themselves at the top. They then define themselves as having the primary right and responsibility to guide and protect their children's social and academic development. They then delegate responsibility and allocate resources to family members in accordance with their norms and the children's capabilities.

In two-parent families, the power relationship between the husband and wife on matters of household role responsibility is not heavily weighted in favor of the father.[5] Since conjugal power and authority tends to be shared by parents, mothers feel more worthwhile and enjoy more autonomy in their roles of educating the children. Mothers use this conjugal role arrangement to define the central issues in the home. These maternally defined issues typically focus on the primacy of the needs of the young people in the family. Therefore, the children, not the parents, are frequently the central characters around which family decisions are made. At the same time, the children are told exactly how their parents' love for them has been translated into frequent parental decisions to set aside personal wants in favor of the children's needs and the needs of "the family." "Family needs" are broadly defined as being material and emotional resources that will improve the family members' sense of well-being. The parents also show genuine interest in hearing what the children have to say about family activities. These children respond to parents' displays of affection and concern by establishing close psychological attachments with parents and readily internalizing parents' admonitions on school matters. Other studies have found that parents have the most effective academic influence over adolescents when the children accept as legitimate the parents' decision-making authority within diverse activities and when they strongly identify with the mother.[6] Indeed, superordinate-subordinate relationships in these homes are reasonably nurturing and agreeable, even during the child's adolescence.

The parent is accepted as the supreme authority in the child's life because, in the eyes of the child, adult status holds an intrinsic legitimacy that is based on legal and ascribed statuses (e.g., adult patriarchal and matriarchal laws) as well as achieved statuses (e.g., primary caretakers, providers). In other words, the child has in the past learned the wisdom and benefits of following mama's or daddy's instructions. As long as these conditions exist, there are few challenges to parental decisions.

One of the most significant patterns among high achievers is that they have received multiple opportunities to play leadership roles—roles in which others are required to rely on them for assistance—while engaged in home academic tasks, leisure tasks, and household—maintenance tasks. This type of routine leadership role enactment enables the child to develop greater skill in accepting and meeting adult expectations, while learning to adjust to a more expansive variety of role responsibilities.[7]

By carefully organizing and clearly explaining the child's roles and functions for particular activities in a way that the child perceives as legitimate, parents are actually (a) helping the child to interpret, integrate, and internalize family social norms, (b) helping the child to cope in other institutions and social settings that require superordinate or subordinate role behavior, (c) enabling themselves, as parents, to function better as socializers, and (d) helping family members to gain clarity about family objectives, goals, and standards.

Sibling Group Structure and Interaction

What a person learns in the home will depend on the kind of information received, and each person may receive the same information through a somewhat different set of lenses. That is, the same event (such as a family discussion) will hold different meanings for each family member because each person's goals and perceptions are tied to their particular status position in that event. Parents of high achievers are sensitive to the individual differences in status and knowledge among their children. Parents, therefore, use their own power to delegate responsibility to other family members so as to structure and support the *organization* of orderly and cooperative status relationships among siblings.[8]

One technique they use to build the students' status in the home is to provide valued information before other family members are informed. The newly obtained information gives the child some temporary power, since other family members (the older as well as the younger members) must rely on the information-bearer to share these resources with them. Another technique parents use is to give each sibling certain nicknames and labels. A child might be known as "the reliable one," "the smart one," "the cute, nice one," "the perfect one," or, on the other side, "the troublemaker," "the slow one," and "the liar." These evaluations of siblings are normally based on parents' perceptions of the child's personality, abilities, and accomplishments while engaged in home activities (e.g., plays the piano, performs schoolwork well, or converses well with parents). These evaluations serve the function of bestowing honor on the siblings in an unequal manner, which directly shapes the structure and quality of sibling interaction.

Quite frequently, parents will make evaluations about individual children based on factors such as (a) perceived individual differences, (b) child's gender, (c) child's ordinal position in the family constellation, and (d) parental needs, goals, norms, and values. In this process, parents impart values and attitudes about age-role and sex-role behavior between siblings. Parents are especially effective in encouraging constructive communication between cross-sex siblings in a diversified set of home activities. Boys, for instance, are taught, "Never hit your sister." Girls are taught that "little girls should act like little girls" when playing games with boys. This training is reinforced by modeling and imitation of conjugal behavior and by parents' sanctions. In these ways, then, parents help establish and maintain the child's status position and, thereby, his or her interpretations of family events.

Parents typically set role prescriptions for siblings which give the firstborn higher status. The eldest boy and the eldest girl usually are assigned the task of "looking out" for the other siblings. Older siblings are sometimes given the authority by parents to enforce family rules by sanctioning the young children in the parent's absence. Although the firstborn child is likely to be given more surrogate-parent responsibilities, her actual authority to enforce her will on others is negligible in comparison with the parents' power. The firstborn child does, however, tend to hold a status advantage over the other siblings as a consequence of that child's own pioneering efforts in school. For example, being the first one among the siblings to learn how to read and write confers automatic status on that child in homes where literacy is prized. Similarly, esteem is gained through other pioneering out-of-home activities that bring positive attention to the family, such as being the first offspring to do fractions, learn multiplication tables, win a classroom award, graduate from school, or visit new places.

Oftentimes in large families children are born in clusters or "sets." Each set of two or more children is relatively close in age, with at least three years' difference between the youngest child of one set and the oldest child of the next. This type of family constellation usually facilitates a greater sharing of values among siblings of one set than occurs between siblings born into different sets. And, in general, the youngest opposite-sex siblings are least affected directly by the values and attitudes of older siblings. Older siblings may, however, serve as "an example"—whether as models to emulate or as "proof" of what pursuits to avoid.

Positional shifts in the sibling constellation are typically anticipated and prepared for. These may occur as children leave the home, when a new baby arrives, and when extended kin (such as cousins) begin living with the family. The middle child may suddenly be the eldest child, or the firstborn may suddenly be the second-eldest in the family. Gains and losses in sibling rank and status are likely outcomes of these shifts in ordinal position. Family conflict and turmoil may occur at these transition times as the family equilibrium is upset.

We need more research in the sadly underdeveloped area of sibling structures to uncover the specific ways sibling groups function as educators during different stages of the life cyle. This effort can tell us much more about life course trends in the *extent* to which high achieving students observe less conflict in the mother-father dyad, hold high status positions in the sibling hierarchy, and enjoy greater interactions and involvements with their parents and siblings.

Some research evidence indicates that the power distribution in the family can condition the way students respond to interpersonal relationships in external systems, such as school cultures and work cultures.[9] The role arrangement of specific home activities apparently places the children in varied interpersonal situations that require the use and development of emotional and mental structures for coping with, and growing from, affectively based superordinate statuses they hold in other settings outside the home.[10]

Parents' Child-Management Strategies

Parental Control Patterns

The way in which parents perceive their own responsibility to the family members stimulates the formation of the family's role relationships during home activities. These dispositions help parents make decisions about *how* to use their powers of delegation to teach the child how to prepare for life's responsibilities and rewards. The particular type of management method parents employ is shaped, in part, by parents' own upbringing and by their perception of supports and constraints in the community and in the home.

In order to have been able to impose their particular standards for parent-child relationships and home activities on their children for a period of seventeen or eighteen years and to limit the degree of conflict, these parents early on had to assert their "legitimate right" to set house rules, demonstrate their ability to delegate role responsibilities for each child, and consistently supervise and monitor the children in the performance of these activities. Perhaps most significantly, parents had to come up with creative approaches for enlisting children's voluntary (and enthusiastic) adherence to "the rules," standards, and expectations for responsible behavior.

One of the most striking patterns was the parents' supervision strategy. All of these parents had the presence of mind to set rather definite and consistent limits on the child's behavior while in school and other community settings. The high-achieving student had a routine daily and weekly schedule which included certain before-school activities, after-school activities, evening activities, and weekend activities. Generally, the parent had, early on, taken a strong hand in structuring the child's time. As one parent said, "An idle mind is the devil's workshop." Even when parents are unable to provide sufficient household supervision (e.g., as a result of long working hours) relationships were cultivated in which responsible youth and adults helped the parents monitor and impose sanctions on the child. The effectiveness of this strategy depended on clear, consistent communication between the parents and the surrogate authority figures.

Parents were aware that although their children had spent a great deal of their time in the home with other family members, an increasingly high proportion of the adolescent's time would be spent in social settings outside the home. These parents addressed this reality by carefully setting rules defining "socially acceptable" out-of-home environments and activities for the child. Parents' enforcement of these rules was based on their own perceptions of the quality of the environment ("Is it acceptable to my moral standards? Is there adult supervision?") and their perception of the child's level of development or maturity ("You're too old for that kind of thing and, besides, girls don't play football"). Parents expected the student to act in a responsible, self-reliant, and honorable manner when participating in school-related activities, athletic and sports projects, shopping, certain dance parties, and church activities. Sometimes parents believed a child would behave maturely in a questionable setting (e.g., a party with neighborhood punks) but would still refuse permission to go. In these situations, parents were censoring how much of the "bad elements" the child would be exposed to.

Apparently motivated by a desire to shield the child from negatively perceived community forces, parents refused to allow these teens to "run the streets all the time." Instead, parents monitored and restricted the child's social activities and general mobility in the community in an attempt to protect against "devilment" and the nonproductive activities that "might make a good kid turn bad." Gangs, criminals, and delinquents, alcohol and drug use, violence, police brutality and abuse, persons who are "up to no good," certain social gatherings, abusive working conditions (if the child is employed), and other deviant community influences are labelled as "off-limits" by parents, because they are believed to encourage moral and social misconduct.

Parents in large cities find their monitoring job extremely difficult in disaster communities of high unemployment and despair. These parents tried to avoid acting out their job frustrations on family members. They reinforced their wishes by regularly communicating to the child that as long as the child remains in the home, family goals and norms take precedence over suspicious social settings. Also, other siblings, neighbors, and friends are solicited by the parents to keep an eye out for the student. The child is given advice for self-protection against all kinds of intimidating situations, including physical attacks, thefts, rape, robbery, and threats.

The higher achiever was more likely to associate with age-grade cohorts and adults from diverse social class, religious, and ethnic groups. His or her friends were usually in the same age category, although they were sometimes slightly older than the student. Usually less than twice a week, the student was in telephone contact with these friends.

The student's "friends," "buddies," "girl friends," and "associates" are observed, questioned, and screened by the parents to detect the "problem children" and "troublemakers." Mothers were particularly wary about their boys spending time in gangs and their girls associating with girls who were pregnant or who were already mothers themselves. Whenever possible, parents attempted to get to know the child's friends' parents. They would tacitly evaluate these parents' environment and habits as they determined whether or not to support a continued friendship between the children. If the "friend's" parents appeared to be poor role models, the student's parents discouraged further contact with the "shady" or "funny" family. Objections by the child were met by parents' forceful assertions: "I don't care if every parent on this block lets their kid do that, you are not going to do it."

Parents of high achievers had held onto the ideology that it was their "legitimate right" and responsibility to set limits on the children's decision-making powers. The parents' basic strategy had been to label children's first conformity to parents' wishes as the "good" and "right" thing to do. The parents usually explained that the salience of their own decisions could be justified by the fundamentally "good" ethical standards on which they were based, as well as on the parents' superior knowledge of such matters. Ironically, while the child was being tutored in certain moral and ethical standards which stressed the intrinsic primacy of parentally defined "right" behavior, parents showered the child with verbal and physical signs of affection, praised the child's personal worth to the family and provided liberal emotional support. The early result had been that the child started to feel solid acceptance of the ways of the household and to make a personal commitment to behave in a responsible, trustworthy manner. These parents had been very effective in inculcating the child with this particular set of psychological dispositions and behavioral habits. They then proceeded to use their authoritative advantage to structure activities for the child while in the home and away from the home. While operating in this mode, parents were able to monitor the child's comings and goings closely and effectively.

Disputes and conflicts were usually given due process so as to resolve them in a fair and loving way. Parents attempted to "get to the bottom" of conflicts and trace the source of the conflict to the child's needs. On those occasions when enforcement of the rules was needed to get the child "back in line" with his or her role responsibility, parents would warn the child of impending punishment or actually mete out the punishment. The two types of warning that parents used were: verbal, such as, "If you keep it up, I'm going to spank your booty-cake," and nonverbal, such as (a) using distraction techniques to draw the child away from undesirable experiences, or (b) quietly staring at the child with disapproving looks or "the evil eye" which the child had come to understand as being the precursor of a more direct form of parental confrontation. When more direct sanctions were required, they were used sparingly. Three types of corrective feedback sanctions were typically used by these parents: temporary withdrawal of privileges, spanking and occasional "whipping," and face-to-face talks with the child about the behavior in question.

The parent routinely enforced most major rules while other "less important" rules were sometimes ignored. While developing their strategies for home management, these parents were consistent in their expectations and made sure that the student was highly functional and well-integrated into the family activities. Within prescribed parameters (determined by parentally approved norms), the student was allowed flexibility and was encouraged to be creative and to grow. In their state of emotional connectedness to the general family cultural pattern, through task-oriented involvements, these students tended to be generally amenable to supervision and sanctioning.

The Danger of Overcontrol

We could say that within well-defined parameters these parents were exercising an "authoritative" guidance of the student's use of time and space. Baumrind found this same management style in families of White middle class instrumentally competent youth.[11] The studies of Dr. Baumrind and her colleagues are among the most carefully conducted researches on parental control with preschool children. She describes the authoritative parent as one who tries to:

> direct the child's activities but in a rational, issue-oriented manner. She encourages verbal give and take and shares with the child the reasoning behind her policy. She values both expressive and instrumental attributes, both autonomous self-will and disciplined conformity. Therefore, she exerts firm control at points of parent-child divergence, but does not hem the child in with restrictions. She recog-

nizes her own special rights as an adult, but also the child's individual interests and special ways. The authoritative parent affirms the child's present qualities, but also sets standards for future conduct. She uses reason as well as power to achieve her objectives. She does not base her decisions on group consensus or the individual child's desires; but also, does not regard herself as infallible, or divinely inspired."[12]

The evidence she has amassed, when linked with the findings of this study and studies such as those done by McClelland, suggests that parents of competent American students may use similar management styles, regardless of family ethnicity or social class.[13]

The research of Baumrind and her colleagues at the University of California reveals that a child's "instrumental social competence" is most enhanced when parents are *not* primarily authoritarian or coercive (or too permissive) in their relationships with their children.[14] In some of the families we have discussed, parents were struggling to discover and peacefully pass on "survival knowledge" to their developing adolescent sons and daughters ("But, I'm doing it for your own good") in order that they might seize available opportunities in an often hostile resource marketplace. Students sometimes felt pressured and put-upon by the parent's ideologically conservative style of "sponsoring" the child into this knowledge. As peer group influences increased (and as new reference groups became more crystallized), the students often started to view themselves as victims of excessive parental demands. Students saw parents not as *providing* opportunities, but as restraining them from the opportunity to grow up, to "come out," and learn to play mature, "adult" roles on their own. Girls might even consider actively seeking a husband or boyfriend and/or pregnancy as a way of establishing "independence."

Parents were sensitive to the child's complaints and to their lowered morale in the house since they did, indeed, recognize the importance of allowing the adolescent to "grow up" and prepare for the realities of surviving as an independent adult in a generally nonsupportive ("every man for himself") and regularly hostile, conflict-ridden world. These parents were ultimately able to keep a modicum of control and maintain a reasonably healthy, cooperative, consensus-based relationship with their adolescent children in the face of these delicate tensions by showing patience, and providing plenty of opportunities for personal (and personable) communication, sharing, and decision-making, while continuing to seek voluntary compliance and avoiding a direct conflict of wills with their children.[15]

Nurturance and Support Strategies of Management

Parents were able to get voluntary compliance with their authority-derived demands by encouraging a generally pleasant mood in the household and never allowing the parent-child affectional bond to deteriorate into irreparable discord or hate. This was accomplished by engaging the child in regular communication rituals and traditions that involved verbal comforting, praising, hugging, kissing, smiling, showing, helping, instructing, questioning, and responding behavior. Rituals such as hair grooming and styling, nail cutting and polishing, bathing and massaging, dancing and singing, storytelling, television watching (especially programs that portray Blacks in positive roles and relationships), grocery shopping, cooking favorite foods and baking cookies and cakes, dressing, serving and eating meals, and joking sessions served as ideal activities for sharing affection and "good times." These same events became excellent situations for discussing personal fears, distresses, criticisms, complaints, and other feelings. At least one parent regularly "strokes" the student by (a) verbally validating her importance as a person, (b) expressing to the student that she is loved, appreciated, and understood, and (c) soothing, reassuring, guiding, and protecting the student. In two-parent homes, both parents supported the child in these ways. The child's resultant *perception* of being loved became the intrinsic reward.

Holiday rituals are family affairs at which love and happy times are the order of the day. Helping to make the dressing or the pies, decorating the Christmas tree, dyeing the Easter eggs, choosing a Halloween costume and creating "trick or treat" lines, preparing a dish for the Kwanza celebration, and picnicking on the Fourth of July, these are the ways the child learns to celebrate, to enjoy, and to appreciate what family life and traditions are about. Parties, birthday celebrations, receptions, and other events occur to celebrate successes and good fortunes of family members. School graduations, any improvement in the family economic status, and release from the armed services are considered times for celebration and happiness. The student learns to associate *successful* times with *happy* times. These celebrations reinforce the sense of accomplishment and bolster the student's belief that intensive activities were worth doing.

Funerals, family reunions, weddings, baptisms, and routine home visits are ceremonies where aunts, uncles, and grandparents get in on the act by offering advice and other assistance to the parents and children. These kin often provide direct positive reinforcement to the achieving child by giving verbal praise, encouragement to "keep on pushing," and inexpensive gifts.[16]

Family Activity Structures

Organizing Learning Activities in the Home—A Conceptual Statement

Parents are legally and socially endowed with the right to delegate tasks and duties and thereby act as the central possessors of power and influence in the home. It is this power to delegate tasks and to allocate resources that gives parents the opportunity to make a difference in their children's education, because the parents can decide exactly what activities the child will engage in, and can select roles the child will play within these activities. The pedagogic work performed during these routine activities in the home will shape children's cognitive structures. The underlying logic here is that what a person spends time doing will determine what he or she does best.

All home activities function as structured contexts for the transmission and enculturation of specific interpersonal skills and information to family members. Since these structured contexts or situations serve to control the flow of knowledge to family members, home activity structures are the ultimate home determiners of the quality of a child's mental structures. Also, activity structures which have the fullest inculcative effect on children's cognitive dispositions are those that have become routinized or ritualized into the recurrent, everyday practices of the family.[17] For all these reasons, the study of home activity patterns holds a special potential for helping educators understand how children learn in the home. In Figure 5.1, I present a typology of home activities and their pedagogic functions. This typology is useful in addressing the question "What are the types of activities that parents of high achievers typically encourage in their children?"[18]

Every household is unique with respect to (a) parents' and children's activity patterns (home maintenance activities, home recreational activities, and instructional-informational activities), (b) the degree to which they engage in specific activities, (c) the developmental sequence in which these activities are performed, and (d) the individualistic nature of children's contact in these contexts. Our theory holds that children are instructed in specific knowledge by participating in different kinds of activities, although specific *modes* of knowledge transmission vary from family to family. Further, families differ in the frequency with which they engage in particular activities. Families also differ in the variety and substance of material resources that are used in their activities. For example, one family may play a game of chess with a standard chess set whereas another family may play the same chess game with a home minicomputer.

For another example, the parents' communication style may be characterized predominantly by a pattern of highly monitored home recreational activities during the child's preschool years, but minimally monitored home maintenance activities during the child's preadolescent years. The family next door, on the other hand, may have engaged their very young children in minimally monitored home recreational activities but then used a large amount of home time during the children's preadolescent years engaging in highly monitored, instructional and informational activities. Families also differ in the degree of established strict, specific rules they have about *when* and *how* such activities should occur. A carefully

FIGURE 5.1
Typology of Pedagogic Modes and Activities

Home Maintenance Activities	Informational and Recreational Activities
Housekeeping, cooking chores	Studying, homework
Caretaking, babysitting	Watching TV
Managing bills and business items	Listening to radio and records
Personal grooming, hygiene	Reading (aloud, quietly; alone, collectively)
Praying, meditating	Problem-solving discussions
	Educational-occupational talks
	Games (e.g., checkers, cards, word choices, reasoning games)
	Home computer use
	Hobbies (e.g., art, photography)
	Letter writing
	Memorization exercises
	Social etiquette practice
	Celebrations, traditions (e.g., "coming out" events, birthday parties)
	Telephone conversations
	Rap sessions, storytelling
	Playing, singing

monitored activity would be seen if a parent insisted that the child make the bed every morning "without a wrinkle," whereas this same activity would be less intensely monitored if the child occasionally performed it without a lot of attention to detail. Another carefully monitored activity might be watching particular television programs with the child in the home at particular times of the day, on a regular basis.

Activities that occur in and around the house and that directly contribute to the aesthetic and hygienic maintenance of the household and its members are covered by the home maintenance activities category. As with the other activities, families differ in the frequency of their engagement in the specific behaviors listed.

Home recreational activities are all those interactive encounters that participating family members define as done primarily for leisure and entertainment. The participants in these activities might be able to see an intellectual value in the activity, but their purpose for engaging in it is essentially nonacademic. Since the classification of these activities is based on the family member's expressed or intended purpose for the activity (whether basically for recreational purposes or basically for cognitive academic development), we may see the same activities as serving different purposes for families. All "recreational" activities could be listed again in an instructional category. The actual cognitive consequences of family activity patterns depend, in part, on the family member's *intended purpose* when engaged in a particular event. Every home activity that is seen by family participants as *primarily* providing them with specific academic information, knowledge, or academic skills could be classified as an indicator of deliberate pedagogy. Those activities family members do not engage in for the principal purpose of increasing their scholastic, intellectual, or literacy development are indicators of implicit pedagogy.

Processes of Deliberate Pedagogy in the Home and Neighborhood

Most deliberate home pedagogy is directly overseen by parents and is aimed explicitly at training the child for some competent action inside or outside the family. In high achievers' families, this parentally guided pedagogy frequently takes the form of preparing the child to behave responsibly in the classroom and in the wider community. Parents specifically impart information to the child about how to prepare for the teacher-peer-pupil relationships in the school environment, how to handle themselves in socially complicated (e.g., racially mixed) situations, and, later how to handle courtship. The communication modes used by parents and children include dialogues, study sessions, routine verbal labeling of events, objects, and concepts, and observation of selected television programs with the child. (The television viewing is frequently mediated by parental interpretation of the events being enacted on the screen.) The family's approach to these role training tasks is crucial.

During the child's preschool and early school years, parents attempted to prepare the child for school tasks during home conversations, study encounters, and other activities that called upon the child to speak, read, spell, and solve challenging problems. Activities involving sensory stimulation, learning by rote, sorting, classifying, and memorizing dominated the parent's early style of communication with the child, but progressive pedagogical techniques (e.g., discovering the child's interests; encouraging learning by doing; systematically drawing upon past experiences to solve current problems empirically or logically) were soon incorporated into the parent-child communication encounters in an attempt to pass on knowledge about the dominant culture as well as knowledge about community institutions (including schools) and family matters.

Children eventually developed their own interests and ideas for intellectual exploration. For example, sometimes a television program or a newspaper story would motivate the child to read further on a topic. As the need for specific knowledge grew, the high achiever purposefully sought (and discovered) answers to the question, "Where can I find more information about my problem?" The student was then shown how to teach himself by using the dictionary or encyclopedia to find answers to homework questions. Homework and study skills have enabled the achievers to internalize more permanently what they have learned from direct knowledge pursuits.

These home lessons are sometimes preplanned but are more often offered spontaneously as the children demonstrate natural readiness for more complex learning tasks in the home. They are encouraged to initiate enjoyable home activities that will expand their vocabulary through speaking, reading, and listening. These progressive home communication techniques are effective in providing the students with opportunities to practice home problem-solving tasks and enable them to develop skills applicable to challenging problems in classroom settings as well. The child is soon able to work alone at home and to continue to develop useful classroom skills for greater success with school tasks. When the student claims, "I don't have no homework, the teacher didn't give us any" for days at a time, the parents often assign their own homework. What the parents assign depends on what skills they believe the student needs to improve. The students engage in some type of reading activity almost daily. Writing assignments of a paragraph or more are done several times a week. Library visits generally occur at least once a month during the school year.

Homework and study are regularly performed, almost ritualistic, activities in the home. Homework generally is done in early evening hours, and reading is often done just before bedtime. The student has accepted responsibility for completing homework assignments since elementary school on. Parents usually monitor homework closely, including work with flash cards, art projects, research projects, reading, and writing assignments, in the child's first school years, while slowly urging self-regulation in these activities. Parents vigilantly guide the children's study efforts in the home until they exhibit a modicum of self-sufficiency in correctly completing homework assignments before they are due. At this point the parents' homework-monitoring role usually becomes less directive and more suggestive.

Parental expectations for successful completion of school assignments tend to ensure that students will devote ample time and thought to school responsibilities. By the time the children reach junior high school, they have learned how to observe, analyze, generalize, and verify phenomena. The parent has, in effect, used a scientific method of instruction to help the child develop a scientific method of inductive and deductive reasoning.

Routine family dialogues are frequently used by parents as occasions to stress to the student that schooling is important. Formal and informal home dialogues between parents and children are regular occurrences. These events reinforce the student's awareness of parental attitudes toward schooling as parents teach their children the proper way to record events that occur in the classroom. Children's school conflicts and crises are discussed and used as opportunities to reaffirm the importance of going to school and "doing your work." Parents admonish the student not to "be scared to explore the environment" and "learn from everybody." The teacher's role is explained as "a person who is there to help *you*, because she already has her education."

Even when parents express reservations about the child's school program, they view school curricular offerings as potentially providing essential knowledge for success in specific occupational fields. Family members frequently share information and views about the behaviors and motivations of workers in every profession they know something about. Parents and children discuss the strategies parents have used in their own quest for self-betterment and family betterment.

Beginning early in life, these youths are taught important lessons in "interpersonal diplomacy." Most often, lessons for adult-child communication are transmitted in an inductive, matter-of-fact fashion when parents discuss their work environment and comment on their on-the-job and off-the-job relations with Black, White, Hispanic, and Asian American co-workers. On these occasions, children receive knowledge about discriminatory practices that parents and others have encountered in the marketplace. Parents explain their status inconsistency to the student in the context of American social relationships as they have personally experienced them.[19]

Parents demand that the child exhibit common sense and positive "home training." They also expect that interactions with some teachers, social welfare workers, bill collectors, repair persons, and others will not be fair or "right." But parents tell these youngsters to "look at people and speak your mind when you talk to them. Don't look down or away. Don't be afraid." The child, in turn, displays skill in social etiquette, a talent that tends to foster positive evaluations from significant adults. Parents repeatedly tell about their own struggles for survival and the "sacrifices" they have made because of low incomes brought on by discrimination in the labor market. The child receives the lesson well; limited monetary resources will mean fewer clothes, fewer class trips which require money, and fewer material possessions.[20] During these discussions the child learns firsthand about social roadblocks (such as racism and discrimination) and is able to assess and verbalize strategies for circumventing these obstacles. This conversational activity stimulates the student's interest in what happens in the larger environment.

Perceiving these dialogues as forms of parental encouragement, the student approaches schooling purposefully. Education is regarded as a key avenue to economic advancement as well as having its own intrinsic value. Lifelong participation in the educational process is viewed as providing inestimable benefits for self, family, and community. These students are also more aware of the multiple practical uses of schooling for everyday living.

Kitchen-table talks have also had the effect of increasing the student's acuity at asking productive questions and articulating rational answers to the questions of others. The talks socialize the student into an achievement-oriented modality by functioning as a vehicle for transmitting those communication skills and social norms needed to function confidently and successfully in the classroom environment.

In the school environment, these students are goal-directed and success-oriented during classroom activities. They avoid classes in which disinterested teachers assign "baby work" or no work. Their sense of identity enhances their competence in teacher-pupil relations. Specifically, they display good judgment, empathy, cooperation, and autonomy in their interpersonal relations at school. They know when to initiate actions in the classroom and regularly ask questions in class.[21]

Processes of Implicit Pedagogy in the Home and Neighborhood

Implicit pedagogic activities in the home consist of maintenance chores and recreational activities, such as games, hobbies, and light reading. Parents generally develop habits in performing the tasks themselves and then find occasions to teach them to the child and simultaneously to impart wisdom and moral codes about how the child can use the skills to make his way in the world. Hobbies such as woodcrafts, electrical repairing, fashion designing, photography, playing a musical instrument, sports, games (such as crossword puzzles, riddles, jokes, word games, chess, checkers, dominoes, card games, Monopoly, Life), museum trips, picnics, walks, car rides, reading books and magazines about sports, gossip, or physical grooming are routine activities which enable these youths to use their powers of reasoning, creativity and language. The children are encouraged by the parents to take reasonable risks ("Go ahead! You might win") and to have confidence in themselves as worthwhile people.

Housekeeping, planning for holidays, shopping, cooking, repairing broken items, assisting siblings and parents, babysitting, and similar home activities are performed primarily by the mother and children.[22] As a preschooler, the child is expected to understand and accept involvement in the household division of labor by being responsible for some family chores. Everyone is expected to clean up after himself and this expectation begins early, often by four years of age. The moral motivation for this norm is linked to a sense of group support. ("When you play and tear up, you have to clean up.") Parents' expectations for the child's involvement are high as parents teach leadership skills, time management, money management and budgeting techniques, reading skills, and trouble-shooting or problem-solving skills. Also, the complexity of decision-making tasks increases as the child grows older.[23]

Some students hold part-time jobs after school. Others have been employed in summer work programs. Employed students are involved in home maintenance activities to a lesser extent than the unemployed. Parents provide opportunities for the child to learn entrepreneurial roles—as well as consumer roles. Students involve themselves in such parentally sponsored activities as holding garage sales, setting up snowball and candy stands, selling Christmas cards, holding Tupperware parties, selling cookies and spices, and so on. These marketplace activities are particularly fertile environments in which the child learns: (1) leadership skills as typified by "responsible" behavior and an attitude that success results from planning, hard work, and good fortune, (2) job-hunting and job-keeping skills, (3) an ability to follow directions and maintain schedules, (4) an ability to function in routinized jobs, (5) an ability to work in a group, that is, to follow a chain of command and play superordinate and subordinate roles (e.g., entrepreneur and consumer), (6) an increased ability to read, write, comprehend, and speak, (7) the skill of sticking with a difficult or frustrating task, (8) an ability to accept and respond to a job supervisor's praise or criticism, and (9) how to interact with co-workers of diverse racial and ethnic groups.[24]

These teenagers express responsible independence while releasing bottled-up emotions at dance parties (disco and soul), concerts, church affairs, sports gatherings, listening to music, and other purely social activities. These social functions appeal to their affective needs and are viewed as occasions for "releasing tensions" and for expressing the self. Not wanting to be totally traditional, since that is perceived as "square" or imitative, these youngsters are pleased that they are given permission to occasionally to "cut loose" and act "freaky" and "wild."

Social Contact Patterns with Schools

This study was done to learn more about the psychological and social realities of students' home lives. Because of this focus, we collected data systematically on only two aspects of the interface between parents and neighborhood schools: (1) parents' perceptions of the school's effectiveness, and (2) parents' participation in PTA and school social activities. Two basic patterns emerged.

The first pattern refers to parents' perceptions of the school. These parents of successful students show great concern about the school's success, or lack of success, in educating its clients. They usually are not satisfied with the school's educational program and occasionally express the wish that their children had been enrolled in a better school, or that the school would find ways to enhance the children's opportunities for learning. They tend to believe that it is *possible* to get sound training from the neighborhood school, but that this requires parental input. They also believe there are better schools somewhere, where teachers and administrators are better at implementing learning programs.

The second pattern concerns parents' contacts with the school. Owing perhaps to these parents' perceptions of their children's schools, they are likely intermittently to visit the school, ostensibly to check on the child's progress. At these times they also, of course, check on teachers, counselors, and administrative personnel. In some instances, the parents, especially mothers, are involved in parent-teacher groups and other school activities. Students perceive these visits as evidence of continued paren-

TABLE 5.1
Psychological Structures and Social Behavior Patterns in Families*

A. Psychological and Emotional Orientations (Accounts of Situations)
   1. Parents' personality structure (salient past and current issues of concern; aims and aspirations; role identities; senses of power)
   2. Student's personality structure (issues of concern; aims and aspirations; role identities; senses of power)
   3. Ethics, standards, and moral dispositions in the home
   4. Parents' perception of own needs and child's needs (and talents)
B. Intellectual Ethos: Values toward Knowledge Acquisition and Learning Norms in the Family
   5. Parents' rule-role norms for guiding the child's learning
   6. Rule-role norms for child's own support of his or her learning
   7. Parents' perception of child's responsibility for obtaining postsecondary education
C. Educational Processes during Family Transactions
   8. Strategies of teaching and learning during literacy activity rituals (type and degree of pedagogic action)
   9. Strategies of teaching and learning during maintenance and leisure activity rituals (type and degree of pedagogic action)
D. Status-Stratification Structures
   10. Family rules and regulations (rights and responsibilities that are delegated and enforced during activities)
   11. Status positions and role boundaries: parent-child authority structure (labels and negotiated role definitions; division of labor; perceptions of who's in control)
   12. Sibling group organization and interaction patterns
E. Management Strategies
   13. Strategies of affective nurturance and support among family members during activities
   14. Parents' strategies for control of children (monitoring and sanctioning during activity rituals)
F. Community Support (Contact Patterns with Mediating Structures)
   15. Family-school contact patterns
   16. Family-workplace contact patterns
   17. Family-kin/friend/contact patterns
   18. Family-consumer agency contact patterns

*Categories A and B are concerned with cognitive, attitudinal, and affective aspects of home life. These categories represent the "senses of reality" that "energize" and "govern" the structure and processes of family interaction. Categories C, D, E, and F refer to the social organization of face-to-face interactions between family members during daily social situations. These interactions provide opportunities for family members to develop cognitive skills and social etiquette.

tal expectation of their successful school performance and of parental acceptance of some responsibility for that performance. These parent-initiated contacts with the school also reinforce the students' identification with teachers and their acceptance of the student role.

Summary and Postscript

The categories of family patterns in Table 5.1 represent my psychosocial classification of family structures and discourse areas. Discussion of these family patterns has appeared in the preceding pages. These categories represent concepts of family psychological orientations, household intellectual ethos and learning themes, status-stratification structures in the home, child-management styles, home activity structures, and family-school contact patterns.

All of these families are functioning in the face of severe hardships and daily challenges to their physical and psychological survival. Even though there is a low quality of life in their neighborhoods, these parents and students are still interested in pursuing achievement, and still believe achievement is possible. Knowing the future will bring new conflicts and failures, the students still show a patient determination to do their best in school. Their manifest payoffs will be a good job, access to basic material resources, and the opportunity to provide their own children with a better standard of living. These parents and their success-oriented offspring believe, in short, in upward mobility through education and hard work.

6. The Family Life of Low Achievers in Two-Parent Homes

> "I can conceive of no Negro native to this country who has not, by the age of puberty, been irreparably scarred by the conditions of his life. . . the wonder is not that so many are ruined but that so many survive."[1]

The Coleman report showed that most minority students in urban schools are low achievers in terms of their measured levels of achievement on standardized tests.[2] The cases in chapters 6 and 7 highlight the family worlds of such low-achieving students, living in the same communities as the high-achieving students. These cases may be compared with the high achievers presented in chapters 3 and 4, in terms of their familial contexts.

Life in less successful families is typified by fewer social and material options and greater despair, pathos, lethargy, and psychological confusion. Parents in these families are often hurt, embarrassed, and ashamed about the circumstances of their homelife. A very telling indication of the serious problems these families have is their general disinclination to talk about their lives. One mother who hesitantly participated in the study expressed serious concern that I (or others) would laugh at her because of her homelife.

Owing to the fact that these families were generally not as cooperative or receptive to this research, the data were more difficult and time-consuming to gather. Although the target students were always cooperative, many parents either refused to be totally cooperative or they responded to my queries and statements in a restricted language mode. Their comments were typically terse. Their unspoken behavior and body language were clear cues that they were suspicious and uncomfortable as we talked about what went on in their homes.

The emotional *spirit* in some homes was truly depressing. I was frankly surprised and elated to get *any* cooperation from some of these high-conflict and multiproblem families. The five family worlds that follow are descriptive of life conditions in one- and two-parent families of some less successful twelfth-grade students. In chapter 6, I will present three case studies representing two-parent homes in which the student is a low achiever at school. These cases are marked by three distinctive patterns. First, both the mother and the father have been struggling unsuccessfully for many years to become upwardly mobile. There is a terrible sense of frustration and distress that exudes from the adults in these families. A second pattern is the father's lack of involvement in child-rearing activities. Mothers in these homes are trying to manage a huge assortment of home tasks and responsibilities while the husband hardly ever participates. As with most family patterns, this pattern has been functioning in this way for many years. The third key feature of these families is the mothers' almost total sense of helplessness, aimlessness, and resignation to their economic and social lot, though this is somewhat less true of the mother in the Wilson family.

The Gaineses

The Family Theme

Often after a family has struggled together for years only to see themselves regressing financially and still struggling for survival, it is difficult for the parents to effect any sustained control over their children's life styles, including their school habits. Psychological and emotional turmoil occupy a much larger position in the parents' mind-set than do harmony and peace. Argument and sarcasm are frequent; large doses of parental apathy are inevitably transferred to the children. Often a child is perceptive enough to see what is happening to his life as a result of the family dynamics but is virtually powerless to do anything about it. The child rejects the life-style of the parents. Not knowing any alternative life-style, the child chooses to sit back and watch life become ever more badly entangled. Under these circumstances, the child exhibits fortitude by staying in school at all. While Rhonda Gaines, our subject, does not meet our definition of educational success, the fact that she has reached the senior year of high school under negative home conditions is clear testimony to her innate capabilities and talents.

The Gaines family is large (11 children) and poor. Mr. and Mrs. Gaines have lived in Chicago for 17 years. They migrated to Chicago from Macon, Georgia. For the past 12 years, the family has lived in the same high rise project facility in one of the city ghettoes. Though they do not like their environment, Mr. and Mrs. Gaines feel "stuck." They can see no way out of the mire.

Inside the four-bedroom apartment we see the standard public housing decor. Steel-brick walls are painted a simple blue, white, or grey. The tiled floors are waxed and shining in a way which suggests they have been recently cleaned in anticipation of the researcher's visit. (With eleven children engaged in continual activity, a floor would seldom stay as spotless for even a few hours.) Immediately upon entering the front door, there is a kitchen to the left, and a dining area with a kitchen table to the right. There is a window next to the kitchen table. Straight ahead we see the living room. In it there is a plastic-covered couch, a console with trophies on top (basketball, boxing, and track), record albums, a cocktail table, and an armchair. There are two pictures of Jesus on the wall and a picture of the oldest girl (the only high school graduate in the family) on top of the console. There is also a small end table with a lamp on it. All furniture reflects a parental attempt to make reasonable, aesthetically pleasing, but inexpensive purchases. There is constant activity in the home. Yelling, crying, interruptions at the door, and telephone ringing seem to occur simultaneously. At the time of our visit, neither Mr. or Mrs. Gaines is working. They were initially unwilling to participate in the study but relented only after Rhonda's strong insistence that they become involved.

Mr. Amos Gaines, Rhonda's father, is 41 years old and a graduate of the seventh grade. Although currently unemployed (laid off), Mr. Gaines works in a factory. His job is to lift boxes onto large wooden palates. In a field note he is described:

> Mr. Gaines is a dark-complexioned man with deep facial creases and sagging eyelids. His demeanor is resigned, complacent, almost nonchalant, as he states, "I [care] but what am I gonna do? I'm not gonna kill myself." He expresses himself poorly, although he seems to be able to read and write slightly better than his wife.

Both Mr. and Mrs. Gaines initially appear extremely inarticulate. When closely listened to, however, they show that they are capable of intelligent thinking. Mrs. Johnetta Gaines can hardly read at all. While in the South, she managed to acquire a fifth-grade education. She describes herself as physically resembling "Moms Mabley," a fifty-ish Black comedienne. Mrs. Gaines is 38 years old. The mother of eleven children, Mrs. Gaines views herself as a housewife and mother.

Rhonda Gaines is the third oldest child in the family. She is an attractive 18-year-old young lady who obviously cares for herself. At one time she considered becoming an airline stewardess, until she learned that she was not tall enough. While in the home, the researcher made the following note:

> Rhonda is an attractive, cute girl of about 5 feet in height. She is light brown in complexion and has full expressive lips. Her teeth are even and white. She wears her brownish hair in a 6-inch Afro style. She is a moody person who sulks (worries) a lot. She also sleeps a great deal. I wonder if there is any connection between her sleeping and an attempt at "escapism."

Rhonda is a quiet, watchful person. In the presence of others, she handles herself with an even, intelligent disposition. When responding to her parents, she often appears irritable and cynical.

Both of Rhonda's parents initially decided to come to Chicago because of perceived "opportunities." Sharecropping and odd jobs were the only sources of employment in Georgia. Each of them worked on a farm. Before long, they decided that Chicago life could be no worse. Mrs. Gaines relates:

> It was better up here in ways and you know, it got hard down there. It got so there wasn't nobody much doing sharecropping; there wasn't nobody doing much at all. But they say it's better down there now. It was a little better than this life now 'cause you could raise some of the food and stuff.

Products of poor families themselves, Mr. and Mrs. Gaines had to make a living for themselves when they were married. Mr. Gaines was 18 years old and his wife was two years younger.

Married life for the Gaineses is not pleasant these days. Six different arguments ensued during my visits to the home. Threats of physical assault freely passed between Mr. and Mrs. Gaines ("If you ever get me involved with something else, I'm gonna break your neck"). Criticism was liberally presented. One example follows:

RC: How long have you all been married?
MRS.G: Oh, about 23 years.
RC: That's a very long time.
MR.G.: [*Laughs*]
MRS.G.: I'm about to get rid of him now.
MR.G.: Yeah, and I'll be glad.
MRS.G.: You better get him a job.
RC: Well, it's good to have a man around, don't you think?
MRS.G.: Well, I don't see no difference. [*Laughs*]
MR.G.: The reason why she say that is because she's never been without one. That's why she say that you see. But when she get without one, you'll see.
MRS.G.: Oh, it wouldn't make no difference, I need you for the groceries, that's all.
[*A small argument ensues.*]

While the strife in the Gaines's home may have many origins, lack of money appears to be a primary concern. Mr. Gaines receives criticism because he is not bringing money into the home. They find it difficult to be happy when their basic needs are not being met. Mr. and Mrs. Gaines cannot ensure their own survival; nor can they ensure the survival of their offspring. Applying for welfare will be the next directon for Mrs. Gaines. They are presently in a state of despair.

MR.G.: Yeah, it's been hard.

MRS.G.: In the last year or two especially. This year has really been hard.

MR.: You can figure out for yourself with 11 kids it's hard to make it, anybody know that.

MRS.: It's just started to get hard in the last two years. It ain't been hard all the time. I mean times is hard for everybody, not only us but everybody. Even people who ain't got no kids. Things is usually hard for po' people anyway.

The fact that no money is coming into the home exacerbates the schism between Mr. and Mrs. Gaines. Under these conditions, happiness and harmony seem impossible. Mrs. Gaines requests that the reader not laugh. She states:

You made me say some things. Now they gonna be talking about those things for a year. I didn't want to give you all nothing to laugh on.

Early Child-Rearing and Familial Practices

Mrs. Gaines has seldom had housecleaning expectations for Rhonda through the years; neither has she ever provided any sustained assistance with Rhonda's school-related tasks. Though Rhonda's older sister provided intermittent assistance during the elementary school years, no sustained effort has been made to guide Rhonda's academic work.

Rhonda's mother does not feel equipped to provide the academic or social guidance her children need. There is little evidence that Mr. or Mrs. Gaines has attempted to instill any strong moral value system in their children. Although unbridled, the children are not surly or insolent. Mrs. Gaines has attempted to teach the girls what she knows—how to manage a home. Academic training is not included in her home management program. Mrs. Gaines remembers, for example, when Rhonda was learning her multiplication tables.

Yeah, I remember once when she was in grade school, she was in I think the sixth grade, and those time tables, she didn't even know her time tables. [*Laughs*] She just didn't know them, that's all I can say, she didn't know 'em. I thought she knowed 'em. That's all I can say, I thought she knowed 'em.

From her comments, Mrs. Gaines appears to be at once interested in seeing her daughter achieve, while ignorant of her own role in producing this achievement. Her own early developmental years in the South and her early years with Mr. Gaines had been without sufficient information sources. Mrs. Gaines feels she has done the things she should do—basically, feed and clothe the children. "The rest," she feels, "is up to them."

Mental Health: General Values, Attitudes and Personality

When asked what three wishes she would make if she knew they could come true, Rhonda named the acquisition of "money, a good man, and a car." These are the major things she has found to bring her happiness in the past. School, peer relationships, and family living have been basically void of positive meaning for her. She expresses a desire to help others who are poor and downtrodden. Black activist Angela Davis is a positive image for her "'cause she did help people and stuff."

Although Rhonda maintains she is afraid of nothing, she tends to shun competition and challenges. Past school experiences have served to make Rhonda critical of classroom competition. A person who basically likes herself, Rhonda hesitates to engage in activities in which she is a continual loser. This attitude tends to make her nonaggressive and unchallenging in school. Support is not sought from home. She feels that those at home can provide none. School successes, however, do enhance her mental attitude. Her nonchalance, then, can be viewed as a reaction to repeated instances of failure. She speaks with happiness about one instance of success:.

RC: What's the highest grade you ever got in [school]?
RG: A B, in English.
RC: How did you feel when you got it?
RG: I was happy. I felt good.

Social factors in the home are important influences on Rhonda's psychological orientation. Whenever she is in the home, Rhonda spends most of her time sleeping. Her interpersonal contact with her parents is thereby reduced. A physically healthy person, Rhonda sleeps almost from the time she returns from school and eats dinner until the next morning. Sometimes she awakens to watch a late night television movie, but later she falls back to sleep. Mrs. Gaines cannot understand Rhonda's behavior. She feels that Rhonda is simply "lazy." "Sleep. Sleep. That girl just like to sleep. She don't work." Since Rhonda expresses feelings of objection about the family interactions in her home, we may view her sleeping habits as an escape valve from the unwanted experiences in the home.

Rhonda's own views on marriage and children provide some clue to her perception of her future. A woman, in her opinion, should stay in the home and care for children. The male, predictably, should be a working man making good money. Marriage is viewed as a situation that will occur "in a few years."

Rhonda's social identity is that of a female student who strongly identifies with her friendship and kinship roles. Her major life goal is to complete her high school education. The Gordon Persons Conceptions System profile data further show a strong psychic state of unhappiness tempered by mixed feelings about her own competence and determination.

In-Home Living Patterns

In the Gaines home, roles are traditionally defined; the husband serves as breadwinner and the wife is charged with managing the home. It is her job to organize roles and responsibilities for performing house duties. General care and guidance of the children is a concomitant responsibility for Mrs. Gaines.

Mrs. Gaines has very little control over the home activities of her children. There is almost no indication of order and routine in the children's living patterns. The teenage children leave and return home virtually at will. When in the home, the children function almost totally independently of the parents, in that parental guidance and supervision are minimal. It is evident that it has been a long while since either parent was able to dictate terms to the children. Both parents, while concerned, demonstrate an attitude of futility. The following field note was made during a visit to the home. Notice the effect of the household dynamics on the researcher:

> I feel frustrated as hell. I have a great urge to put some eggs in my shoes and beat it out of here. The continuous physical movement of bodies into and out of the house; my feeling that I cannot keep an eye on all the activity around me; a frustration with a certain resignation in Rhonda and her parents. The five-year-old continues to pull at, sit on, and play with my tape recorder and other equipment; though he obviously is putting a hole in the cover, there is no parental attempt to stop him.

In this excerpt we see the influence of these household dynamics on the researcher. This phenomenological experience caused the researcher to feel confused, due to the chaotic home environment.

Peace and tranquility in the home were achieved by Rhonda only when she slept. Trust between Rhonda and her family is slight. Money is kept in her personal possession. Of the members in her family, Rhonda feels the most respect for her oldest sister (20 years old) from whom she has received some encouragement. Although she is pessimistic about her family, Rhonda nevertheless maintains a belief in herself.

RC: If you could be like one person in your family, who would that be?
RG: None of them.
RC: Why is that?
RG: [*Laughter*] I want to be better than that.
RC: Do you think that you will be?
RG: Yes.
RC: Why is that?
RG: They ain't doin' nothin', just sitting around. You see, I know I could make it if I tried. As long as I ain't got no kids or nothin' like that to hold me down.

The number of "kids in the home" is the reason Rhonda wants to leave home. She would prefer to live in her own apartment but knows that is impossible to do without the money. By moving away, Rhonda hopes to realize a modicum of quiet and order. In her own mind she is running away from the home situation, not from her parents. Indeed, she loves her parents, but she feels disillusioned because she does not feel proud of her homelife. Some of these dynamics are seen in the following field note:

> Rhonda, Mrs. Gaines, and I are talking at the kitchen table. Mrs. Gaines is very nervous. She says she "can't stand to sit in one place too long." Her sister, who lives in the building, knocks on the door and enters when one of the children opens the door. Mrs. Gaines walks around the kitchen area apparently deciding her next move. Rhonda taps her fingers on the table as she watches her mother.

Duties and responsibilities in the home fall to Mrs. Gaines and the older girls. Since there is no systematic schedule of duties, Mrs. Gaines ultimately finds herself doing most of the housework. Mrs. Gaines does not expect much work from Rhonda. This sometimes creates arguments between Mr. and Mrs. Gaines.

> MRS.G.: She's got some responsibilities around the house, but now the menfolk, they don't do nothing.
> MR.G.: What about you? Do you have any responsibilities? Do you do anything? She washes dishes and you call that responsibility?
> MRS.G.: Working and keeping house is a responsibility. What else is she going to do? She go to school all day, and she don't have time to work. She keep up with her classes. This is responsibility. Housework is responsibility. That's like any other job. To keep it clean so you can live here is like any other job.

Mrs. Gaines's comments reflect her generally flexible, nondirective approach to her children. To Mrs. Gaines, school activity is "work" which is so involved that additional expectations for housecleaning are unreasonable. Until two years ago, Rhonda was not expected to perform any household tasks.

Time and space orientations are largely determined by the children themselves. While Mr. and Mrs. Gaines expect the children to come home at night, their expectations are loose and inconsistent. There are few, if any, punitive measures taken by the parents to enforce time and space expectations. No firm guidelines exist to shape the children's lives in any particular direction. Mrs. Gaines, primarily responsible for child rearing in the family, feels wholly inadequate in directing her children's activities. This fact is highlighted in her thoughts on Rhonda's school future.

> I think she could graduate if she'd put her mind to it, but she won't do it. When they get a certain age you can't tell them nothin'! They

ain't gonna do anything they don't want to. That's why she behind now and taking so many credits this semester. I can't do nothin' with them if they don't wanna do it. But yeah, I look for her to go. I look for all of them to go.

Mrs. Gaines wants her children to be successful in school. Like most mothers, she hopes to live to see her children do well in life. But her insistence that she "can't do nothin' with them" is a reality which appears to have developed before the children got to be "a certain age." She faults Rhonda for her unsuccessful school performance. Mrs. Gaines feels children are capable of ordering their own lives. Thus, any limitations experienced must be made the responsibiltiy of that individual. By placing the responsibility in the hands of the individual, Mrs. Gaines feels able to function better as an individual in her own right. She refuses to "let them worry [her] to death."

Educational Orientations in the Home

Rhonda Gaines is a D student in school. Though a senior this year, she is not at all certain that she will graduate. She must first repeat some of the classes in which she received F grades. Right now, her biggest asset is her attendance. She goes to school most of the time. According to her teachers, classroom participation is minimal.

Rhonda's oldest brother dropped out of high school in his senior year. He is now twenty-one years old and works as an auto mechanic. Her twenty-year-old sister graduated but is now at home "doing nothin'." For the past few years, Rhonda's friends have also been influential in her rejection of an academic orientation, choosing instead to miss classes and "get high." Still, Rhonda maintains her interest in school. At her senior level status, Rhonda now has the distinction of being the most highly educated among her group of friends. To achieve this distinction, she found it necessary to avoid interacting with them.

Mr. and Mrs. Gaines are not operative in Rhonda's schooling pursuits. Mr. Gaines argues that he is busy making money for the family; Mrs. Gaines expects the children to fend for themselves "because they're in a higher grade than I went to." To her, higher education is a dilletante's endeavor. Mrs. Gaines sees marriage as a realistic alternate route for her daughter. She attempts to encourage Rhonda in this direction by warning her that "if she don't hurry up, she ain't never gonna get married. She can't keep no boyfriend long enough." Since marriage does not seem to be forthcoming, she expects Rhonda to get a job. When asked which she preferred, "money" or "education," Rhonda quickly stated "money."

Rhonda expresses aspirations for a career as a secretary. Such interest as she has in school achievement can be attributed to her belief that more schooling leads to better jobs and better jobs lead to money. She believes that school represents an obstacle to be overcome. But since she has found it difficult to overcome, she states:

> I'd rather be working. I'm just tired of sitting around [school] doing nothing. Plus I ain't gonna get nothin' if I don't work for it.

School success is a goal that Rhonda would like to have attained. She feels it would have increased her interest in education. Her past and present experiences, however, have not been encouraging. As a result, she now wants simply to graduate.

Mrs. Gaines, as previously stated, prefers not to involve herself with her children's schooling. Her visits to school for Rhonda are few. She has visited the high school only once in almost four years. When she did appear at the school, the occasion was prompted by a telephone call from a teacher requesting her presence.

There are no regular homework or study rituals in the Gaines's home. Rhonda's parents have no expectations for homework activity in the home; they defer that activity to school personnel. Rhonda admits that she only studies around test time. "No, I don't study a lot, only when I have to, like when I have a test or something."

With no educational games, rituals, talks, and the like, in Rhonda's home, she finds it difficult to perform well in her studies. Indeed, were it not for the low academic standards at her ghetto school she probably would not graduate this year. Still, she hopes to have the basic skills necessary to be functional in society.

The Jacksons

The Family Theme and Background

Even when a two-parent family is able to sustain itself at a minimal but stable financial level, educational success for the children does not automatically result. For the parents, the rigors of day-to-day urban existence are difficult and exhausting. After over 25 years of marriage, the conjugal relationship may be problem-laden. Parental bouts with alcoholism may effectively prevent any systematic home management. Strong parentally devised educational support systems for the children under such circumstances are rare. Neither time nor circumstance has afforded the parents the physical and psychological wherewithal to be adequately effective in their children's educational pursuits.

Our exploration into the Jackson family constellation includes data provided by all members of the family except the father. Mr. Jackson was never in the home while the researcher was there. His repeated unavailability was attributed to the long work hours he spends at a cabinet making factory. Mrs. Jackson informed me that it was probably better that her husband not be in the home during our visits since he might be antagonistic to our inquiries and he seldom spends much of his free time in the home anyway. During one of our visits, Mr. Jackson called home and after being told of the researchers' presence, insisted to his wife that the researcher was her lover and that she was "covering" for him. He asked to speak to the researcher and immediately began questioning the motive behind the research. He asked, "Are you the police?" Response: "No, why do you ask that?" His response: "'Cause you act like the police." After the purpose of the intrusion was carefully explained, Mr. Jackson softened and promised to join in on the following evening "after I leave work." He never showed up. Mrs. Jackson explained that her husband is an alcoholic fighting to control his drinking.

The Jackson family has lived in the projects for over eleven years. They had previously resided in slum tenements. Mr. Bob and Mrs. Mattie Jackson migrated to Chicago from Mississippi in 1949. There are ten children in the family; they range from 19 to 6 years of age. Our subject, Jerry Jackson, is eighteen years old and the second oldest sibling. He will be the first person in the family to graduate from high school. Mrs. Jackson finds it impossible for the family to live adequately on her husband's yearly income.

Mrs. Jackson is a tall, angular woman whose arms and hands reveal large veins indicative of having worked hard. A product of a conservative southern Christian family, Mrs. Jackson was not prepared for the stresses and strains of urban life. While in the South, most of her time was spent "working and going to church." At the age of seventeen she was married and moved with her husband to Chicago. Then the trouble started:

> So when I came to Chicago I went a little astray and just stopped going [to church] and started to drinking heavily—something I wasn't used to doing. So I finally stopped going to church. I haven't been at all for about a year and a half. It's not that I don't wanna go, it's just one of those things.

Mrs. Jackson feels that "money problems" have been the central cause of most of the family's other difficulties. She professes to hold to the religious teachings of the church. She currently describes herself as "sanctified." Early childhood appears to have been the happiest period of her life. She relates:

> I was raised up in church. You know, my grandma, she was a Christian lady, she's been dead about 2 years, but when we was down South, we'd go to church *every* Sunday; Sunday School *every* Sunday, and if there was a service during the week, we went to church. . . down South there's so much to do. I was trying to explain to my children, they don't have anything to do but go to school, but there we had to work the garden and the field and the

house, and then go to school. We got as well educated as we could, especially the poor peoples, we got what we could. I went through the 8th grade, and I tell my children, some of them be in 8th grade and they don't know nothin'. When we went to school, we learned. We wasn't playing around. Those teachers down there, they learned us. Sometimes my children tell me their teachers have a half pint and act high. We didn't go through all that.

Mrs. Jackson speaks nostagically of the days when she enjoyed a moral, conservative life-style. She doesn't understand the teacher and pupil behavior often found in big city schools. Disorderliness is something she seldom encountered before her marriage.

Jerry is a slight youth about 5 feet 7 inches tall. His face is narrow with long, sharp features, and his complexion is dark olive. He wears square-framed, horn-rimmed glasses similar to those worn by the late Malcolm X. He is a personable youth who appears to recognize the limitations within his school and family. An aggressive lad, Jerry feels he is "lucky" to be graduating in June, since he had often come close to dropping out. He wears stylish, "in" clothing and shoes with three-inch heels. In many ways he impresses one as a man-child.

Early Child-Rearing and Familial Practices

Jerry's early years in elementary school are characterized by his parent's laissez faire approach to his academic behavior. Many of Jerry's time-space choices were not parentally guided. While religious moral values were stressed, there were no systematic home educational requirements presented. Mrs. Jackson did, however, insist that Jerry attend school classes. She also urged him to "grow up and make something of yourself." However, Mrs. Jackson never suggested or dictated how Jerry should occupy his time each day. Jerry remembers having had "more time to fool around."

Because of Mrs. Jackson's drinking bouts, she was not always able to supervise her children's behavior. Thus, young Jerry regularly had to act "independently." Accepting this responsibility, Jerry made determined efforts to "do what was right," despite the lack of parental supervision. Mrs. Jackson recalls that Jerry's efforts were entirely different from his siblings':

He was the only child I didn't have any trouble with going to school. I don't care how cold it was, or what happened, he was going to school, and his report card was always beautiful.

Mrs. Jackson was pleased with the passing grades Jerry received in school. Though Jerry was not an A or B student, Mrs. Jackson was pleased with his grades because he was not failing. Since he appeared to be self-motivated and successful, Mrs. Jackson found no reason to dictate to him.

According to his mother, Jerry was a private child, often choosing to be alone and away from his siblings. She noticed that he often appeared disturbed during parental arguments and shunned conflicts with family members.

> Jerry is kind of a hard child to figure out. He's always been like that. When he was a little child, he never played with the rest of his sisters and brothers. He like to play by hisself. He's kind of a strange child. He's concerned about people, but if he can't help he seems a little worried.

Mrs. Jackson attempted to provide her children with love and understanding. She has always been concerned about their welfare. Often, however, her approach to child rearing placed a tremendous responsibility on the children for their own lives. In a gut-level, survival-oriented environment, this lack of parental direction may easily have negative consequences. Mrs. Jackson speaks of her years in the housing projects with sorrow.

> Well, I had some terrible times, seem like the worst time in my life. When the children all begin to grow up and everybody would [need money] at one time, that's a bad time. And when you ain't got it to give them, honey, that hurts. It really does. My boys would say we gotta have this or we want this. I would try to figure my way out whether you need this, gotta have it, or you just want it, because spending unnecessary money I couldn't afford it. But I would give them some money—$5 or $10 or $15—to buy what they have to have. I was doing this because going to school, not working, not old enough to work, you know the value of money. You want money. If you don't get it, you might go out there and try to "take" somebody. That was the thing I was trying to avoid with my children, like sticking up. They had a lot of boys over here on Fridays that would just scare me to death sometimes. I guess the Lord heard my prayers. I used to pray so much for them and cry. The boys would go out to the train track and take stuff and the police would be out there and they'd be shooting and I was afraid they'd get hurt.

We see that Mrs. Jackson perceives she has successfully reared her children, since they have not become juvenile delinquents. In this instance, a strong push for educational excellence is necessarily considered secondary. The horrors of the urban ghetto have been a continual source of anguish for her. Home visitors were allowed in the hope that her boys would want to "stay out of the street." Again, Mrs. Jackson encouraged Jerry's self-direction and independence through her lack of direct confrontation. With all the other children needing attention, Mrs. Jackson felt she could only devote limited time to "watch over" him. Realizing the effort that is involved with raising even *one* child, Mrs. Jackson feels her accomplishments with the children would never have been possible without the help of God.

Mental Health: General Values, Attitude, and Personality

Jerry's chief personality characteristics are his independence, determination, and amicability. Described by his mother as a person who "likes to figure things out for hisself," Jerry studies his environment in search of his truth. Over the years he has been expected to learn on his own. As a result, the learning process has often been slower and more difficult.

A strong-willed determination is another of Jerry's qualities. His mother has often seen that "if he's got his mind made up to do it, he would." Mrs. Jackson recently discovered that Jerry reads the Bible. She found the Bible in his room. When asked, he admitted to his mother that he reads it regularly. He also practices "mind control." Jerry exudes a healthy confidence in his ability to overcome obstacles. He relates:

> Well, you see, I'm more of an independent person now, psychologically independent, you understand what I mean? And I saw mistake after mistake, and I realized the damage it does. So I go the other way, which is uphill, and the results would be good for you. I tell my partners I'm not going to get into it so they're not going to come to me with the bag they used to come [with] to try to influence me.

Jerry's ability to act autonomously with his associates highlights his self-motivation. Welcoming classroom competition, Jerry believes he can now perform much better than he has in the past. He feels a strong moral sense of right and wrong; being successful in school is considered "right." Mrs. Jackson tells him "whatever you do, it better be the right decision," thereby further emphasizing moral considerations.

Jerry's sense of independence is balanced by his belief that listening to the advice of others is virtuous. He feels that it is harmful to act totally independent of others. To listen to the advice and ideas of family and friends, he feels, may aid him in making his own decisions. Because he is psychologically mature, Jerry is able to view his academic and social limitations realistically.

> I feel I'm not up enough, my level, as far as my rap with someone about any subject; it's not good enough.

Since Jerry is open to self-improvement, he will probably continue to develop. Having experienced many family hardships, Jerry is aware of the meaning of struggle. He is willing to continue struggling and sacrificing to do the things he has been taught are "right."

Jerry has slowly developed a more serious attitude about life in the past two years. One major event that prompted his attitudenal change was seeing his oldest brother Larry go blind. What began as a case of cataracts quickly developed into something more serious. Larry first lost the sight in one eye and, soon after, lost his vision completely. This process had a profound effect on Larry and Jerry. Mrs. Jackson recalls:

> [Larry] used to sit by hisself a lot. I guess he was just trying to get it together to adjust, so finally he just came out of it and acted like normal, just like everybody else. Jerry would take him out in the back and show him a few pointers [in basketball]. Jerry, you can never tell bout him. He never seems to let things worry him too much. He used to talk to me about it; and Larry. He used to question me about it when Larry was going to the hospital. Most of the time when something bothered Jerry, he'd just sit by himself. I guess he'd just concentrate or be wondering. He very seldom asked me a question. He'd just try to figure it out for hisself.

The psychological effect of seeing his brother slowly go blind was particularly strong for Jerry. He admits undergoing a period of introspection and bewilderment. Out of this trauma came a stronger sense of purpose. He was more committed to self-improvement and development. Indeed, he wanted to change his life-style. He says:

> In school, people were looking on me in the wrong way, as a person who demonstrates drinking wine. And I didn't like this kind of thing at all. I'd like people to look on me in a better way.

After years of problems within the family and peer group, Jerry is attempting a gradual change in his behavior. He now feels he truly understands what it will take to "make it." Most of his psychological energies appear headed in the "right" direction.

Jerry's Gordon Persons Conceptions Systems profile indicates strong identification with friendship, student, and kinship roles. His political orientation is conservative and he perceives his family as primarily working class. A major goal is the attainment of security. Jerry registers a relatively high level of unhappiness with his present life circumstances. A self-sufficient and determined young man, Jerry looks to the future for self-improvement.

In-Home Living Patterns

Societal pressures have contributed to the excessive drinking habits of Mr. Jackson, and, during certain periods, of Mrs. Jackson. Mr. Jackson is seldom in the home to interact with his children. When he is home, Mr. Jackson spends a great deal of time to himself. Although Mr. Jackson loves his children—he is the undisputed "boss" of the house—he seldom becomes deeply overtly involved with them. Jerry relates:

He used to give me some money [but] it seemed like he didn't have too much to say. He acted like he wasn't interested as far as talking to me was concerned but he's shown me he was by being a little more strict on me, he'd do it that way.

Through his stern demeanor, Mr. Jackson has expressed his concern for the welfare of his children.

Mrs. Jackson has the primary responsibility for the guidance of her ten children. At best a difficult task, these responsibilities seem to Mrs. Jackson almost impossible to fulfill. Because she has not divided and assigned household chores to the children, Mrs. Jackson finds herself continually saddled with a multitude of duties to perform. She feels it is appropriate that children have an option as to whether they will clean or not. Moreover, Mrs. Jackson maintains that she does not mind cleaning.

Jerry keeps his room clean, but I have to do a whole bunch of gettin' it together before he get it together. When it's getting the house clean, I usually have to do it. Like most families I promise [them] an allowance if [they] do clean; "if you don't, I won't give you an allowance." Usually when I get up in the morning, if I have something to do like washing or something special to do that day, I get up early and I get my dinner on and watch my stories. I like to work outside. When it gets warmer, I plant flowers. I like all that stuff. I like to keep myself busy. If I sit still, I think too much.

Mrs. Jackson's willingness to perform almost all the household chores for ten children has meant that she has less time to supervise the children actively. This has had a particular impact on the degree of maternal control over the children, which we will discuss below.

Jerry feels a closer psychological tie with his mother than with his father. He has noticed that his mother trusts his reasoning ability much more than his father does. Jerry insists "she believe in me more than my father do." Nevertheless, Jerry is appreciative of his father and other family members. He knows that they have all contributed something to his survival. He states:

I understand what my mother did for me, my sisters, my father. I've been helped because of the good advice.

All the family members have provided sources of love for Jerry. Even during the daily parental arguments of the past, Jerry detected in his parents a sense of concern for their family. It was this sense of family cohesiveness, and a perception of his parents as victims themselves, that caused Jerry to continue to support the family. Still, consistent organization and control are not easily detected in the household. The younger children often ignore Mrs. Jackson's commands to "come help clean up." Only after repeated, energy-exhausting admonishing is Mrs. Jackson able to get the children to obey her requests. Still she describes herself as "strict."

> I'd say I'm strict, but it don't help. Yes, I am. I try to tell my children just the natural facts about it and if they don't do it what's going to happen to them. They don't all agree with me but they know they usually don't have no choice, just Larry. If they don't do it they're going to get punished. I don't have to punish my children because they say, "We're sorry, we ain't gonna do it again." I take their allowance away for a month or get the broomstick. If they go some place I say to be back at a certain time, they do just about what I say. They're a little slow at doing the housework, and I have to get at them quite a bit about that.

While Mrs. Jackson obviously attempts to monitor the behavior of her children, the limits on her control are broad. She is seldom able to perform her household duties and simultaneously supervise ten active human beings. On weekends, Jerry admits he stays out with friends until the next morning. When at home, he is almost totally free to use his time as he sees fit.

Whenever Jerry isn't in school, he is either in the neighborhood interacting with friends, or he is at home watching television or in his bedroom "just thinking." Mrs. Jackson will question Jerry about flagrant abuses of time and space expectations. For example, whenever Jerry stays out most of the night, he knows his mother will mildly scold him. At these times Jerry tells his mother that she makes him feel "like I'm a child." Mrs. Jackson, attempting to develop her sons into men—not children—usually feels ambivalent about her expectations. Jerry feels that since he is not "in the street" on most nights, his mother should really "have nothing to say."

While Mrs. Jackson makes strong attempts to supervise her children, her requests to them often go unheeded. She thus spends considerable time and energy monitoring her children and still has little truly effective control over their usage of time and space. Mr. Jackson does not attempt to discipline the children at all because of the merciless beatings he has occasionally given while inebriated. For Mrs. Jackson, the result of these circumstances has been heightened personal stress and tension. Her recourse, then, is religion, that is, "to leave it in God's hands."

Educational Orientations in the Home

Even though Jerry Jackson has a high motivation to achieve, the behavioral processes within the home do not strongly encourage this desire for achievement. Jerry receives hardly any academic assistance from members of his family. Though verbal encouragement is offered by his mother, that alone cannot be considered an adequate support system for successful educational performance. Most often, Jerry has had to search within himself for answers to the academic problems he has encountered.

While there is no real evidence that the family has served actively or consciously to discourage Jerry's educational efforts, it is clear that education has not been stressed in the home. In school, Jerry has tremendous difficulty with subject matter appropriate for his grade level. His teachers rate him as a poor student who has good attendance. Primarily because of his attendance and his willingness to exert effort, Jerry will graduate in June. His grades average out to a D+. Test scores are similarly low. Still, as Jerry pursues schooling, he feels job and money opportunities will be more readily available. For him, jobs and money will be necessary if happiness and satisfaction are to result. He articulates this attitude clearly.

I want to live successfully. To live successfully is to live satisfactorily. I want to be satisfied. I have to have what I want in order to get what I want. I have to have a good future and go on to school. Right now I think I'll do three or four years in school.

Jerry's quest for schooling is a result of having observed the direction of friends and kin who chose not to pursue schooling. He has developed a strategy for sustenance in his adult years. He continues:

I know the only way to get success in life is to graduate first of all, because you can't just jump into something if you don't have a diploma, that is, if you want to make something out of yourself, if you don't want to just live, you know what I mean.

For Jerry, too many of his years on earth have been spent "just living." He would now like to begin to create a better future.

At this time Jerry is making efforts to solidify his goals and aspirations. Mrs. Jackson maintains that, at present, Jerry does not know exactly what he wants to do after graduation. Jerry sometimes speaks of a possible career in cabinetmaking like his father. At other times, he talks about continuing his schooling in a college. Jerry's chief attribute with respect to his goals is his belief that he will be successful in whatever he decides to pursue. He says over and again that:

I don't think anything can hold me back, not if I make up my mind.
If I did the best I could, I feel it would be a complete success.

This sense of determination can be considered a result of Jerry's attempts at "mind control." As long as he believes he can do it, the thinking goes, there is always the possibility that he will do it.

Jerry's parents have not urged him to continue his education beyond high school. Mrs. Jackson expresses pride at seeing her son close to graduating from high school, but she makes no effort to suggest his next course of action. Her thinking is that he is going to do what he wants anyway and "there's nothing [she] can do about it." Mrs. Jackson is not certain that her son's future ambitions will be successful, but she wishes him the best of luck. Whatever will make him happy will also make her happy. She says, "If he's satisfied, I am too."

To Mrs. Jackson, "things have worked out beautifully." Jerry is graduating on June 14, his birthday. Mrs. Jackson has encouraged Jerry by stressing the principle of self-reliance. She states:

> I tell him he's got to help himself, and he should try to help somebody else. I always told him if you try to help yourself, I'll be right with you, but if you don't want to be anything, ain't anything I can do.

Because of numerous other responsibilities, Mrs. Jackson has found this self-help emphasis to be successful for her. In a family like the Jacksons, for example, a high school diploma always represents a certain achievement. A person who manages to attain it must be considered successful.

In the Jackson family, direct parental involvement in the children's schooling is almost nonexistent. Visits to the school are virtually never made. A school visit is viewed as an indication of trouble, not as a preventive measure. It is with pride that Mrs. Jackson asserts, "I never had to go to school for him, believe me, never." To Mrs. Jackson, the fact that she has seldom visited Jerry's teachers is a positive comment on his school performance (and school behavior). He has managed to stay out of trouble. Academically, however, Mrs. Jackson hardly knows what is going on with her son. She accepts whatever Jerry tells her about his poor academic situation, since he is, she feels, more knowledgeable about the technicalities of school, grades, tests, and the like. She states:

> I don't see his course book [grades]; once in a while I do. I ask him about it. If he did something wrong with it, he won't let me see. He'll sign it and take it back, so I asked him about it. He'll bring it to me and I question him about it and he try to give me some kind of explanation because he knows I don't understand. He's always got some kind of excuse. The things he tells me I don't want to believe, but he puts it so I don't know what to do about it.

Again, Mrs. Jackson's interest is apparent but there is some lack of influence and trust, and her active involvement in school (e.g., making an attempt to learn the meaning of grades and test scores) is nonexistent. She relies on her son for school information with full knowledge that he will attempt to explain away unfavorable results.

In the home itself, homework, study, and reading rituals are not seen. Jerry cites a lack of privacy as the most important reason for his poor education habits at home. A part-time job is also cited as a deterrent to home study. A third explanation is that social interaction with peers has frequently diverted attention away from school subject matter. Whenever homework is done, Jerry receives little assistance from other family members. Again, Mr. Jackson defers to Mrs. Jackson, and she defers to school personnel. She says,

> If I couldn't explain [homework] to him right, I'd tell him, "Jerry, I don't quite understand this; I think you'd better ask your teacher so you can get a good understanding." So he'd do that, and sometimes he'd say I was right.

Mrs. Jackson is not able to provide the home assistance her son needs. Similarly, Jerry has seldom been able to receive the intensive assistance needed at school. Already overcrowded and archaic, school facilities make further school support unlikely. His recourse has been a practical one: "Just do the best I can."

Seldom does Jerry talk with his parents about school, education, or his future. According to his mother, he has never talked with her very much about anything. Jerry is actively interested, however, in discussing educational opportunities. After our research was completed in the home, Jerry stated that he now had an even stronger interest in going further in school. This case serves as an example that academic help is not always available (in school or at home) just because it is desired. A devastating occurrence such as the blindness of his older brother may sometimes be the crucial spark needed to ignite the power and determination within. Although Jerry is educationally "less successful," he feels his future is still very much his own.

The Wilsons

The Family Theme

It may sometimes happen that highly authoritarian parents, strongly interested in the school achievement of their children, will help produce an educationally unsuccessful, rebellious, and troubled child. By disallowing a maturing child the necessary level of social independence while simultaneously encouraging conflicting goals, these parents can produce a negative influence on the child's educational direction. Unable to adjust to parents' dictates, the child may perform academically only to the extent that it is absolutely necessary. Achievement levels are low, since motivation has been diminished by a high level of parent-child conflict.

The parents in these situations, sometimes unwilling to admit to familial effects, may place the blame on the school. Though these families may consist of two parents (and be as financially secure as a low income family can be), educational success for offspring is elusive. Instead of seeing their child become eager to achieve in school, they observe him becoming anxious to leave home.

The members of the Wilson family are: Mr. Carl Wilson, 65 years old; his wife, June, 52 years old; Carlene, 20; Carl, Jr., our subject, 18; Cynthia, 17; and Ray, 15. The Wilsons have been married 21 years and have resided in a public housing facility on Chicago's far South Side. Mr. Wilson is a man who has obviously taken work seriously all his life. He is a conservative, "family type" man from Mississippi. Three years ago he retired from his job at the steel mills. During his employment there, he was never able to amass enough money to move his family into a family home. After the first encounter with Mr. Wilson, I made the following field note:

> Mr. Carl Wilson is a 6-foot-tall, solid handsome man, whose body-build alone would place him in his fifties, rather than the 65 years of age that he is. He has a light complexion, a mustache, and short grey hair covering his entire head. He is not overly muscular, but he appears unmistakably powerful. A distinguishing feature is his suspicious approach to people, which is manifest by his sharp, darting, wary eyes and head movements. His image is that of a strong, rugged man who could probably command considerable attention in a room of people. Mr. Wilson is usually terse in conversation, often seeming to hold back his innermost thoughts. His forceful bass voice and his to-the-point challenging demeanor initially made me say, "Why does he act like this? It is easy to see how others may perceive him as 'overbearing.'"

Mr. Wilson is a very strong father figure in the home. When he speaks, the children almost jump to attention.

Mrs. Wilson is a dark-complexioned, slightly overweight but very well kept woman. Her personality is outgoing and, on the surface, aristocratic. She takes great pains to keep up her appearance. She currently works as a home interviewer for a community-based poverty project.

The Wilsons live in a home which has a relatively nicer appearance than many of the others in the neighborhood. Mrs. Wilson has lived in these same projects since 1944. The apartment shows a great deal of effort and some expense in its interior decorating. In the living room, a sectional couch is covered with plastic. Across from the couch is a color console television, a square thick glass cocktail table, and tables with large figurine lamps, an all-purpose carpet, dark red curtains and wall paneling throughout. The kitchen-dining room is next to the living room. A homemade sliding partition separates the two rooms. The upstairs decor is much simpler than the downstairs area. Carl, Jr., shares his room with his 15-year-old brother.

Our research subject, Carl, Jr., is a big fellow, about 5 feet 11 inches tall and weighing about 200 pounds. He has a bulging stomach which hasn't yet quite gotten out of control. An athlete, Carl is a "serious" individual who gives the appearance of being older than he is, partly because of his physical size. He is light-skinned in complexion, has large facial features, a very large Afro hairstyle, and often talks with his tongue resting on his lower lip. Like his father, Carl exhibits a cautious demeanor, hinting that he may be bottling up his inner emotions.

Mr. and Mrs. Wilson have both worked almost their entire lives. Born in 1909, Mr. Wilson went through the 8th grade in Biloxi, Mississippi, and traveled to Chicago in search of opportunity at the age of 27. Since that time, he has worked in a variety of factory and labor-oriented jobs. His longest period of employment was a thirty-year career at the steel mills. Mrs. Wilson was born and reared in Chicago in a two-parent family. She recalls both of her parents working, even during the Great Depression. Mrs. Wilson values the work ethic and is proud of having "been working practically all my life." Her parents encouraged these values during her high school years by insisting that she work after school. The Wilsons have been married for over twenty-one years. The marriage is Mrs. Wilson's second, the first having ended in divorce some years earlier. It is Mr. Wilson's first marriage.

Early Child-Rearing and Familial Practices

When Carl, Jr., was born, his mother was fully prepared to provide him with the proper nurturance. At the time of Carl's birth, Mrs. Wilson was raising two teenage children born during her previous marriage. Mr. and Mrs. Wilson reared their son in a highly disciplined fashion. He was expected to be obedient and always to remember "his place" as a child. Mr. Wilson describes his son as having been significantly "cooperative" during this early period. This cooperation was obtained through consistent parental observance of Carl's activities. Both parents spent time with young Carl, but Mr. Wilson guided his son with a firmer, stricter hand. Carl states that he often felt the "pressure" of his father's will and he did not like it. But, he says, "I was young and had to accept it." Because of his father's stern approach, Carl's social behavior was effectively curbed away from delinquent activities. Carl always tried to avoid the wrath he knew his father could project.

Mrs. Wilson continually scolded her son about his homework responsibilities. Sometimes she worked with him on difficult assignments. Mostly, Carl was expected to tackle his homework independently. Mrs. Wilson seldom checked his work to make sure he completely grasped the concepts being taught. Carl remembers that he felt considerably less pressure from his mother. His social behavior was being monitored a lot more closely than was his academic behavior. His parents' gravest concern about his schooling centered on social aspects, not academic aspects. They were most concerned when Carl was once suspended for fighting in school. But as long as Carl came home with mostly passing grades, his academic performance was never brought into question. He was not necessarily expected to get the higher grades, as long as he passed his subjects.

Mental Health: General Values, Attitudes, and Personality

Carl manifests a strong interest in sports and athletics. He derives much of his ego strength from his physical accomplishments on the field. Gang activities are consciously avoided. Instead, Carl favors dating and party activities. Carl does not particularly like movies, because the images are not "real" for him. He would much rather spend his leisure time playing basketball or football or talking with friends.

Carl is an independent young man who understands that he is responsible for his own behavior. Many of his friends are allowed much greater mobility than he. Although his friends do not have a strong academic orientation, they are generally considered fair students in school. Many of these young men play on various school teams. Carl has had many long, sometimes violent, disagreements with his father about his associates. Carl feels that his father has no right to restrict his associations and reminds his father that "they can't force me to do anything I don't want to do."

Raised in a strongly moral environment, Carl believes in treating others as he wishes to be treated. He may be considered a humane person, but Carl is not a religious person. Churchgoing is an infrequent activity in the family. Carl expresses no strong racial or political commitments. Rather, at 18 he is much more interested in the same things as his peers: sports, girls, and planning a life that allows him to be independent of parental rules.

The Gordon Persons Conceptions System information reveals that Carl, Jr., identifies with his student roles, although he fantasizes about professional sports-oriented activities. Short-term gratification is achieved largely through sports and recreation. He expresses concern for his personal autonomy and reveals psychic states of happiness *and* unhappiness with his life. He would especially like to improve his level of status and prestige. A feeling of immediacy toward life goals can also be detected. Carl, Jr., thinks highly of himself and looks to the future for a better life.

In-Home Living Patterns

To Mr. and Mrs. Wilson, the ideal family setting is characterized by mutual respect, harmony, sharing, and love. The father is viewed quite traditionally as the household head and the mother is perceived as his assistant. Urged by Mrs. Wilson, the family strives to live together in a spirit of peace. Mrs. Wilson, as wife and mother, mediates disagreements between the father and son. Largely because of Mr. Wilson, the household is run in a conservative manner. Movie-going is discouraged because it is felt that most modern movies are "too vulgar." The children are not allowed to stay outside the house past 10:30 P.M. on weekdays. Some of Carl's friends are not allowed in the home, since Mr. Wilson doesn't like their demeanor.

Home activities involving noise are kept to a minimum. The interaction between Mr. Wilson and Carl, Jr., is minimal. They seldom say anything to each other. An air of tension can be sensed whenever they are in the same room together. A year ago, after a long series of father-son arguments, Carl packed his bags in preparation for leaving home. His eventual decision to stay was the result of the mediating efforts of his mother. To this day, the tension between Mr. Wilson and his first son is still present. The following field note captures some of these dynamics:

> Mr. and Mrs. Wilson just walked in the house from the kitchen door carrying some groceries. They are coming in from shopping. It is 5:00 P.M. I see them from my place on the couch in the living room. They don't say anything. Mrs. Wilson speaks to Ray, telling him to go clean his room. She then talks to her daughter, Cynthia, who is helping remove food items from a bag. Mr. Wilson doesn't say anything to anyone. It is pointedly icy between Mr. Wilson and the children. Finally, after about five minutes had elapsed, I said, "Hi, how are you Mr. Wilson, Mrs. Wilson?" She greeted me cheerfully. Mr. Wilson muttered a greeting over his shoulder to me. From that moment till I left two hours later, I did not see him say anything to his kids except once. Speaking to the fifteen-year old, he said, "Ray, turn that TV down."

Although Carl, Jr., was in full view of Mr. Wilson, no acknowledgments were made by either person toward the other. Carl began fidgeting and nervously shaking his leg when his father entered the home. Mr. Wilson's gruff, authoritarian demeanor seems to be at the root of the children's anxiety.

Mrs. Wilson can be described as liberal in contrast to her husband. While maintaining certain expectations of her children toward household duties, she attempts to show love and affection through her maternal concern for their well-being. She also tries to be flexible with the children, not pressuring them to behave perfectly. Mrs. Wilson functions as the household organizer. She assigns all household duties and supervises the children's performance in carrying them out. An active, energetic, robust woman, Mrs. Wilson gives the instructions, but with a tacit understanding that Mr. Wilson will have the final word. Mr. Wilson has no household duties; Mrs. Wilson says his "duty" is that of "breadwinner." Mrs. Wilson feels that responsibilities are necessary to effect family cohesiveness. She states:

Like I said before, it's more or less teamwork, everybody has a part to play, to maintain a home it takes that. It can't be a one-sided thing.

It is largely because of Mrs. Wilson's efforts that certain family members have not heretofore severed ties with each other. Carl, Jr., is still uncomfortable in the home and hopes to move away shortly after graduation. He feels that his father's requirements are too "old-fashioned."

Mr. and Mrs. Wilson unquestionably have most of the power in the Wilson home. Together, they effectively control much of their children's time and space. Carl, Jr., is most upset with their control, a control he feels affects his entire life. He wants no more of it. He states:

Yes, I want to be on my own. Like when I get out [hesitates], I just really want to be on my own anyway. That's what I want.

Carl, Jr., speaks cautiously about "when I get out" because he wants to camouflage his distaste about living at home. While he loves his parents, he simply loves his freedom more. He states further:

I don't mind living with them. I'm not too much where I can't live with them, but you can do more when you're under your own roof than you can when you're under your parent's roof, with your parents around. You see, if you live with your parents you gotta go with their rules, too. See there has to be a limit, and when you're on your own there's no limit.

Carl, Jr.'s parents have prescribed limits on his time and space which, when followed, make him feel like a "square" next to his friends. During the week, his time is filled with school and work. If he isn't working, he must report his whereabouts to his mother. On weekends, he cannot stay out past 11:30 without encountering an argument with his father upon returning home. Indeed, he must account for nearly all his activities.

Sometimes Mrs. Wilson will allow Carl a modicum of mobility. He is periodically allowed to drive Mr. Wilson's automobile on a weekend date. On these occasions, he is usually expected to call home bi-hourly. Carl interprets this parental expectation as an indication of their low level of trust. He states:

What she thinks is I be going out to different parties and stuff all the time but I don't. You see like sometimes I just go to Butch's house, like he play the drums, and then sometimes we'll go out and go over to our girl friends' houses, not run the streets. Like whoever I go out with be a close friend and the girls usually are friends.

To Carl, Jr.'s parents, their restrictions are mandatory if he is to avoid the negative forces in the community. In contrast to the achieving students, Carl disagrees and claims his parents are too cautious and that he is big enough to take care of himself. He views his parents' actions as treating him "like a baby."

One possible effect of this strong paternal restrictiveness may be seen by observing Carl's younger brother. Ray is usually in the home when required and presents very little argument to his parents about their other demands. He shares a bedroom with his older brother. However, Carl does not like Ray. They constantly throw verbal jabs at each other. In the following field note we see this process:

> Ray is 15 years old, 6 feet tall and weighs about 240 pounds. He talks and acts in a very effeminate manner. Carl seems upset or disturbed whenever Ray enters the room. As Ray talks to one of his friends in the kitchen, Carl and I talk about his football trophies. Carl interrupts our conversation and asks Ray to lower his voice. Ray ignores him. Carl begins giving Ray angry, mean-looking facial expressions and finally yells, "Ray, can't you talk lower? Can't you keep the voice down?" Ray, who has been talking at a whisper for the last 10 minutes, jumps up and says in a childish-girlish tone, "Oh forget you, I'm not talking loud." Something about this statement makes Carl angrier. It appears that Carl is angry for at least two reasons: (1) Ray's insolence and pomposity, and (2) Ray's peculiar mannerisms.

Carl, Jr., looks upon his young brother with a perturbed, disgusted attitude. Seldom did we discuss anything having to do with Ray. Perhaps Ray's personality is the result of being oversheltered and overprotected. Carl, Jr., is doing all he can to avoid acting like (or interacting with) his brother. This further contributes to a breakdown in the family cohesion that Mrs. Wilson so strongly desires.

Educational Orientations in the Home

Carl, Jr., is primarily interested in sports and athletics while schooling is perceived as a secondary goal. Carl believes that the only reason he is currently in school is because of the opportunity to play on the teams. Similarly, his sporadic thoughts about going to college revolve around his desire to play football and/or basketball at the college level. Although he reported his grade-point average as C level, a check with one of his teachers revealed that he is in the bottom half of his class and averages D+ grades. His older sister graduated from high school two years ago and now attends a community junior college. Mr. Wilson finished the eighth grade and Mrs. Wilson has completed a few classes at the community college. All of Carl's friends are involved in sports but not in scholastic activities. He admits that academically oriented people are not among his friends. Although Mr. Wilson discourages it, Carl plans to continue interacting with these friends.

Realizing there is a possibility he may not be successful in competitive college athletics, Carl embraces aspirations to learn computer programming in college. His ultimate goals are "a lot of money" and "success in life." He sees education as a key to his future independence. Education, he feels, will be necessary for him to maintain himself financially. Money is the motivating factor for Carl, Jr., right now. He feels that without it, independence from his parents will be impossible. He states:

> The way things are going, it isn't going to be enough to have a high school diploma to wash dishes. Nowadays you need some kind of degree in just about everything, so I would have to go to school first before I could deal with life.

Carl, Jr., badly wants to "deal with life," which to him means being his own person and making his own decisions, comfortably. For Carl, the college degree represents not having to "be out hustling and scuffling all my life."

Carl's past school performance may be described as "fair." Not satisfied with his present level of performance, Carl feels that the teachers should give him more guidance in his learning pursuits. Carl is capable of doing better in his schoolwork but feels it takes up too much time. To Carl, only bookworms and people whose parents always keep them home are able to "keep their heads in books." Carl is proud that he is not in that category. He feels that a *reasonable* school effort is pretty close to his present effort.

Mrs. Wilson tried to attend classes part-time at a community college but dropped out because of the difficulty she encountered trying to be a mother, wife, worker, and student. She now rationalizes that "it wasn't really what I wanted to do anyway."

Both of Carl's parents express high expectations for him in his school endeavors. Carl remembers once in elementary school receiving a whipping in front of his friends, because he had gotten a failing grade. But his parents have not been consistent in their expectations. While Mrs. Wilson focused on classroom studies, Mr. Wilson has repeatedly stressed sports to his son. Mr. Wilson states:

> Like any father, I'd like to see him on the field. Regardless, if you go to school you should participate in sports.

Carl has found it difficult to please both parents. By making stronger attempts to excel in sports, Carl satisfied his father. His grades were not severely criticized as long as they reflected a passing score. Mrs. Wilson encourages her son to "get the high school education and [maybe] go on to college."

Mrs. Wilson has maintained contact with the school through the PTA over the years. She is very critical of the quality of education the students receive and believes the school is the major obstacle to her children's school progress. Interestingly, she seldom communicates with Carl's teachers directly. She has not attempted to find out what specific teaching strategies she should use at home to complement the school's efforts. Instead, she has concentrated on the larger school issues of teacher qualifications, school discipline, and curriculum content. This type of parental "school involvement" has not been productive for Carl.

The educational rituals of homework and study are only intermittently performed. Carl now spends about one hour each week at home engaged in homework or study activities. Mrs. Wilson seldom inquires about his homework requirements and she never checks his homework efforts. Still, she has always expected her son to satisfy his homework responsibilities. During his early years in elementary school, Mrs. Wilson "made" her son fulfill these requirements, but after fourth grade she slackened her efforts at home to devote time to "the community." This community work, when linked with her other responsibilities, has presented a tremendous burden for Mrs. Wilson.

Carl, Jr., does not like to study at home. He says that the environment is not conducive to any serious reading or studying pursuits. He believes the noise and home tension make it difficult. Carl hardly ever reads at home and is sensitive about reading in school, because "the students will be laughing." Throughout the last four years, only once has Carl studied seriously for a test. On that occasion, he spent three hours one night in preparation for the next day. Furthermore, there is an absence of talk rituals in the home. Schooling is sometimes discussed but never in such a way as to clarify goals that would enable Carl to develop his educational direction more firmly.

While he is not failing in school, Carl has not pursued his studies with the intensity to qualify him as an educationally successful student. Sporadic, piecemeal, and inconsistent familial efforts have contributed to a sporadic, piecemeal, and inconsistent educational performance. Various interpersonal problems among family members have added other difficulties to be overcome. In the future, with a more diligent effort (and with some assistance), Carl may change his educational direction.

7. The Family Life of Low Achievers in One-Parent Homes

The intrafamilial characteristics so evident in the lives of high achievers are almost totally lacking in the following single-parent families. The mothers are still working through deep personal traumas from their own childhood and young adult years. As with the intact families of low achievers, it is clear that these families need help, and they need it *yesterday*. To watch these families going through their daily existence, even for a few days, is to be struck by a reality that is difficult to digest or forget. Seeing these families almost literally holding on by their fingernails is a testimony to the remarkable ability of the human spirit to survive in the face of overwhelming odds.

Of particular concern to us is the effect of the home environment on school performance. Our young women, while unsuccessful as students, are still basically level-headed and searching for something better. They still love their families. These cases demonstrate the degree of home abuse one can withstand at various stages in the life-cycle and still be considered legally sane. Let us visit the Joneses.

The Joneses

The Family Theme

A married couple with children sometimes finds that the family can accrue a greater financial advantage if the father "officially" leaves the home. The mother can then become eligible for welfare benefits and thereby provide the necessities which the uneducated, sporadically employed father cannot. Although the father is "officially" absent from the home, his actual presence is very much a reality. Instead of living in the home, however, he may operate in the role of "boyfriend." He is then able to live alone elsewhere but visit the family whenever he wishes. The family, then, is labeled "single-parent," because the mother is the only parent regularly in the home.

These parental adjustments may appear to their children as an indecisive and unsettled life-style. The child may wish both parents were permanent household members, or the child may feel that the father should have no voice in the matters of the home. The behavior of the children, it may be felt, is out of his domain, since he does not regularly provide for the children. In these instances, the child may interact with both her parents in a spirit of hostile dependency. That is, the child may grudgingly accept what is perceived as parental intrusion in the home. Family cohesiveness is, at these times, difficult to maintain. For the parents, effective educational encouragement of the child is almost impossible, since the child has little respect for the parents' character and life-style.

Mrs. Sadie Jones is 40 years old and the mother of seven children. The oldest is 18 and the youngest 9 years old. The others are aged 10, 11, 12, 13, and 15 years old. Alice, the oldest sibling, is our subject. She is a high school senior anticipating graduation in June. Mrs. Jones is a native of Arkansas, having migrated to Chicago in 1953 soon after her own graduation from high school. After her arrival, Mrs. Jones soon met, became pregnant by, and married Mr. Wiley Jones. She was 21 years old when Alice was born. Mrs. Jones has been a welfare recipient for the past 9 years.

Mrs. Jones is a very heavy, generally unkempt woman. She seldom moves from one place to another in the home and hardly ever leaves the home. Her hair is short and straightened. She has no teeth, and sometimes saliva collects at the corners of her mouth when she talks. A pleasant enough person, she speaks in a slow, resigned drawl.

Alice Jones is about 5 feet 6 inches tall and weighs about 140 pounds. She wears a dark brownish, short Afro hairstyle. It is apparent that, unlike her mother, Alice makes attempts to keep her appearance up. Her demeanor is easygoing. She speaks with an air of practicality and resignation.

The Joneses live in a public housing facility situated in the middle of a large ghetto area. They moved here four years ago from another poverty-stricken area nearby. The four bedroom apartment is noisy, untidy, and too small for the family. The furniture appears old but functional. Each child shares a bedroom with at least one sibling. The basic apartment design is consistent with the standard public housing apartment format. There is a noticeable absence of pictures on the walls.

Mrs. Jones does not like her apartment even though it represents an improvement over the deteriorating tenement she moved from. More than anything else, she longs for a private home. For the time being, though, the present surroundings must be tolerated. Mrs. Jones remembers worse times growing up in rural Arkansas in a poor, single-parent family. In Chicago it has been easier for her to fulfill her girlhood dream of marrying and having a family. She never considered college, since her mother was too poor to provide financial assistance. Also, college was never a family expectation. The North seemed to offer the best possibilities for personal improvement.

Early Child-Rearing and Familial Practices

Two and one half years after her arrival in the city, Mrs. Jones was married and the mother of a baby girl. They named the baby Alice. Then, as now, making a living was an inordinately difficult endeavor because of the low-paying jobs available to Mr. Jones. A native Chicagoan, he had dropped out of school in the ninth grade. Together they were able to maintain themselves at a minimal level of existence.

Mrs. Jones attempted to provide the basic needs for her little girl. Food, clothing, love, nurturance, and moral development were all provided by the young Mrs. Jones. Academic needs, however, were not considered, since it was felt that the school would provide everything in this area. Mrs. Jones did not place any particular stress on Alice's intellectual development. Exposure to cultural and intellectual events was not provided. Mrs. Jones says that she did not know at the time "that all that was necessary."

Mental Health: General Values, Attitudes, and Personality

Alice Jones has developed a low concept of herself. Prone to self-blame, Alice often appears overly critical in her self-appraisal. At times she expresses feelings of worthlessness, although she is not fatalistic in temperament. Alice feels that all her school problems are her own fault and that her own "lack of smarts" is the true reason for her poor school performance.

Alice functions in a spirit of independence and freedom, but she is also extremely cautious and does not claim any person as her friend. Instead, she describes her close social comrades as "associates." Mrs. Jones encourages this attitude in her daughter by regularly telling Alice about the problems "friends" can cause. To Mrs. Jones, friends are likely to "steal your money and your man" if given the opportunity.

While Alice questions her own ability to act on her world in a positive way, she still has a desire for self-improvement. However, she feels alone in her pursuits. Her mother does not know how to help in school affairs, and her father is someone she would prefer to avoid. A respectful young lady, Alice believes that people should be civil toward one another. She is not at all convinced, however, that adults automatically deserve ascribed status. Through her contacts with her parents and teachers, she has learned that "they can be wrong a lot."

Pessimism and doubt describe Alice's attitude toward the classic American work ethic. Education and hard work, she feels, will not necessarily result in a better set of life circumstances. Still, she is not willing to stop trying, since her sense of hope is all she really has. Alice believes in God, but, like the other family members, never goes to church. From her mother she has learned that it's easier to stay home.

Race, politics, and social equality are not strong themes in Alice's value set. These areas have not had the same impact for her as have such immediate concerns as getting additional money through part-time employment. Sex and dating are infrequent activities for Alice, perhaps because she is overweight.

The Gordon Persons Conceptions System data reveal that Alice has an extremely confined sense of social identity even though she registers strong in the student-role category. Major life goals are to attain security and, to a much lesser extent, education. She finds very little that is gratifying at the present time. Unhappiness is a chief characteristic of her present psychic state. She appears to care about herself and wants to improve.

In-Home Living Patterns

Mrs. Jones is always in the home. She is very obese and sluggish in her demeanor. Although Alice, the oldest offspring, lives with her mother, she is displeased with the inactivity she sees at home. Mr. Jones is at present unemployed but seldom stays with his wife in the home. Since he is only occasionally available to act as a father figure and provider to the children, the older ones refuse to respect his authority. He sometimes dictates his requirements for behavior to the children only because Mrs. Jones encourages this by telling the children to pay attention to him. Alice resents this. She is especially resentful of his attempts to mete out different kinds of punishment. She feels that he has no rights in the home, and that she is "too old to be taking whippings from him."

The family almost never goes on outings together. Seldom does the entire family participate in family picnics, moviegoing, and other activities. It has been a few years since either parent felt inclined to do these kinds of things. Alice is not unhappy about this neglect, since she prefers to avoid contact with her father. She describes him as being authoritarian, arrogant, and without much love. When asked if she would risk her life to save her parents from a catastrophe, she replied "yes" for her mother and "no" for her father. The level of family cohesivenss is not as strong as Mrs. Jones would like it to be. Sibling relationships appear to be more amicable; Alice admits that she identifies with and cares about her brothers and sisters. She says they have a reciprocal feeling about her.

Mrs. Jones reveals that her husband performs most of the disciplinary duties when he visits the home. She believes he is more restrictive (and therefore more successful) in monitoring the children's behavior. She prefers not to "bother with it." Mrs. Jones assigns the household cleaning tasks to include all her children. As the oldest child, Alice is allowed to provide some guidance and direction to her siblings. The younger children are expected to do as their big sister says.

Most of the control over the children in the home rests with Mr. Jones. Mrs. Jones feels she has pampered Alice too much. She describes her daughter as now being "out of control." She states that Alice "runs over" her.

R.C.: Do you think that you babied her too much?
MRS.J.: Yeah, I do. I really do.
R.C.: How did she respond to this?
MRS.J.: Take advantage of me. They take advantage of me.
R.C.: What do you mean?
MRS.J.: I don't know, you know, well maybe I can't describe it, but you know they . . . if I tell them to do something they won't do it. So I just think they take advantage of me, you know, by my being too nice to them. I think I'm too nice to them. I don't really lay the law down too much, I say.

We see that Mrs. Jones does not feel that her child-rearing techniques have been effective with her children. Very little time and space control are possible under these circumstances. Whatever expectations she has for the children are presented in a casual, languid spirit and are interpreted that way by the children. The pattern has persisted for so long now that it may be virtually beyond alteration.

Alice has been allowed a wide latitude in her mobility in and away from the home. She is one of the few teenagers I encountered who is allowed to smoke cigarettes at home. "Associates" are regularly escorted in and out of the home. Whenever Alice wants to leave, she simply does so. As long as she has returned before 12:00 that night, she will not encounter any serious parental scolding. Since Alice's father is often elsewhere, he cannot always be on hand to monitor her activities.

Educational Orientations in the Home

Alice has never performed well in school even though, in my opinion, she is capable of tackling her school work adequately. A young woman with the ability to learn about and survive in the often fast-paced ghetto environment, she seems capable of learning school subject matter. Still we find that Alice is a poor, almost failing, student who is only graduating because of questionable school policies. Alice is not happy with her own performance. Her reading and English skills are at the elementary school level. Her mathematics scores are similar. In school, her teachers mostly observe her sitting nonchalantly and staring into space.

Alice admits that school has been a bad experience for her. Hardly ever has she had enough success to make the experience a pleasant one. Now, she questions her own intelligence and ability (and, ultimately, her worth as a person), preferring to "get it over with" quietly by graduating in June. The classroom dynamics have been equally unkind to her. She states:

I don't like to be called on, and then you have to go to the board and stuff like that. I don't like that. And then I get mad if I have to go. And then somebody start laughing at me; [the teachers] don't be asking me too many questions, I just sit there and listen. That's all. We just sit there and do whatever we have to do. If we have to do some work in a book, I do that and give it to them. Now if I know the answer I don't mind answering some questions, but if I don't know it, then it's her fault 'cause she don't know when I know it and when I don't know it. They just don't ask me too many.

Unwilling to humiliate herself time and again in the classroom, Alice has become more protective of her ego and less concerned about her ability to perform school tasks well. Her entire demeanor sends the message to the teachers to leave her alone or risk encountering an insolent response. She perceives school as a boring experience, a chore which will one day end.

Alice has no plans for further education after high school. College is considered an impractical goal, although she secretly wishes to attend. On a visit to a girl friend at a midwestern college, Alice was impressed by the relatively peaceful, serene existence she observed. She considered going then, with thoughts of getting away from home and changing her environment. This thought quickly passed, however, in favor of another kind of thinking. She states:

A.J.: I just like the way they do things on their own, things like that. But I still don't think I would really want to go.
R.C.: Why not?
A.J.: I'm not ready for it.
R.C.: What do you mean?
A.J.: I'm too slow for college for one thing, and I don't like school for another thing, and let me see . . . I don't like school that much.

Alice's goal is to complete high school. She does not wish to pursue schooling after this semester. She even feels that she will drop out completely if for some reason she cannot graduate at the end of the term. At this point in her life, Alice does not feel aggressive enough to pursue higher goals. She states:

I don't like anything that's hard, and me being lazy, that much studying, no.

Alice's own feelings of inadequacy in school are now dominant and provide the biggest clue to her scholastic future. She has plans to pursue hairdressing, perhaps as a career. Her major goal is to leave the projects one day and obtain a home in which to live. She does not see education as being a significant variable in her plans.

Parental encouragement and expectations are almost totally absent from the home. Mrs. Jones is not attuned to any of her daughter's school endeavors. She has been away from school for 20 years and finds that a "lot of things have changed" during that period. Alice seldom speaks with her mother (the only parent she expresses love toward) about school problems. Recently, however, Alice mentioned to her mother that she might drop out of high school.

> She considered dropping out now and taking a GED course (high school equivalency test). I told her she was almost here, she should go ahead and try to make it here.

This parental encouragement at a crucial time aided in Alice's decision to stay in school. These kinds of incidents tend, however, to be the exception. Alice has usually been left to steer her own academic course. There are no academic models in the family (or among relatives) that Alice can consult. Whatever assistance she may receive is a chance occurrence. The only reason Alice has not made a final decision to drop out is that her father has warned her that he won't allow her to "lay around doin' nothin'." Alice is disgusted:

> I'd probably have to listen to a whole lot of fussin' and they might put me out. I don't know. Tell me to get a job and be saying I'm "stupid" 'cause I ain't goin' to school. I think my mother she'd probably cry but my father he might put me out and tell me to get a job.

Both of Alice's parents are obviously interested in their daughter's successful completion of high school. The encouragement they have sometimes offered, however, has been more threatening than encouraging. Alice has not responded positively to this approach.

Alice's mother would like to see her become a secretary or a hairdresser. Her father sometimes tells her to do better in school. They both expect Alice to do the best she can. But very little assistance is provided by them. They don't know how to bring this expectation about. Alice knows little more. Mrs. Jones seldom comes to the school for any reason. She has absolutely no contact with Alice's teachers about academic concerns. Once, when Alice was sassing a teacher, Mrs. Jones was asked to come to the school. This was her only appearance.

Educational talks, games, homework, reading, or other activities are not performed in the home. Alice almost never discusses grades, homework assignments, or any other aspect of school with her parents. She does homework when it becomes absolutely essential. Other times, she is happy simply to forget about it. Even when homework is necessary, she does it in school, working on it "just before the class starts." None of the younger children were observed doing homework or reading in the home.

Instead, watching television programs and socializing are primary activities. Mrs. Jones does not encourage her children to participate in any academically oriented rituals.

The Harrises

The Family Theme and Background

In some single-parent, poor families, past years have been characterized by a series of dashed parental hopes and dreams. Hardship and heartache have continually made life experiences less than pleasant. Fighting an urge simply to "stop trying," the parent may engage in a continual search for a strengthening agent to assist her through troubled times. Additional amounts of money, education, and social status are viewed as unattainable, except through some type of "luck" or "fate." Success is perceived as the ability simply to survive. The church, at these times, often serves a crucial function by providing spiritual food to nourish these embattled persons. God is seen as the only relief available for the psychological and emotional turmoil experienced by the family. Through religion, this parent may find the inner strength to cope. Attempting to keep the family together, the parent may involve her children in church activities. Still, genuine happiness is improbable because of the day-to-day struggle to provide for the family. Economic and social realities almost ensure that family functioning will be extremely difficult. Adequate supervision of the children becomes a formidable task. Since the parent knows little about education, she is unable to guide her children effectively in these pursuits. Usually, an inability to control the children is a concomitant characteristic.

Mrs. Betty Harris is a 39-year-old mother of six children, five of whom are still in the home. Frank, the oldest child, is 20; Sharon is 18; Dee Dee, our subject, is 17; Bobby is 15; Craig is 13; and Sharon's baby Marilyn is 2 years old. Mrs. Harris separated from her husband over ten years ago. The Harrises have lived in the project for twelve years, moving here from another ghetto area on Chicago's South Side. Mrs. Harris has worked as a nurse's aide since she first left home to get married at age eighteen. She is a member of a Baptist congregation and attends services all day on Sunday. Sometimes Mrs. Harris also attends week–night services. An active churchgoer, she strongly encourages her children to participate in church-related activities. They variously serve as ushers, choir singers, and Sunday school students.

Dee Dee Harris shares one of the three bedrooms with her two sisters. A high school senior, she has attended neighborhood public schools since kindergarten. Today, Dee Dee is a 5 feet 3 inches and of medium build. An attractive girl, she has chocolate brown skin, full features, and black hair with a brown tint. Her mother asserts that Dee Dee has been a chronic source of problems for her over the years.

Mrs. Harris was brought to Chicago by her parents from Augusta, Arkansas, in 1934. She was one year old. After attending school for eleven years, she dropped out to get married and start a family. As the oldest female child (second oldest of ten) in her family, Mrs. Harris was expected to handle many of the home and child-rearing responsibilities. Her decision to drop out of school was made when she began to feel that she "understood life."

All of Mrs. Harris's seven brothers are alcoholics. She remembers that they were never expected to attend church or school as youths. Mrs. Harris' mother was a public aid recipient during her growing years. When Mrs. Harris reached her teens, her mother (Mrs. Smith) had begun relying more heavily on her service in the home. Mrs. Harris began attending school with decreasing frequency. Finally, she decided to quit completely. Mrs. Smith "didn't say too much" about it. Mrs. Harris felt that while Mrs. Smith needed her services in the home, she was not happy about seeing her drop out. Because of the need for additional home assistance, however, Mrs. Smith did not object.

Mrs. Harris recalls that she has always enjoyed attending church. When she was a child, her mother and sisters would laugh at her because of her regular church attendance.

> I always did go to church and if some of the Jehovah Witnesses
> came by, my mother and sisters would say, "I don't have no time to
> go, someone will save me," and I'd say, "There's no use talking
> about it, we really don't know who's right, and we really don't know
> who's wrong," and I always figured church was within yourself.

Mrs. Harris remembers receiving no family encouragement in her religious pursuits. Her Bible study slowly waned, but she "still believed there was a God." The early adult years (20–30 years old) were spent, "going out and having a good time." Then, about five years ago after coming close to death, Mrs. Harris experienced a religious reawakening. She recalls the event:

> MRS.H.: I always did believe in the Bible, believe in God, but now I
> seem to get a lot more out of it than I did before. Understanding, I
> read the Bible more often than I ever did before in my life.
> R.C.: Why was that? What brought that about?
> MRS.H.: Because it seemed like when I was sick in '69, something
> came over me.
> R.C.: Spiritually or physically sick?
> MRS.H.: I think it was both. I was sick physically and really begin-
> ning to think. Something happened to me in the operating room. I
> had surgery in '69, and some people say they don't believe in reading
> the Bible, but there were two voices talking to me.

R.C.: Was it an actual voice that you heard or was it a feeling you had?

MRS.H.: It was actually a voice.

R.C.: A male voice?

MRS.H.: Yes, it was.

R.C.: And can I ask you what it was saying?

MRS.H.: Well, I was going into shock and the doctors couldn't get no pressure, and they'd call another doctor and he'd take my pressure, and he couldn't get any pressure, and at the time it seemed like I was going to give up. At that time my kids were in grammar school. They hadn't graduated yet. It seemed like I could see their graduation, and some of the kids said, "you're not going to be here," but it seemed another voice said, "Let go, you can make it" and I had a vision of the graduation and all the other things I wouldn't be here for. And another voice kept saying, "I'm here with you always, don't worry about it, let go" and when I woke up I was in recovery. I woke up in the morning and I was in recovery. That happened on Sunday, in July of '69.

Most of her energies today are spent working, providing for her family, and praising God. She seldom engages in social activities. In the sparsely furnished home, two pictures of Christ can be seen on the living room walls. The children, however, are not as religiously involved as their mother.

Early Child-Rearing and Familial Practices

Mrs. Harris's own childhood did not necessarily teach her to insist upon obedience from children. In her home, she served as a helper and assistant. Her brothers and sisters functioned fairly independently of parental dictates. Strong moral and educational training did not exist. With her own children, Mrs. Harris developed a somewhat stronger, but similar approach. Moral training was provided through her requests to her children to attend church. Schooling was seen as important, but it was not emphasized as being imperative.

When Dee Dee was in elementary school, she remembers being engaged in a life-style of disarray. While her mother was away from the home, Dee Dee and the other children would leave the house to play with friends. Over time, the children started exploring numerous avenues to occupy their time. Dee Dee describes some of these avenues:

We used to fight and go down to that other building down there, and we used to fight and carry chains and carry brass knuckles and put them around our fist and go down there and beat the girls up and shoot at them and all that. Yes, I did a lot of it; that's why all these scratches are on my face. I mean, you know, that's when I was in grammar school and a little bit when I got in high school. We started busting girls' heads with pop bottles, beating them up, hitting them with knives, cutting them, and everything else. Now most of [the girls] got pregnant; they got pregnant and they wouldn't get married and like most of my friends are young.

Dee Dee was associating with a gang of girls who engaged in acts of neighborhood terrorism. She still speaks fondly of those days although she claims that now she "don't hang around with my friends too much."

Mrs. Harris was surprised when Dee Dee's social behavior first became known to her. Dee Dee was a freshman in high school and insisted on staying out late for dates, cutting classes, and so forth. Mrs. Harris was not aware of many of her daughter's activities. As a result of her long hours away from home, the children had the opportunity to become involved in a variety of behaviors of questionable legality. Seldom were parent-child interactions totally peaceful. Mrs. Harris was always exhausted from her duties at work and at home.

Mental Health: General Values, Attitudes, and Personality

Dee Dee is described by her mother as "selfish, lazy, stingy, and fast." Dee Dee describes herself as "independent," perceiving herself an adult. To her, it is her "right" to monitor her own behavior. She states emphatically:

I don't want someone running my life for me. I want to do it all by myself.

Dee Dee is an active, gregarious young lady who likes to "party." She likes to "boogie" and "have a nice time." Her opposite-sex peer relationships further reflect her strong-willed, independent stance. Past experiences in the neighborhood have convinced her of the necessity of being "tough." She states:

Like I tell dudes where I'm at. Like I met one dude. He say, "you be good to me and I be good to you." I told him, "Hey, you know." I told him that before we start talking, having any conversation, I want him to know that I'm gonna be me, you know. Like I was dealing with this young man when I was living on the 13th floor and he tried to throw me down the steps, you know, and hit me all in my eye and my brother took up for me then. He kicked his behind and all that. Like see, he had brought me into the hallway and this was before my mother got home. There was nobody home but me. And see like I was a dummy then 'cause he said, "Come here," and I came. I came out in the hallway to see what he wanted. And I went out there and as soon as I opened up the hallway door he hauled off and hit me in my face; and I just started beating that nigger to death and I told him when I got on top of him, I said, "Look, I got to show this in public, and don't you ever hit me in my face." I said, "Don't you never raise your hand at me." So one day he came back and he started pleading with me, telling me he was sorry. I said, "No brother, when you hit this, you got messed up," and so I told him, "No," I told him to go about his business and get the hell out of my face. So he went down to the 11th floor right after that and he got his eye shot out; like him and his friends were playing around with a gun, you know.

A number of incidents similar to the one above were cited by Dee Dee to explain her position that she is capable of handling her own life. Parental assistance is viewed as interference. Although she is well liked by her peers, an aggressive, stubborn, asserting demeanor has developed in Dee Dee's personality.

Comparing Dee Dee with her older sister, Mrs. Harris describes the difference as being "like night and day." Mrs. Harris is concerned about Dee Dee's constant "cussing around" when things don't go her way. According to Dee Dee, her mother and older sister tell her to cleanse her soul.

My mother told me that she had a vision that I had 7 devils in me and my sister told me that she had a vision that I had 12, but I don't know."

Dee Dee admits that her behavior could be immensely improved. She states that she has not been happy with herself. In the last two years, Dee Dee has been attempting to change her life. She believes in her mother's alarm about "devils" because she has had similar dreams and visions.

Dee Dee appears to be in the process of waging an internal battle with herself to enforce better morals. She has avoided her old peers, opting instead to devote more effort to her high school studies. Realizing that graduation is near, she hopes to have the necessary credentials to receive her diploma. Churchgoing has become a regularity for her. She is sorry for much of her past attitude and behavior. She states:

I don't know. Like I'm trying to be a young lady most of the time. I don't think it was right of me being around mostly all the young mens', getting high, and it would just be me, you know, so I stopped it, you know, I looked at myself, I thought of it. I'd say it's not too late. I mean like the things I'm trying to accomplish I'm getting slowly and slowly trying to be good. [*Laughs*] Let's see, I've been to church about two years; I like going to church. I would say it give me a place to go. It seems like really when I go to church I get something out of it. You know. I mean like, I'll put it like this; the things I used to do, I don't do it no more.

Adolescence has been a turbulent stage of life for Dee Dee. Now that graduation is drawing near, she feels it is necessary to take a look at her future. What will it be like?

There are no strong political or racial attitudes to be detected in Dee Dee's profile. On sexuality she believes that sex is good but pregnancy should be avoided. She does not believe in aborting a baby. She has thought of getting married, but she hesitates because many of her married friends report negative experiences. She states:

Nowadays, the way things are, I'd rather just stay with a man cause you know there ain't too much to marriage.

Dee Dee asserts that she has been "lucky" not to have become pregnant already. She plans to avoid conception carefully for the next few years while she determines her life path.

Another important influence on her new attitude comes from Dee Dee's father who has recently visited with her. He is remarried but still occasionally talks to his children. She has become more motivated to finish high school since he told her he was "happy" and "so proud" of her coming so close to graduation. Now that her father expresses some semblance of concern when she calls him, Dee Dee feels that her home situation is improving. The missing pieces to the puzzle are being found.

Dee Dee identifies most closely with her female roles while strongly accepting her kinship, student, and friendship roles. Her major life goal is security. Her transcendental concerns are not particulary religious; they are given the neutral label of "unreligious." Her psychic style appears to be a basically opinionated one in her interactions with others. She scores high in the social awareness category but does not register high in the social responses area. The data further show that she has a moderate sense of self as measured by her verbal responses. Levels of autonomy and independence are not registered. Future concerns are most central to her present thought processes.

In-Home Living Patterns

There is a lack of parental control in the Harris household. The parent-child relationships are at an impasse: the children say and do what they wish to the mother and vice versa. Exhausted, Mrs. Harris often ends her scoldings by referring the children to the Bible. The oldest son is at this time out of jail on bond for purse-snatching. The fifteen-year-old is on probation for neighborhood vandalism. The sibling interrelations are accentuated by rivalry, disrespect, and disharmony. Moreover, there is very little mutual trust between family members, especially where money is involved.

Mrs. Harris has long ceased being shocked by her children's behavior. Of Dee Dee, she states:

She's easily upset and slams doors and you can't tell her nothin'. And when I try to make her understand, like with Craig, he and Dee Dee were very close, and she pops him upside the head and hollers at him, and I tell her she should feel more for him than she do, that I have to go to work and she should see the small kids get up and get dressed and she spends an hour in the bathroom putting on make-up and eye shadow and false fingernails.

And she describes her fifteen-year-old:

Bobby's a little out of hand too. Bobby's more sassy than Frank. Frank's 20 years old. He don't talk back to me, but Bobby's something else. Bobby don't like to be told nothing even in school. He always thinks somebody's picking on him, when they tell him something. He don't like to be told nothing. Even at church if somebody tell him to stop talking he'd get mad and walk out. This what his probation officer found out. His whole problem is he don't want the teacher to say anything to him. He'll get smart and curse. He's just got a big mouth, that's all.

We can clearly see the children's lack of respect for the mother. All the children have had problems. Mrs. Harris is least critical of her oldest daughter, Sharon, perhaps because she can identify with being the oldest daughter in the family. Mrs. Harris was also the second child and the oldest daughter. Sharon gave birth to a baby girl two years ago. Her pregnancy came as a surprise to all the family members since she was previously considered "quiet" and "sweet." Dee Dee describes the dynamics surrounding Sharon's pregnancy.

I'm not trying to talk about Sharon, you know. She quiet and everything [but] it turned out Sharon was sneaky, boy. And the dude came and told my mother that he felt his [personal needs] was more important than having a kid, you know. That's what he told my mother. He said that taking care of his self was like taking care of 5 people, like taking care of 5 kids.

Dee Dee and her sister love each other, but they do not get along. Indeed, there is hardly any trust between family members. Some of the children have been known to take money from their mother's purse as well as from each other. Mrs. Harris's many admonitions almost always fall on deaf ears. The children have decided simply to do what they want. They will avoid certain activities, however, so that their mother will not be "hurt." Dee Dee, for example, maintains that she has attempted to avoid becoming pregnant primarily because she knows it will hurt her mother.

Still, Dee Dee carries a basic lack of respect for her mother. To Dee Dee, her mother could not possibly know what was best. She says, "My mama thinks she know me but she don't know me." Mrs. Harris relates, "I'm 'always wrong,' I 'don't know what I'm talking about,' and the other person is 'always right'." In many instances, the "other person" is a friend or associate of Dee Dee's. Over the years, peers have had a great influence over Dee Dee's behavior. Mrs. Harris views herself as being in competition with these friends, for the mind of her daughter. Again, we see that Dee Dee's psychological orientation is away from home; she is not home- or family-oriented. She still prefers to be "in the street" with friends.

Almost all of the housework and chores are performed by Mrs. Harris, since it requires tremendous effort to make the children help her. Sometimes Dee Dee cooks dinner, because Mrs. Harris often refuses to do it alone. If the children want to eat, they must assist in the meal preparation. Most often, a parental request for Dee Dee's assistance is met by voluble reluctance:

> Dee Dee don't do no more housework than she has to do. Dee Dee don't do pots and pans on the stove, and when she do the housework, she's constantly fussin, "get that outta here," "put that down," "stop bugging me."

Mrs. Harris now most often prefers to do the housework herself, and thereby curtail the "static." She rises every morning ("even if I'm not working") at five o'clock and occupies her time performing home duties. She admits that she is "so used to using my hands, I don't want to keep still."

While there is parental concern for the children in the Harris household, there is little parental control over the children. Speaking of her oldest son, Mrs. Harris says:

> He's so hardheaded, he won't listen. He's not really what you call a leader, he's a follower, and easygoing. If I tell him not to let his friends in, he's so weak he lets them on in, but he don't listen to me.

Mrs. Harris seldom demands, anymore, that her children listen to her. She realizes that her control over the older children's time and space slipped away some years ago. The older children discipline the younger children, often without Mrs. Harris's approval. The younger children have now begun doing as they wish. The fifteen-year old started asserting his autonomy about a year ago. Mrs. Harris relates:

> He started by coming in when he got ready. He had come in at two o'clock. He did it twice. One time I met him at the door. I think it was last week. I was in the closet when he came in the door. He thought I was in bed, and I broke my pot on his head.

Mrs. Harris is desperately trying to maintain control over the children's behavior as long as possible. She has not "given up" completely only because she derives further strength from her church activities. The trend toward unruly behavior has become more evident with her younger son.

Dee Dee tells her mother to stop "showing off" when her mother scolds her in the presence of guests. Mrs. Harris describes the events on one such occasion:

> I told her, "If I were in the grave, you would always give me the respect." She says, "You always trying to show off in front of my man." I tell her, "You have to get up early the next morning," and she'll always make excuses. She told me one time, I said, "Dee Dee you got a watch," and she said, "See, there you go again, you're just trying to show off." It was 11:30 at night.

Dee Dee is very much in control of her own time and space. In the home, she stretches the parameters as far as she wishes. Mrs. Harris's only recourse with her children now is to beg, plead, and try to "reason" with them. Because she loves her children and views them as her responsibility, she tries to keep them in the home.

Boys are continually brought into the home by Dee Dee. Once Mrs. Harris caught Dee Dee in the act of serious petting in the kitchen. Mrs. Harris tried to explain her position as a mother to the boy. Dee Dee became angry. Dee Dee states:

> My mother says I'm living a fast life and like I told her what I wanted. I wanted to have my own room. I told her how I wanted to have my hair fixed and she says I'm trying to look too old. I said, "I'm sorry but I'm doing this my way because I feel this is going to be the best time in my life." It's going to mean everything. And I say "Mamma, when I go with my friends, don't listen for me, I might be gone 3 or 4 days. I'll call you and let you know ain't nothing happening to me and I'm all right. I don't want to be smart with my mother, just live my own life. I don't want anyone to run my life for me.
> There are some things I want to do by myself.

We see that Dee Dee is continually attempting to broaden her freedom of movement. Almost none of this movement is directed toward educational pursuits. Rather, Dee Dee is occupied at this moment with trying to "live life."

Schooling is not considered a high priority in the home; the maintenance of order and peace is a more immediate necessity for Mrs. Harris. She tries to do the best she can to provide for her family so that they don't have to rob and steal. She is still smarting from the distress of having her oldest son arrested for robbery. To her, success will be to see her children become decent adult citizens. She prays daily for this goal.

Educational Orientations in the Home

Consistent with other aspects of the family pattern, there is no continual, disciplined commitment to educational achievement in the Harris home.

Educational goals are seldom discussed and deliberate educational rituals do not exist at all. Dee Dee decided to complete high school only after repeated urging by an older friend who had previously dropped out. Dee Dee considers school "boring" and something "to cope with." Her school experience has been extremely difficult, in part because she is not equipped with a strong academic foundation in reading and math. The highest grade she has ever received in high school is a C. Because of the unwritten policy of her school to promote students for attending classes, she will probably graduate in June. Dee Dee's oldest brother dropped out of school after his freshman year. Her sister, Sharon, born only ten months before Dee Dee, will also be graduating in June. Fifteen-year-old Bobby attends a school for children with serious behavior problems. Mrs. Harris consoles herself with the fact that at least two of her children appear to be headed for graduation.

Mrs. Harris has no idea what Dee Dee plans to do after graduation. There have been few discussions of career possibilities and options. Dee Dee now works part-time as a file clerk in one of the community hospitals. Although she has not told her mother, Dee Dee has made inquiries to a Black college in the South. She does not expect to attend, however, because of anticipated admittance problems and unavailability of financial assistance. At this time she leans toward a career in nursing (like her mother) or secretarial science.

Although Mrs. Harris is concerned about Dee Dee's education, she is unable to exercise the necessary control for helping her daughter. Mrs. Harris' own school aspirations involve her desire to become certified someday as a registered nurse. But she has not attended school in over twenty years. Right now, family obligations make the notion of additional schooling an impractical one.

Whenever Mrs. Harris attempts to assist her daughter in school concerns, she is accused of "interfering." Dee Dee refuses even to show Mrs. Harris her end-of-term grades.

> Once I asked to see her grades and she said she'd passed, and I told her she hadn't passed nothing. She asked me how I knew and I said I was there. They don't bring the course book home; they give out these little sheets of paper with their grades on it. The counselor had the carbon copy, and I said that's what I read. I don't tell her when I'm coming to school but I comes.

The fact that Mrs. Harris must come to school to learn about Dee Dee's grades is again indicative of her lack of power and influence in the home. This action also suggests, though, that Mrs. Harris is concerned about her children's educational performance. Mrs. Harris's willingness and desire to make contact with the school demonstrates a concern that might not be immediately apparent. Unable to demand any particular behavior, Mrs. Harris can only ask her daughter to "do better."

Mrs. Harris does have expectations for her children's schooling. She expected her oldest boy to complete high school. When he did not return to school after his freshman year, Mrs. Harris was extremely hurt. With Dee Dee, Mrs. Harris would like to see her pursue a nursing career and "settle down."

Dee Dee admits that her mother has done more to encourage her to finish high school than anyone else has. Illustrating this process, Dee Dee states:

> [She told me] "You better take you ass over there 'cause you're going to need an education, get to school," and all this and that.

Mrs. Harris feels she must constantly resort to giving direct orders when she wants something accomplished because only then do the children perceive "that [she means] business."

One of Dee Dee's girl friends, a 24-year-old woman with four children, was responsible for Dee Dee's decision to attend summer school. Without these summer school classes, Dee Dee could not hope to graduate in June. Dee Dee's friend had returned to school and graduated last June at the age of 23. This proved to be a key motivation for Dee Dee, who would sometimes study with her older friend. Together, they provided one another with encouragement and support. Without her friend's assistance, Dee Dee maintains, she would have dropped out a year ago.

Apparently Dee Dee is entirely capable of exerting the energy necessary to achieve her chosen educational goals. By calling upon her inner resources, she has managed to do just enough to remain on the school rolls. As she discusses her potential, she laughs:

> I just say that I'm going to try as hard as I can, you know, I'm just going to give it all I've got, and when I do, you know, I come through.

Other singular experiences in school have convinced Dee Dee that she is capable of doing the work. She has simply not been adequately motivated to perform.

Mrs. Harris asserts that she "very seldom" has observed Dee Dee studying or doing homework at home. Dee Dee's defense is:

> You can't study here, you've either gotta go to one of your friend's houses. We just can't study and hear record players, the record player was so high everything on the wall was just shaking. I felt I couldn't study at home. There was so much noise, you know. And I'd probably be jumping off into whatever my family was doing and forget about my homework.

Ritualized study behaviors have never been implemented in the home. Because of her lack of control, Mrs. Harris is not able to sit down with her children to discuss schooling and career plans. In the absence of reasonable decorum, study becomes unlikely. Mental fatigue and general disinterest are more natural behaviors under these conditions.

Dee Dee claims that she receives little help from school personnel. She once visited her counselor to discuss ways to improve her grades, but she was told she couldn't be helped. She states:

> He'll start talking about something else, you know, or either he'll tell me he too busy, and he's supposed to be my counselor, you know, and you're supposed to go to your counselor and explain to them your problems and all this. [*Laughs.*] He be off someplace. Like he be on a cloud that ain't even got here yet.

Perhaps Dee Dee's school problems are too extensive to be solved by her rare visit to the school counselor. Perhaps her limited exposure to educational orientations in the home has continued over too long a period. Her desire to graduate in June suggests that she certainly believes that schooling can be beneficial in some ways. Although she has been defined as "educationally unsuccessful," her drive toward graduation must be kept in mind. Dee Dee will make efforts to do schoolwork, but effective vehicles in the home, and perhaps the school, clearly have not been provided to promote these efforts.

8. An Analysis of Dispositions and Life-Styles in Low Achievers' Homes

The low-achieving students in our study are academically marginal and have low grades but they show varying degrees of achievement motivation. Almost always in the lowest 20 percent of the senior class (based on grades and class rank), these students are members of families with a history of psychologically devastating experiences and a myriad of current social and economic problems. Family members seem to have been psychologically and emotionally scarred by their life experiences. Most of them "just can't see how" they can do any better. Success in this social context is measured by one's ability to *survive*.

Although all of these parents are interested in their children, they seem suffused with a sense of powerlessness about their children's school performance. "I can't do nothin' about it" is a standard response among parents in this group. These parents regularly express despair and voice chronic complaints that external forces (e.g., lack of decent jobs, educational opportunities, unsupportive relatives) have been "keeping [them] down." Indeed, there is little happiness and much misery in these homes. Because the social influences of family and nonfamily factors are intertwined, it is not possible to ascertain precisely the degree to which societal impediments shape these parents' psychological orientations. What we know for sure is that most of these "low-achieving" students are the first ones in their families to reach the twelfth grade. Let's examine the patterns of family interaction in these students' homes.

The parenting style that characterizes parent-child interaction in these households is akin to the one Farber describes as an "unsponsored independence" parenting style.[1] This style is marked by relatively loose social ties between the parents and children and by less parental vigilance in the teaching and supervision of the child. Some of the interpersonal and social patterns that are associated with this style are described in the categories below.

Parents' Early Experiences in Family of Origin

Parents of low achievers were raised in a home environment that was filled with stressful life events. Many of these stressful events have remained unresolved over the years. The mothers of these mothers had undergone "bad" marriages and had survived under extremely destitute circumstances in the South. Intimate family support networks had been almost nonexistent for these limited-resource families. Parents spoke mostly about their trials and little about "good times." Though their trials were not always qualitatively worse than those of the parents of the successful, the sense of powerlessness and hopelessness was markedly different.

Students' Early Experiences in the School

Students had generally poor quality social and academic experiences in kindergarten through twelfth grade. Two related patterns of school behavior typified the classroom experience of low achievers. First, these students recalled few occasions when teachers had provided strong, sustained encouragement in their school efforts. This was tied to another classroom pattern, the child's background of limited success in classroom discourse. When the student was unclear about subject matter, teachers had not managed to reach him or her through careful instruction, corrective feedback, or reinforcement techniques in the classroom. The classroom experience had helped to foster a negative self-concept regarding school success and defensiveness against failure.

Parents' Early Socialization Behavior toward Child

During the child's first ten years of life, the basics of food, clothing, shelter, and a certain degree of emotional support had been provided. However, the parents found themselves unable to sustain their performance of routine child-management functions because of their own psychological-emotional turbulence and their recreational-leisure activities (which helped them temporarily escape from the high-stress problems confronting them personally). Parents held no expectations that the child would regularly engage in home academic activities and they had provided almost no standards or guidance directed toward deliberate literacy learning at home. These parents were interested in the welfare of their children but lacked the ability to foster achievement-oriented behavior in their offspring. They appeared to use their overburdened psychic energies to perform their parenting roles as best they could. Limited awareness of their role as educators, early debilitating social experiences, and contemporary constraints in the home and marketplace were the major contributors to these parents' tendency toward sporadic emotional and cognitive nurturance of the child.

There is, of course, no one parental pattern among those families with low-achieving children. In one family the attempt is made to set limits and to discipline. But this is not set in a context of the good of the child, and thus becomes a tug of war, a contest of wills, with authority and not success as the end and with the offspring ultimately seeking to escape. In several homes there are almost no limits at all, the parent or parents having given up because "it don't do no good." In these instances, the teenager has been left to determine his or her own direction, under the influence of peers and unique life events (such as the blindness of an older brother). In other homes the emphasis is on good character and morality, but not on achievements and school endeavors. The key difference, then, is not between one- and two-parent families or between control and freedom but between parents who build up their offsprings' self-esteem, treat their children and the school with respect, and encourage learning activities, and those parents who do not. When the child fails in school, however, the parents of low achievers tend to blame the child, whereas the parents of high achievers tend to blame the school, thus keeping the child's self-esteem intact.

Differences within Family Units

The quality of life in low achievers' homes, we are saying, is different from that in the high achievers' families. When we look at the form and substance of the same psychosocial elements that guided the analysis of home life for high achievers (Figure 5.1), we see that the nature of low achievers' home psychosocial patterns is substantively different. The sharpness of these differences is indeed remarkable when we consider the fact that all the families in this study are low-income families living in the same neighborhoods. A comparative content analysis of low achievers' family patterns reveals differences in the nature of role stratification, activity patterns, and the perceptions of family members. I shall briefly describe the substance of the psychosocial structures in the low achievers' homes. The main purpose in doing this is to establish the context for a normative comparison of high achievers' families with low achievers' families.

Low Achievers' Parents' Personality Structure

Low achievers' parents have experienced severe, psychologically debilitating events at earlier stages of their lives. Past (and contemporary) experiences in their own family of origin and in the marketplace have had a "trickle down" effect which has left mental scars so deep as to have rendered them unable or unwilling to stay deeply committed to quality parental functioning. These parents have undergone repeated trauma, they have sustained immeasurable strain and pain, and they now have an impoverished human spirit. Sensing little hope of a better tomorrow, their greatest efforts and concerns are directed toward their family's immediate physical and emotional survival. While these parents have made strong commitments to their families and are willing to make personal sacrifices, they have not enjoyed the degree of social reward they need to make it seem worthwhile. Most of these parents miss the emotional support of adult spouses and kin, and their children can provide only limited support.

Students' Personality Structure

Students in these families have surprisingly good conceptions of themselves, *except* in their literacy abilities. That is, these positive conceptions do not include school success and achievement. Even though these low achievers have gone through twelve years of mediocre-to-poor personal school experiences, they still have a desire to improve themselves in preparation for the labor market, but they do not see schooling as the prime means to that end. Many of them have made inquiries to teachers, counselors, and acquaintances about opportunities for education but have received little assistance. It appears that they are already being prepared (and are adapting themselves in different ways) to the social constraints they will probably undergo after leaving school.

Parent's Perception of Family Responsibility for Their Children's Education

All of these parents are concerned about their children's educational and maturational progress. They seldom see, however, how they can do more than they are already doing. A large amount of the responsibility for the young child's education is placed squarely on the child. When school failures occur, these parents do not see this as due to their own lack of involvement or the inadequacy of the school. Rather, as noted above, the child is seen as not having fulfilled his or her own school responsibility.

There is little parent-child communication and agreement on matters having to do with schooling and education. Parents are likely to have little knowledge of students' grades, test scores, learning styles, and so on. They say that they are not aware of the extent of their children's school problems. In fact, these parents frequently perceive their children as having done "just fine" in their school experience. Believing that a student's upcoming graduation from high school is "proof" of success, parents may express vague and happy remembrances of the student's early years. (I personally found this a rather odd parental perception, since many of these students were unable to read most sections of the daily newspaper or school materials designed for high schoolers.)

Parental Expectations for Child's Postsecondary Education

Parents of low achieving girls generally express the hope that their daughters will have an early marriage, and parents of boys hope that their sons will get jobs or "do something useful with themselves." They tend to feel that the student's real talents and interests are not in education but either in marriage or in a job. Though parents do not intend to impede the student's efforts, they seldom provided the child with direct help or encouragement on school matters. They usually have little to say to their children about postsecondary education, because they have had no orientation into it (for either themselves *or* their offspring).

Family Norms, Rules, Expectations, and Morals Training

Rules for household conduct, when they exist, tend to be nebulous and contradictory or sporadically enforced. Parents frequently make verbal pitches for "good" behavior. But it has not been established that particular goals, standards, and norms are absolutely essential. Parents even have a hard time enforcing rules that they feel strongly about. Perhaps so much of their experience in the marketplace makes "rules" about "right" and "fair" seem cheap and unenforceable. Still, parents try to enforce the rules that do exist. Even when they are in the home, these parents have been ineffective in establishing standards that all family members abide by. While parents do hold to certain perceptions of right and wrong, they are not able to generate the sustained commitment of the children to these norms. It appears that even when the parents have worked at establishing home decorum and rules, the "bad" behavior of one child causes severe mental anguish for the parent and weakens his or her internal strength to exercise patient communication with the other children. This pattern of communication breakdown then feeds on its own inertia as parents limit their concern to the daily struggle for survival.

Status Positions and Role Boundaries in the Home

The parents of low achievers have little control over the creation or maintenance of the status of family members. They have allowed group relations to proceed as if there was no need to identify specific positive roles and positions for each family member. Sometimes the parent has a general conception of the appropriate shape of family role relations but has not made the effort to define role expectations to each other family member. Existing role expectations tend to operate on a covert level and are infrequently made explicit or else they are reinforced sporadically and inconsistently.

Fathers in the two-parent families are held in low esteem by others in the home. Mothers are frustrated over these fathers' inability to fulfill either their provider role or their parenting role adequately. Feeling very put-upon and put-out by their expanded home responsibilities, these mothers suffer from the effects of role overload and give in to feelings of helplessness and ineffectiveness.

Patterns of Explicit and Implicit Pedagogy in the Home

There are no consistent, regularly performed learning rituals in these homes. Reading of school materials, writing, and homework are seldom, if ever, done in the home. Although parents sometimes "remind" the students of homework obligations, there are no parental attempts to supervise or check the student's progress. Parents find time for television soap operas, but seldom hold family dialogues, except during arguments. The student may have tried to find the right answers to school questions but, not succeeding, has sought short-cuts and other ways to "get over." Ultimately, the student tends simply to lose interest in the study activity, perceiving it as being unimportant to survival.

Parents do not expect students to be responsible for home chores. Home duties may have been assigned by the parents, but the student is seldom held to a regular routine of completion. Parents very often end up doing the chores they initially assigned to the youngsters, thus fostering irresponsibility. Indeed, the student spends very little time engaged in parentally required responsibilities and duties. The child undoubtedly has picked up messages through these interactions that his or her parents do not expect the child to complete tasks, including school tasks.

Patterns of Parental Control and Support

As we have said, these parents exhibit a sense of helplessness over the children's behavior. In matters of child rearing, these parents feel incapable of imposing strong guidance or control over their children. Instead, they impose inconsistent limits or no limits at all. This is largely due to the fact that parents lack control over their own lives. Neither can they nor their children count on any reliable support from others. Sometimes, the people who were most willing to give support (e.g., other relatives) are embroiled in the greatest conflict with these parents.

These parents may have some vague idea of the student's school performance; they may know that their child is being only minimally productive, but they feel powerless to help the student improve or to control his or her behavior. Instead, they feel that the child's staying in school is an accomplishment in itself. Their attitude is that the child should be praised for being a twelfth grader. As one mother said, "If the school lets her graduate, she must have done OK."

Although there is currently little parental effort to supervise or channel the student's time and space (e.g., *where* the student goes; *when* the student goes or returns; with *whom* the student goes, etc.), parents sometimes "remind" the student of such responsibilities. More often than not, these students were members of groups in which "unlimited" leisure activity is valued, and norms for excelling in school are not a high priority. Most of these families conform to Baumrind's "permissive" control style of management.[2] The student, quite simply, does as he or she pleases. Even the infrequent parental "reminders" which tend to be *critical* of the child, however, seem to motivate him or her to maintain at least a minimal level of productivity.

The inconsistency of parents' sanctioning and support patterns is tied to their own coping threshhold. Having experienced severe role overload and frustration over an extended time, these parents sometimes use indiscriminate or inconsistent physical punishment and incessant criticism, ridicule, rejection, derision, or berating of the child's behavior and attitudes. These rejecting behaviors are almost always seen by parents as attempts to *help* the child, but frequently have an obvious opposite effect on the child. The more parents use these methods, the more the child repeats the undesirable behavior, because the child perceives the parent as not understanding and not supportive, and as an adversary—someone to be "bested." This invariably leads to a sense of unintended, but mutual confusion and antagonism between parent and child.

Finally, some mothers provide certain "stroking" behaviors for the student, but they are usually performed *only when the child* overtly makes it clear that he or she needs comforting. Parents have established relatively few family fun rituals which provide family members an opportunity to enjoy themselves and other kin routinely. The parents themselves feel a lack of support and control over their lives and activities and are simply emotionally beaten down.

Family-School Contact Patterns

Finally, parents almost never visit the school, except in response to the school's request resulting from the child's misbehavior or poor work. The parents express few complaints about the quality of education being provided. Unsolicited, impromptu visits, just to see how teachers and counselors are operating on their child's behalf, are virtually nonexistent. These parents are likely to say they "don't have time," because of other demands on them, or else to say that they don't understand what is going on at school, so they will "leave it to the teachers." Thus, a positive, reinforcing pattern of school-home encouragement for student achievement is missing.

9. The Family and the Bases for Academic Achievement

Support, Control, and Power: A Theoretical Contribution

Diane Baumrind concluded in 1972 that high parental support and high control, when that control is internalized and based on reasoning and accompanied by a child's sense of power, result in academic achievement.[1] She notes, however, that this might not hold for girls and for the disadvantaged. Rollins and Thomas, in their theoretical review, conclude that Baumrind's generalization about support and control holds for boys but not for girls. Girls, they argue, are made dependent and less aggressive because of a different kind of supportive socialization and (perhaps also by "nature") and thus the toughness required for girls to be academically successful results not from parental support, but from the lack of it. These authors, however, do not refer further to the disadvantaged.

The present study of the Black ghetto family is in a position to add to and alter the generalizations of Baumrind and Rollins and Thomas. High power is important, as Baumrind notes, but not as a *general* condition. Power on the part of the offspring aids achievement only when it is experienced in matters pertaining directly to academic achievement. Anthony's mother, for example, feels she can learn much from her children. She says, "they are my children, true enough, but they can tell me a lot of things to help me." And James Earl Treppit expresses this sense of power: "I think I'm the smartest in my family. I'm the smartest, and I do more studying than any of the others." So, it is not a general sense of power, but power in the intellectual sphere that fosters further school achievement.

As for support and control, the present study finds Baumrind's generalization to be correct for *girls as well as boys*. That is, for both boys *and* girls high support, plus high internalized control, and a high personal sense of (intellectual) power are needed for high academic achievement. The reason this is true for girls as well as boys in a poor Black environment seems relatively straightforward. Rollins and Thomas hypothesized that traditional support socialization for girls makes them soft and dependent instead of tough and competitive. However, in the ghetto the environment *itself* leads to toughness and the necessity of self-assertion, regardless of gender. Thus, if parents have the presence of mind to be supportive of their girls, these girls probably can translate this support, in combination with the resilience or toughness fostered by the environment, into academic achievement. The case studies in chapters 3 and 4 are full of illustrations of the supportiveness and successful control attempts of the parents whose teenage offspring are doing well in school.

It is worth repeating that support and control, in the present study, are not a function of single parenthood or family intactness; they are cultural, not structural phenomena. It is also possible, we should note, that the distinction between presumably middle-class boys and girls reported by Rollins and Thomas is less correct now than it was when the research that they report on in their review was done.

Other Contributions to Understanding Achievement in Poor Black Families

Our research was not restricted to support, control, and power in relation to achievement. We have sought to depict as completely as possible the family culture and processes in these homes. We have assumed, and found, the centrality of parents and other significant authority figures in children's learning experiences. The manner in which parents capitalize on a child's emotional dependence in order to delegate responsibilities and to exercise contol over home learning activities functions as a major stimulant to learning and value transmission in the home. The patterns and styles of contact parents organize into their relationships with their children provide a particular level of parental sponsorship of the child's growth and development. Parents may be said to "sponsor" the child's role enactment or competence (as a student, for example) to the extent that they (1) carefully delegate to children certain duties and responsibilities in literacy skills development activities, (2) provide regular instruction, assistance, suggestions, and coaching during highly affective interpersonal encounters, (3) establish the legitimacy of particular norms, rules, and values (codes of conduct for "appropriate" behavior), and (4) utilize verbal supports, sanctions, and other nurturing reinforcement strategies as mechanisms of social control. These parental behaviors may be enacted during home activities while the child is participating in various interpersonal configurations (parent-child; parent-child-sibling; other significant person; child-sibling).[2] During home educational activities, recreational activities, and health maintenance activities, parents may directly or implicitly convey knowledge and warmth (emotional nurturance) that enhance the child's competence with language codes, moral codes, and behavior codes which are applicable in out-of-home social situations. While the sequence, frequency, and pacing of the child's engagement in these face-to-face home activities will vary, *any* routine engagement gives some practice in using certain cognitive operations. The cognitive operations used during these activities include (a) memorization of rules for particular social encounters (e.g., how to respond in the classroom), (b) mental rehearsal at initiating oral or written communication, (c) practice in self-reflection and clarification of purposes and experiences, (d) reasoning, critical thinking and creative problem-solving practice (e.g., finding solutions to complex problems through role playing in groups), (e) practice at exercising self-confidence, emotional calm, self-direction, self-regulation, and personal control, and (f) exposure to reasoned, mature perspectives and preferences for ways of behaving within a wide range of relationships. The repeated use of these cognitive functions during activities contributes to the creation of psychological dispositions (ways of thinking about or defining a situation) and social habits (ways of behaving in social situations). A major function of this cognitive work is to promote the development of a child's interpersonal competence in the expanding role set of a school-age child. This competence includes the ability to speak, read, write, and understand at a level sufficient to achieve reasonable communication goals during interpersonal encounters in school classrooms.

Table 5.1 presented the general categories for classifying psychological and behavioral learning patterns in family systems. We should note that all of the classification categories can be applied to each of the four family cohorts (e.g., single parent/high achieving). Table 9.1 shows how family values and communication patterns in homes of the high achievers differ in structure and content from those patterns found in the low achievers' homes. Notice that when we compare the high achievers with the low achievers in terms of the *quality* of the seventeen patterns, a clearly contrasting picture emerges. This suggests that when we talk about racial, ethnic, or social background differences *between* families, we frequently are really talking about group differences in the social organization of family units with regard to particular communication processes and rituals, and the resulting cognitive and behavioral differences. That is, we are addressing the *degree* to which families' home environment patterns are the same or different, given the range of personality and behavior variations that families display. Therefore, the form and substance of the family psychosocial patterns are the most significant components for understanding the educational effects of high achievers' families and low achievers' families—not their race or social class background per se. In Table 9.2 we see that seldom are the seventeen achievement-fostering patterns present in the low achievers' families.

Our seventeen patterns, then, serve to distinguish the family success orientation. While we know that these family psychosocial patterns are basic to literacy acquisition, further research is needed to determine the relative *weight* of the pattern categories overall, and for various ethnic, socioeconomic, and gender groups. It is possible that sets (or clusters) of significant patterns may emerge from among the seventeen we have iden-

TABLE 9.1

A Comparison of the Quality of Success-Producing Patterns in Homes of High Achievers and Low Achievers

High Achievers	Low Achievers
1. Frequent school contact initiated by parent	Infrequent school contact initiated by parent
2. Child has had some stimulating, supportive school teachers	Child has had no stimulating, supportive school teachers
3. Parents psychologically and emotionally calm with child	Parents in psychological and emotional upheaval with child
4. Students psychologically and emotionally calm with parents	Students less psychologically and emotionally calm with parents
5. Parents expect to play major role in child's schooling	Parents have lower expectation of playing role in child's schooling
6. Parents expect child to play major role in child's schooling	Parents have lower expectation of child's role in child's schooling
7. Parents expect child to get post-secondary training	Parents have lower expectation that child will get postsecondary training
8. Parents have explicit achievement-centered rules and norms	Parents have less explicit achievement-centered rules and norms
9. Students show long-term acceptance of norms as legitimate	Students have less long-term acceptance of norms
10. Parents establish clear, specific role boundaries and status structures with parents as dominant authority	Parents establish more blurred role boundaries and status structures
11. Siblings interact as organized subgroup	Siblings are a less structured, interactive subgroup
12. Conflict between family members is infrequent	Conflict between some family members is frequent
13. Parents frequently engage in deliberate achievement-training activities	Parents seldom engage in deliberate achievement-training activities
14. Parents frequently engage in implicit achievement-training activities	Parents engage less frequently in implicit achievement-training
15. Parents exercise firm, consistent monitoring and rules enforcement	Parents have inconsistent standards and exercise less monitoring of child's time and space
16. Parents provide liberal nurturance and support	Parents are less liberal with nurturance and support
17. Parents defer to child's knowledge in intellectual matters	Parents do not defer to child in intellectual matters

tified (e.g., parents' expectations and action patterns). Further, it might be fruitful to look at the *number* of patterns that are qualitatively different in their substance within low achievers' homes. Perhaps we can identify certain problem areas that need to be addressed in individual families. For example, parents may have had high expectations for some students who are not high achievers.[3] That is, they wanted their children to achieve, but did not know how to bring it about. The Wilson family, for example, exhibited five of the seventeen patterns found in the high achievers' families but still produced no high-achieving student. Conceivably, the target student in that family might have had a higher achievement level if someone had identified the weak or missing processes and patterns and developed strategies for stimulating and strengthening these particular family social patterns.

A Conceptual Model of Learning Processes in Family Units

Based on an analysis of the case study data, a systematic interpretation of the nature of learning dynamics in households can now be presented. Figure 9.1 depicts a conceptual model of the achievement-fostering process in family units. The arrows represent predicted direct effects of the antecedent variables on psychological and behavior patterns. Components 1 through 6 of this model focus on explaining the causal connection between (1) the family members' past developmental patterns in their families of origin and families of procreation, (2) family members' current social opportunities in the kin network and resource marketplace, (3) parents' current information and assistance opportunities in their children's schools, (4) children's learning opportunities in the classroom, (5) the family unit's surface structure or compositional properties, and (6) family members' psychological and motivational structures. Within this sextet of components, I am *first* postulating that the way in which parents and other family members experienced life in their youth will have a direct effect on (a) parent's contact patterns with kin and friends and with other community institutions (excluding schools), and (b) parent's contact patterns with the child's school.[4] A *second* postulate is that parents' and siblings' historical experiences and parent's contact patterns with kin, friends, community institutions, and school personnel will directly influence parents' and siblings' individual psychological dispositions. Here we are hypothesizing that parents' sense of well-being and efficacy and their academic aspirations and expectations for their children are directly influenced by their contacts within community structures, including schools. Furthermore, these community contacts are hypothesized to influence the level of the target child's own aspirations and expectations. While there is a limited amount of research and theory that addresses itself to the hypothesis that parent contact with kin, friends, and others will affect children's academic orientations,[5] a fair number of school-community involvement studies have reported a positive relationship between parents' school involvement patterns and their attitudes toward the school and schooling.[6]

In the fifth and sixth components of the model we are postulating that family demographic characteristics (such as race and class) will explain *some* of the variance in parents' and pupils' academic attitudes and learn-

TABLE 9.2
Frequency of Incidence that Success-Producing Patterns in High Achievers' Home Compare in Quality with the Patterns in Low Achievers' Homes

	Gaines	Jackson	Wilson	Jones	Harris
1. Child has had some stimulating, supportive school teachers					
2. Frequent school contact initiated by parents		X	X	X	
3. Parents psychologically and emotionally calm with child					
4. Student psychologically and emotionally calm with parents					
5. Parents expect to play major role in child's schooling			X		
6. Parents expect child to play major role in child's own schooling	X	X	X	X	X
7. Parents expect child to get postsecondary education					
8. Parents have explicit achievement-centered rules and norms					
9. Students show long-term acceptance of achievement norms as legitimate	X	X		X	X
10. Parents establish clear, specific role boundaries and status structures with parents as dominant authority			X		
11. Siblings interact positively as structural subgroup					
12. Conflict between family members is infrequent					
13. Parents frequently engage in explicit achievement-training activities					
14. Parents frequently engage in implicit achievement-training activities					

TABLE 9.2—Continued

15. Parents exercise firm, consistent monitoring and rules enforcement			X			
16. Parents provide liberal nurturance and support						
17. Parents defer to child's knowledge in intellectual matters		X				

ing norms. Most of the available family-school research has provided support for this hypothesis.[7] Indeed, it is in this conceptual domain that the majority of family background studies have been conducted. Let us not, however, pass over this point lightly. After all, throughout the present study we have emphasized that family processes and culture, not structural and demographic variables, determine achievement orientations in children. Nevertheless, we must not be interpreted as saying that the appropriate process factors (see Table 9.1) are equally distributed regardless of class, race, ethnic group, and the like. What we *are* asserting is that when class or race differences are found, they can best be explained by the leader variables in the first four components and by the internal dynamics of family life (components 8 and 9), not by the economics of class or the simple fact of race.

The model then indicates a postulated relationship between the general psychological orientations of family members (component 6) and their definition of the family situation (role expectations), their patterns of emotional nurturance, their construction of specific management patterns, and their activity habits in the home (components 7, 8, and 9). The theoretical basis for this psychosocial conceptualization is well established.[8] Very simply put, how we define our situation at a given time tends to stimulate our action pattern at that time. Some work is available that reports a positive relationship between family achievement values, decision-making patterns and activity patterns.[9] However, none of the studies we found has analyzed the entire system or set of normally occurring activities in the home in terms of their relationship to these particular psychosocial antecedents, or in terms of their relationship to achievement outcomes.[10] This study has provided such an unprecedented data set. We have found that parents with greater expectations, higher aspirations, and a stronger sense of well-being (1) enjoy more balanced conjugal decision-making patterns, with a high degree of mutual agreement on decisions concerning the child's intellectual welfare, and (2) engage family members in a wider variety of specific literacy-enhancing activities for a longer

FIGURE 9.1
Conceptual Model Explaining the Development and Maintenance of "Survival" Intelligence through Home and Community Interaction Processes

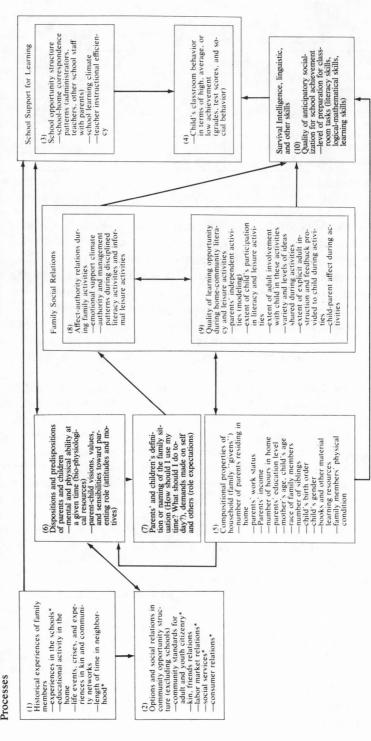

The one-way arrows predict causal relationships; the two-headed arrows indicate there are significant effects in both directions.
*Denotes this variable is important to home social processes but is not directly examined in this study.

period of time. Studies of French elite families provide further evidence of the social impact of these psychosocial patterns.[11]

The eighth, ninth, and tenth components in our model represent our expectation that the organization of the system of learning activities in the family unit will energize or facilitate certain learning (engagement) processes for the duration of the activity. Here we are saying that variations in the way resources (human, material, time, space) are used during any particular activity affects the child's cognitive behavior, interest, and attitude during the activity. These mental processes affect, in turn, the child's level of intellectual development. The conceptual logic for this line of argument is drawn from the findings of "instructional sociology," which have been concerned primarily with pedagogic practices in classroom settings.[12] We know of no published studies that report such data about the instructional dynamics in contemporary large-city family units. Most of what is available is anecdotal or is too peripheral to school pedagogy to have much significance for school boards, school administrators, and classroom teachers.[13]

Specific Hypotheses for Further Testing

Our data strongly suggest the importance of family processes for high educational performance in school classrooms. These patterns should be studied further with other ethnic and social class cohorts in larger, more statistically oriented samples and studies. Hence, it is our intent here to convert some of these apparently key functioning patterns into researchable hypotheses for further testing. The following hypotheses were generated from the case study data reported above:

1. *Early successes* in school endeavors are important for sustained academic progress. Students who do well in school have often had early, relatively pleasant, supportive learning experiences at home and in school. It becomes much easier to continue in school pursuits when one has long been receiving positive reinforcement and support from teachers.

2. The student's attitude toward pursuing *higher education* (e.g., college) influences the intensity with which he or she approaches present study. If higher education is a definite goal, the student is inclined to take high school pursuits more seriously.

3. When parents are actively involved with the school instructional program, there is a greater likelihood of the student becoming academically successful. As *parental visits* to the school are made, knowledge about the student is increased. With this knowledge, parents are better able to assist the school in helping the student to the fullest. Without this knowledge, parents and teachers may be at cross purposes, or may each deal with the young person in ignorance of the other setting.

4. The *regularity* of a student's school attendance is directly correlated to high educational performance. If a student perceives school attendance as a reasonable expectation, that student is more likely to attend classes, thus increasing the possibility of learning.

5. The *intensity* of the student's school pursuits is correlated with academic performance. A student who sets reasonable but challenging time goals for completion of school endeavors will likely carry high levels of motivation and "drive." The student possessed of a sense of urgency is gratified by academic success. The student who has no such feelings of urgency is likely to make schooling a low priority item.

6. *Parents'* perception of their own *coping threshold* affects their ability to stand up to the continual pressures of everyday life. To the extent that parents *feel* helpless to change their social condition, they will not encourage their children to master school material.

7. Certain student personality characteristics are correlated with successful school performance. Students with a *positive view of themselves* are better able to realize their capabilities and potentialities. A student who is reasonably autonomous, independent, assertive, and highly structured will probably not find school classrooms difficult to cope with. Furthermore, if the student feels a sense of power in intellectual matters, at home and elsewhere, this will increase academic motivation.

8. *Parental* conceptions of their own *role responsibilities* (and their children's responsibilities) in the students' schooling endeavors are important to educational outcomes. If parents see family members (including themselves) as determinate entities in the academic progress of the student, parents and siblings will tend to play a supportive role to the student. Without this psychological conception, parents will provide little or no support (e.g., physical, affective, instructional, etc.) to the student.

9. Parental expectations for the student's home behavior are important to academic success. When parents clearly and regularly delineate their *standards and rules* for the student's home conduct, the student is able to understand more easily what to do at home. By knowing how to follow parental instructions, the student finds it easier to understand the instructions and requirements of school personnel as well.

10. Power and *authority* relations in the home affect academic performance. When parents have authority over the student, exercise that authority in the home, and attempt to make that authority reasonable to the student, the student may feel more compelled to follow parental wishes. Deviation from parental requirements is not likely to occur as frequently as when they are seen as arbitrary, unreasonable, or inconsistent. In homes where parental power is too high or too low, students will have limited respect for authority and will not be as likely to comply with parental or school requests.

11. The student's *sentiment* or affect toward his or her parents is correlated with educational achievement. If a student expresses pride and respect for parents, he is more inclined to see their achievement demands as legitimate and to follow parental advice in school matters. In these instances, the parents have usually encouraged the student in educational tasks throughout his family life.

12. The clarity of *role boundaries* between parents and children is positively related to school performance. Incongruent or inconsistent role expectations for home behavior may make it difficult for the student to interact with authority figures outside the home. Not fully understanding proper role norms, students may encounter difficulty in their interaction with nonfamily persons. In school, teachers may have a difficult time attempting to reach or teach this student. However, when the student knows how to relate to others, communication and learning is further facilitated.

13. The degree and quality of *sibling interaction* is positively correlated with academic success (provided, of course, the siblings are academically oriented). When a student has the advantage of having many enriching interactions with siblings, academic pursuits become emotionally and intellectually less frightening. The student derives strength from this family unit support system.

14. The degree of parental influence over the student's *time and space* is important for school success. As parents are able to channel the student into parentally sponsored, academically oriented spheres of activity, the student acquires a sense of self-reliance, home approval, and initiative. If parents are unable to channel the student's use of time and space, negative forces (e.g., gangs) have a greater opportunity to recruit the student.

15. The extent of a student's responsibility to perform *household chores* is important for academic success. By learning responsible behavior in the performance of home duties, the student is better able to contend with those classroom situations requiring diligence, independence, and commitment. Without this home training (parent expectations and child behaviors), the student may become lackadaisical and irresponsible at home and school.

16. The regular occurrence of family *discussions on school issues* is positively correlated with high academic achievement. When parents discuss and explain the benefits and costs of schooling during routine home dialogues, the child is likely to develop a greater appreciation of his or her school endeavors. By experiencing continued familial emphasis on school concerns, the student perceives school achievement as a natural pursuit. As school becomes meaningful and purposeful for the student, school issues become an integral part of the family consciousness. Thus, the student is more likely to be socialized into the family orientation toward academic pursuits, whether that orientation is favorable or not.

17. The *teaching style* of the parents (deliberate or implicit instruction, information sharing, and feedback patterns) is important to school performance. Parents who are able to communicate literacy-enhancing subject matter directly to the student thereby provide an enriched home learning environment. This enriched environment is likely to aid the student in comprehending the requirements of the school curriculum. A parental lack in this area, however, can be partially compensated for by the parent providing other opportunities for the offspring to acquire a sense of power in the intellectual sphere.

18. The extent to which the student performs *homework* is positively correlated with academic performance, provided the homework process is reasonably clear and challenging to the student. When parents insist upon the completion of challenging school homework assignments, the student's academic performance is likely to be positively affected. Since early homework expectations are likely to foster the "homework habit," student's familiarity with the subject matter is likely to be increased. Usually the absence of a homework ritual is accompanied by a general absence of scholarship.

19. The degree and quality of parental involvement in *home social activities* with the student is positively correlated with academic achievement. When parents are involved with the student in leisure activities requiring the use of intellectual functioning capacities, the student is more likely to become acquainted with concepts useful in classroom settings. Exposure to a wide repertoire of communication symbols and codes aids the student in effecting high academic achievement.

20. The supportive or "sponsoring" relationship of parents to students is important for educational success. When parents provide high levels of support, protection, and guidance, the student's educational pursuits become more manageable. Conversely, low parental support will foster high rates of discord and conflict, or a sense of powerlessness. These conditions make educational pursuits more difficult for the student.

We had thought that moral training or the development of a strong sense of right and wrong would also be related to achievement. We discovered, however, that nearly all the families engaged in such training, and therefore this did not distinguish the academically successful from the unsuccessful. This suggests that parents may provide the child with a strong moral foundation but still not see the child become educationally successful. Nevertheless, some aspect of this issue is doubtless related to achievement.

10. Families and Futures

Social Policy Considerations

Frustration with the failures of social programs of the 1960s and 1970s compelled many policymakers to shift the onus of responsibility to the victims of society's mistakes. Nevertheless, solutions to children's achievement problems will inevitably require the full commitment and resources of labor, government (at all levels), media, schools, churches, and other key sectors of society. This type of massive institutional effort is the best (though perhaps idealistic) recourse we have for awakening ourselves to the societal goal of "life, liberty, and the pursuit of happiness" for everyone. Clearly, program solutions calling exclusively for "family strength" or "parent education" will provide limited accomplishments when the family's basic socioeconomic needs are not met. With Black American family median income leveling at about 60 percent of the U.S. family median (and dropping), Black American parents are frequently unable to provide their children with the knowledge resources or "cultural and linguistic capital" that will help to improve their life chances. The economic problems must be solved through the opportunity structure of the larger society; otherwise families like the Treppitts and Farlands may be the exception, when they could be the rule.

More than nine million Black American youths under eighteen are receiving some type of formal education. Millions more Anglo-, Asian, and Hispanic American children will seek status mobility through schooling. Many, perhaps most, of these youths will spend some of their developing years in attenuated families. For social institutions to ignore or misdiagnose the special needs of these youths and their families is to ensure the appearance of more communities of quasi-literate persons, and a further fragmentation and weakening of the American spirit.

At some point, an escalating societal disenchantment with the overall quality of life in our communities will *move* us to address ourselves to the inattention of our public institutions to (1) the hideous degree of stress many parents undergo in their daily psychological and emotional routines, (2) the massive social and economic decline in low-income American families, (3) state-sanctioned stereotypes and assumptions about family cultural patterns and needs (e.g., inaccurately describing family life-styles and customs in the mass media), and (4) the illiteracy in the public schools. Humaneness and common sense must guide our movement toward fundamental social change in these areas.

The moral fiber of the "American Dream" rests on our basic commitment to responsible policy administration and governance that grows from real compassion and support for all American citizens. The problems of the families in this study, even those fostering achievement, are not simply a consequence of family members' behavior. Limited access to needed resources plays a heavy part. As long as there are economic and political incentives for maintaining poverty,[1] "democratic" policymakers will frequently assign a lower priority to the developmental needs of poor families. But these public policy injustices bring inescapable social costs because they are not based on sound principles of systemic growth, efficiency, and effectiveness. It therefore seems intelligent and prudent to acknowledge and confront the existing social problems that hinder our ability to communicate and grow together in a *well* society.

Implications for Parents and Other Family Members

Diana Baumrind, Jerome Kagan, and others have correctly maintained that "there is no such thing as a best way to raise children."[2] A universal formula for academic grooming, equally effective for all developing persons, does not exist.[3] Children are different, families are different, and societies are different. The parents in each family will use their authority to create family life-styles and to encourage the child's intellectual development as well as they can. General child-rearing prescriptions may be inadequate to the needs of the mother who asks "What should I do in my particular circumstances?"

At the same time, we have pinpointed important differences between the family processes of two kinds of ghetto families. Families whose members are emotionally able to love, cooperate, support one another, and find some support outside the home are usually more satisfied with their lives. We were repeatedly struck by the strong mutual support systems and wide range of controlled structured activities in the homes of competent students. Though a certain amount of psychological violence and turmoil seemed inevitable in these high-stress communities, a continual parent-child love bond enabled some families to enjoy a strong achievement orientation and to produce competent students. Conversely, in some families, deep emotional turmoil abounded due to long-term powerlessness, mistrust, discord, confusion, and anger. This situation tended to prompt family members to abuse themselves and one another.

Given a massive commitment to literacy enhancement in "difficult" communities, educators working with families may actually be able to reverse much of the academic impoverishment in large cities by "taking children where they are" and systematically teaching them. Parents should be reminded repeatedly of their role responsibility for teaching their own children, since schools are frequently overloaded and teachers often feel overburdened or "burned out." Parents who expect public schools and other public agencies to take the major responsibility for their children are likely to see their children leave school sooner than they should and with inadequate preparation for social responsibilities.

Evidence in this study highlights the necessity of strong parental involvement and encouragement of children. But, practically speaking, parents in these communities are in dire need of well-conceptualized support programs to offset or "buffer" the tremendous psychic overload they routinely experience. These Black parents also need practical training and information programs that pass on tools which help prepare children for specific classroom lessons. These parents need formal preparation for understanding how instruction proceeds in the school. By learning exactly what education procedures they can use in the home, parents will feel more confident in their ability to improve the quality of their children's classroom learning experiences. For two decades now, the debate over the Moynihan report has revolved around the issue of economic versus structural solutions to problems of success in the Black family. Our conclusion would be that the solution involves *economic* opportunity, public support services, and creative family *processes*. The issue of family compositional *structure* is secondary to, even a by-product, of the other two.[4]

Implications for Schools

Serious legal and ethical questions continue to be raised about how public schools provide equal educational opportunities for all children. The way in which time, curriculum, personnel, and material resources are allocated within neighborhood schools tends to promote the development of a few children at the expense of many other children. Part of the reason for this situation is the general lack of knowledge that school personnel possess about their own clients—the students. Perhaps the principal difficulty in solving the learning problems in urban schools has been the general misunderstanding about how schools teach children and how home and community settings work together to influence children's school behavior. We know from recent research that effective schools are characterized by (a) effective leadership and management, (b) good, committed teachers who know how to stimulate children to do classwork, (c) efficient and active classroom task structures, and (d) many instructionally involved parents.[5] Nevertheless, we are still searching for suitable mechanisms (such as staff development policies and family assistance policies) for transferring the conditions for school effectiveness from one school to another.

While it is true that the education community already knows the pedagogic techniques which produce high rates of literacy in low-income communities, political and social forces have made it difficult to implement the necessary actions on a widespread level.[6] Leaders in the educational establishment have apparently not seen that it is in everyone's interest to meet the literacy problem in our large cities squarely and resolve it. The high costs to society (in terms of high unemployment, welfare, crime, incompetence, poor race relations, apathetic and cynical citizens, and so forth) are gradually forcing us to take notice. Indeed, without a stable social fabric that offers people the prospect of real hope and opportunity, the general economy of business and industry cannot continue to thrive.[7] And, of course, the action of schools is central to the formation of a stable social fabric.

The challenge facing educators today is to create necessary and sufficient circumstances to let teachers and administrators know that they have a personal stake in seeing to it that their pupils become literate in English, math, modern technology, and public etiquette. This perspective would show the teachers why it is in their best interest to teach in a way that compels children to learn. This challenge will be carried out first in the area of ideological warring, where myths and misunderstandings about urban school children and their families will have to be clarified to school professional staffs. This is an essential consciousness-raising step that functions to renew the commitment of teachers and their unions to create quality school environments. Government and school policy must be revamped to serve the reciprocal information needs of schools and households better.

It is time to show administrators and other school personnel how they might use the information in this study (and other studies of community social patterns) in the formulation of effective school instructional programs. The proposed training would enable them to maximize the "fit" between the home and school by showing them how to reach high goals for the acquisition of literacy.[8] This training would focus particularly on how to achieve instructional goals through (1) school policies for hiring, classroom placement, and promotion that boost staff morale, (2) staff development procedures that enhance teachers' instructional skills and home correspondence skills, (3) evaluation procedures that require administrators, teachers, parents, and students to share responsibility for students' learning, and (4) policies, programs, and practices for school-home correspondence that promote the development of the 17 literacy-producing actions in Table 9.1.

This study provides basic home background information which agency administrators, curriculum planners, and teachers will find useful in constructing developmentally effective classroom experiences for all their children, and for low-income Black children in particular. By knowing more about the kinds of psychological and behavioral home processes that are normative for high-achieving and for low-achieving children, the school may provide a pedagogically balanced learning *system* for the child. This learning system would be marked by developmentally successive classroom activities, and cognitively challenging out-of-school activities which encourage higher-level mental processing for more children. For children whose home environments do not routinely provide certain healthy social experiences (e.g., language learning experiences and positive attitudinal and emotional experiences), schools may offer a special sequence of classroom tasks that stimulate the child's acquisition of reading, speaking, and other social skills.[9] This type of instructional sequencing in the classroom may serve as a synergizing force that also improves the quality of family life through the feedback of child to parents, while retaining the basic cultural integrity of the home.

Uncharted Territory in the Study of Learning in Families

Although several important research projects on family learning processes are now being done, there is not enough carefully done research on the role of parents' home teaching practices. Increased knowledge of the home functioning patterns in different ethnic communities will enhance the prospect of (a) developing appropriate school policies and procedures for increasing the knowledge levels of all categories of school children, while (b) preserving the integrity of "the school" and "the home" in each neighborhood.

At this point, we need incisive, statistically significant studies to provide a clear understanding of home academic functioning. As we proceeded through the data analysis for this study, several research questions became apparent. Some of the most needed research areas are listed below:

1. We need statistical studies of relationships between family processes that focus on the specific uses of family time, space, and other resources during specific home activities, and their relative influence on students' classroom role behavior ("process-product" studies) at various stages of the child's school career.

2. Educational and family researchers need to provide improved conceptualizations of parents' perceptions of control and mutual responsibility in their relations with school personnel.

3. More studies tracing and analyzing family educational practices over three generations of a family are needed.

4. We need to discover the patterns of family pedagogy used in the homes of teachers, clergymen, business persons, social workers, construction workers, never-employed parents and so forth. Further, we need to determine the relative effects of work cultures, church cultures, jail cultures, and school cultures on family members' home functioning at various stages in the life cycle.

5. Good empirical research is still needed to document the specific impact of particular family interaction processes (such as sibling recreational interaction or the pedagogic effects of specific television and radio programming) on children's academic achievement. More studies using a wide range of environmental properties as antecedent or intervening variables are needed for analyzing the production of academic talent.

6. Large-sample longitudinal cohort analysis studies which analyze family processes and school processes concurrently throughout the child's school years could be extremely useful for understanding achievement.

7. We also need more research into the *negative* consequences of being a high-achieving student in a community dominated by low-achieving youth.

Further research into intra- and interfamily dynamics and the relative influence of individual families as educators is needed in these and other highly neglected areas. We may then be better able to discover more specific quality-of-life indicators (which are our best clues to the family's future) for use in theory building, family planning, and school planning. Government-, business-, and foundation-sponsored research projects in this area would go a long way toward aiding our analyses of these achievement dynamics in families.

Social workers, psychologists, staff developers, educators, and family practitioners need better assessment and diagnostic tools to help them provide adequately for more families. The results from this study are a beginning in the development of such measures. Under supportive conditions, children who "test low" in early school years can then progress to high achievement. The reliable evidence does not indicate that Black children *cannot* learn; rather available data show that they often *do not* learn what schools want to teach. With more research on family activity processes and school-home correspondence patterns, social service professionals concerned with family support and resocialization will have an opportunity to create more systematic strategies for assisting children's social development in classrooms and neighborhood environments.

It appears, then, that improvement of community, family, and individual conditions through education is an attainable goal. We must, however, be prepared to formulate strategies more carefully—strategies based on accurate, incisive portrayals of family life experiences.[10] We are now responding to this challenge through our current research and program delivery activities with the Los Angeles Family-School Project. The Claremont Graduate School Faculty in Education and the Spencer Foundation are sponsoring this effort. The results of this new work are providing even more knowledge about what children of different backgrounds learn in the home and *how* they learn it.

Suggestions for Family Communication

Our data suggest a wide variety of specific parental practices that may serve well in equipping school children with the comprehensive writing, reading, verbal, and social skills and personal qualities needed for learning classroom lessons and coping with adults and peers. Some of the most important home practices on which parents might wish to focus their attention are presented below.

1. It is important that parents clearly define and fully accept their responsibilities for "parenting." This means being a provider, teacher, nurturer, coach, and source of hope for the child. All family members should routinely try to understand and give "strokes" to one another and actively seek support and assistance when needed.

2. Help the child establish relationships with other achievement-oriented persons.

3. Establish rules for every conceivable social situation by openly discussing "appropriate" behavior for that situation.

4. Parents should use their influence to establish educational activities in the household and routinely monitor the young child's use of time and space, while providing the child with consistently enforced rules for behavior. Nurturance, understanding, and sensitivity to the child's needs and ways of thinking are important in this process.

5. Family members should work to uncover and accentuate the positive characteristics of one another. Criticism should be constructive and meaningful for the child. Dare to make reasonable demands on the child consistently. He or she should receive strong moral training and opportunities for values clarification and evaluation of ethics.[11]

6. Parents should emphasize the importance of *dedication* to tasks for achieving goals. This may be done by providing the child with regular leadership opportunities as part of many everyday family activities. Provide situations for practicing language skills, while exercising responsibility, self-assertiveness, and independence. Involving the child in household chores and consumer decisions is one way of doing this. Letting the child play leadership roles in the family teaches the child the feeling of being appreciated. Constructive part-time work in local institutions is also beneficial. Encourage the child to interact in community institutions (e.g., schools, churches, business establishments, etc.) as producers as well as consumers. Explain the decisions you make to the child and offer other options. The child should be frequently encouraged to learn and practice social skills in *initiating* discourse as well as following the actions of others.

7. Parents should encourage the child to be reasonably ambitious in school and to pursue higher education. Maintain clear, creative expectations for school achievement in the K–12 years. Enroll the young child in supplementary reading, math, and science programs—especially in grades 1–8. At least one evening a week take the child to the library. After a while, vary your

out-of-home experiences with visits to museums, operas, plays, talks, and so forth. (Many of these are low-cost or free.) When parents stress the importance of school while actively involving the family in other educational processes, the child is likely to become academically involved.

8. Insist that homework and other educational activities be regularly performed in the home. Play home games together, especially word games. Conduct family discussions centering on school concerns. Build the child's vocabulary as part of everyday family life by discussing different subjects every day and writing notes to one another.

9. Students should be taught (by example) to love and respect parents and, as a result, other authority figures. They should also learn how to interact with other adults outside the family clan. Allow regular opportunities for value-clarification dialogues and problem-solving sessions as soon as the child can talk.

10. Parents should organize the siblings into a cooperative unit of persons who play, work, and learn together. This will give children more opportunities for intellectual stimulation and growth.

Many of these parent-child behaviors should occur through routine home activities such as at mealtime, while watching television, and during family dialogues. Trips to various support organizations and community agencies are enlightening out-of-home activities for family members. Reading should become a family habit. The daily newspaper provides an excellent means (a) for increasing a student's knowledge about the political-economic processes of our society, (b) for improving literacy skills, and (c) for serving as a point of departure for family dialogues, debates, and intellectual explorations. Family classics, fables, bedtime stories, Bible passages, and short stories with simple moral messages can be used in the home to teach the child about love, fellowship, sharing, competition, brotherhood, inequality, stigmatization, human greed, philosophy, and other concepts facilitating intelligent decision making during social relationships. Parents who share loving, expressive instructional relationships with their children are likely to be successful in passing on survival knowledge for social competence in the student role.

The ethnic family's future will be determined, in large measure, by its ability to take an active approach to family and community problems. This study demonstrates that specific qualities of family functioning are required to prepare children for competent school behavior from kindergarten through high school. The seventeen intertwined and mutually reinforcing pattern categories of the previous chapter represent indicators of the quality of family life in single-parent homes, two-parent homes, and in other family structure arrangements. The substance of these pattern categories provide clues to the social learning process in each home. These clues then provide a context for systematically strengthening the learning patterns in contemporary households and classrooms.

Notes

1. The Issue

1. Robert K. Merton, *Social Theory and Social Structure* (New York: Free Press, 1968), 319, describes this grooming as a process of "anticipatory socialization." This is a social interaction process that prepares a person to adapt more readily the values and habits of a "nonmembership group"—that is, a group to which one does not belong but to which one aspires. Merton explains that by embracing the values and standards of the nonmembership group, the individual will find "readier acceptance by that group" and will "more easily adjust to it." Examples of such "nonmembership" groups are peer groups, work groups, racial groups, scholastic groups, economic groups, and gender groups. To the degree that a person understands and accepts the values and the formal and informal rules of work roles, educational roles and so forth, that person is likely to interact competently with others in these groups.

In this book, I look at how family members pass on knowledge to one another, and how the knowledge transmission process prepares young people to enact social roles in classrooms with a high caliber of social competence. "Social competence" refers to the effectiveness, appropriateness, skillfulness, excellence or convincingness of a person's enactment of the tasks that are essential for goal attainment in a particular classroom, work place or other social setting. Put differently, social competence is the demonstration of normative control over social processes during events. The superior performance of role responsibilities is the major indicator of social competence during the events. For example, most people would judge a fourth-grade student socially competent if the student could meet national standards of "appropriate" fourth-grade student behavior. This behavior includes maintaining one's personal health and safety, showing exemplary reasoning ability, winning at school contests (e.g., grades, test scores), exhibiting strong motivation or drive, possessing a high academic self-concept, showing reasonable patience, taking initiative during lessons, having dedication to academic pursuits, generally showing talent in sending desired messages, finding solutions to problems, staying out of trouble, and normally engaging in peer interactions. The key point here is that social competence is reflected in the quality of role performances, and the nature of these role performances is largely dependent upon the patterns of primary and secondary socialization in the home.

2. Bernard Farber, *Family Organization and Interaction* (San Francisco: Chandler, 1964); Diana Baumrind, "Current Patterns of Parental Authority," *Developmental Psychology Monograph* 4, no. 1 (1971):1–103. Farber introduced the concepts of "sponsored independence" and "unsponsored independence" in this important work. I am indebted to Bert Adams for bringing these concepts to my attention. I have expanded Farber's explanation of the concepts to address the socialization issues in this study.

3. For this argument, see Martin Deutsch, "The Disadvantaged Child and the Learning Process," in A. Harry Passow, ed., *Education in Depressed Areas* (New York: Teachers College Press, 1967), 163–79. See also Norma L. Radin, "Some Impediments to the Education of Disadvantaged Children," in P. H. Glasser and L. N. Glasser, eds., *Families in Crisis* (New York: Harper & Row, 1970), 68–78; Daniel P. Moynihan, *The Negro Family: The Case for National Action* (Washington, D.C.: U.S. Department of Labor, Office of Policy Planning and Research, 1965); Edward C. Banfield, *The Unheavenly City* (Boston: Little,

Brown, 1970); H. Etzkowitz and G. M. Schaflander, *Ghetto Crisis: Riots or Reconciliations?* (Boston: Little, Brown, 1969).

4. Colin Greer, *The Great School Legend* (New York: Basic Books, 1972), makes this argument in his controversial historical analysis of urban schools. There is some evidence, however, that today's private schools frequently produce relatively large contingents of literate persons. See the essay by Andrew M. Greeley, "Catholic High Schools and Minority Students," in A. M. Greeley, *Minority Students and Catholic Secondary Schools* (New Brunswick, N.J.: Transaction Books, forthcoming). The fact is that schooling will probably become even more instrumental in "qualifying" people for jobs as we move ever closer to a "credential society." For a good discussion of this trend, see Randall Collins, *The Credential Society* (New York: Academic Press, 1979).

5. See Collins, *The Credential Society*.

6. See Urie Bronfenbrenner, *The Ecology of Human Development* (Cambridge, Mass.: Harvard University Press, 1979), 210.

7. See H. Cooper, "Pygmalion Grows Up: A Model for Teacher Expectation, Communication, and Performance Influence," *Review of Educational Research* 49, no. 3 (1979):389–410; R. Hoge and S. Luce, "Predicting Academic Behavior from Classroom Behavior," *Review of Educational Research* 49, no. 3 (1979):479–96; Hugh Mehan, *Learning Lessons: Social Organization in the Classroom* (Cambridge, Mass.: Harvard University Press, 1979).

8. These preparatory tasks are essentially learning activities during which pedagogic and cognitive work processes produce images, meanings, and understandings that nurture higher level speaking, reading, writing, and computing skills.

9. Trevor R. Williams, "Abilities and Environments: Another View," 1979 (preprint).

10. Peter M. Blau and Otis Dudley Duncan, *The American Occupational Structure* (New York: John Wiley, 1977), 295.

11. See R. H. Dave, "The Identification and Measurement of Environmental Process Variables That Are Related to Educational Achievement" (Ph.D. diss., University of Chicago, 1963); R. M. Wolf, "The Identification and Measurement of Environmental Process Variables Related to Intelligence" (Ph.D. diss., University of Chicago, 1964); James S. Coleman et al., *Equality of Educational Opportunity* (Washington, D.C.: U.S. Office of Education, 1966); William Sewell and V. P. Shah, "Parents' Education and Children's Educational Aspirations and Achievements," *American Sociological Review* 33, no. 2 (1968):191–209; Christopher Jencks et al., *Inequality* (New York: Basic Books, 1972); Kevin Marjoribanks, *Families and Their Learning Environments: An Empirical Analysis* (London: Routledge & Kegan Paul, 1979); idem, *Ethnic Families and Children's Achievements* (London: George Allen & Unwin, 1981).

12. Coleman, *Equality of Educational Opportunity*.

13. Jencks et al., *Inequality*, 1972, 77.

14. Dave, "The Identification and Measurement of Environmental Process Variables that are Related to Educational Achievement."

15. Wolf, "The Identification and Measurement of Environmental Process Variables Related to Intelligence."

16. Joel Weiss, "The Identification and Measurement of Home Environment Factors Related to Achievement Motivation and Self-Esteem" (Ph.D. diss., University of Chicago, 1969).

17. Irving Sigel and Ann McGillicuddy-DeLisi, *Parental Distancing, Beliefs, and Children's Representational Competence within the Family Context* (Princeton, N.J.: Educational Testing Service, 1980).

18. Boyd C. Rollins and Darwin L. Thomas, "Parental Support, Power, and Control Techniques in the Socialization of Children," in Wesley R. Burr *et al*, eds., *Contemporary Theories about the Family*, Vol. 1 (New York: Free Press, 1979), 317–64.

19. A. B. Heilbrun and D. B. Waters, "Underachievement as Related to Perceived Mater-

nal Child-Rearing and Academic Conditions of Reinforcement," *Child Development* 39 (1968):913–21.

20. Diana Baumrind, "Socialization and Instrumental Competence in Young Children," in W. W. Hartup, ed., *The Young Child: Reviews of Research*, Vol. 2 (Washington, D.C.: National Association for the Education of Young Children, 1972), referred to in Rollins and Thomas, "Parental Support," 339.

21. Rollins and Thomas, "Parental Support," 340.

22. These research studies have variously focused on ethnic background of the family, family social class position, family size, family unity, parents' aspirations for children, paternal role functioning, maternal role functioning, children's home role functioning, and parents' child-rearing patterns. See Bernard Rosen, "Race, Ethnicity and the Achievment Syndrome," *American Sociological Review* 24 (1959):47–60; Robert B. Bell, "Lower Class Negro Mothers and Their Children," *Integrated Education* 2 (1964–65):23–27; R. B. Zajonk, "Birth Configuration and Intelligence," *Science* 192 (1976):227–92; Bernard Rosen, "Family Structure and Achievement Motivation," *American Sociological Review* 26, no. 4 (1961):574–85; Elizabeth Herzog and C. Sudia, " Children in Fatherless Families," in Bettye Caldwell and H. Ricciuti, eds., *Child Development and Social Policy* (Chicago: University of Chicago Press, 1973), 141–232; Louis Kriesberg, *Mothers in Poverty: A Study of Fatherless Families* (Chicago: Aldine, 1970); David A. Schultz, *Coming up Black: Patterns of Ghetto Socialization* (Englewood Cliffs, N.J.: Prentice-Hall, 1969); S. Webster, "Some Correlates of Reported Academically Supportive Behaviors of Negro Mothers toward Their Children," *Journal of Negro Education* 34 (1965):114–20; Urie Bronfenbrenner, "Some Familial Antecedents of Responsibility and Leadership in Adolescents," in L. Petrullo and B. M. Bass, eds., *Leadership and Interpersonal Behavior* (New York: Holt, Rinehart & Winston, 1961) 239–71; H. H. Davidson and J. E. Greenberg, *School Achievers from a Deprived Background* (New York: Associated Educational Services, 1967); Diane Scott-Jones, "Relationships between Family Variables and School Achievement in Low-Income Black First Graders," paper presented at the annual meeting of the American Educational Research Association, Boston, 1980.

23. See Oliver C. Moles, Jr., "Child Training Practices among Low Income Families," *Welfare in Review* 3, no. 6 (1965):1–11; N. Freeberg and D. Payne, "Parental Influence on Cognitive Development in Early Childhood: A Review," *Child Development* 38, no. 1 (1967):65–87; Hope J. Leichter, *The Family as Educator* (New York: Teachers College Press, 1974); Cynthia Wallet and Richard Goldman, *Home, School, and Community Interaction: What We Know and Why We Don't Know More* (Columbus, Ohio: Merrill Publishing Co., 1979); J. Walters and N. Stinnett, "Parent-Child Relationships: A Decade Review of Research," in Carlfred B. Broderick, ed., *A Decade of Family Research and Action* (Minneapolis, Minn.: National Council on Family Relations, 1972), 99–140; Victor Gecas, "The Influence of Social Class on Socialization," in Wesley Burr et al., eds., *Contemporary Theories about the Family, Vol. 1*, (New York: Free Press, 1979), 1:365–403; B. Martin, "Parent–Child Relations," in F. D. Horowitz, ed., *Review of Child Development Research*, vol. 4 (Chicago: University of Chicago Press, 1975). Two especially useful books on the family's role in children's school achievement are Kevin Marjoribanks's discussions of family research studies in the United States and abroad, *Ethnic Families and Children's Achievements*, and *Families and Their Learning Environments*. Professor Marjoribanks provides a good empirical description of several studies of family life in Australia, Canada, Britain, The Netherlands, and the United States. His treatments provide a more global context for understanding how family life contributes to children's learning.

24. Theresa A. Sullivan, "Racial-Ethnic Differences in Labor Force Participation: An Ethnic Stratification Perspective," in Frank D. Bean and W. P. Frisbie, eds., *The Demography of Racial and Ethnic Groups* (New York: Academic Press, 1978), 165–87; Milton Gordon, *Human Nature, Class and Ethnicity* (New York: Oxford University Press, 1978);

220   *Notes*

Tamotsu Shibutani and Kian M. Kwan, *Ethnic Stratification: A Comparative Approach*, New York: Mac Millan, 1965.

25. Collins, *The Credential Society*; Sullivan, "Racial-Ethnic Differences in Labor Force Participation."

26. L. F. Cervantes, "Family Background, Primary Relationships, and the High School Dropout," *Journal of Marriage and the Family* 27, no. 2 (1965):218–29.

27. E. M. Drews and J. E. Teahan, "Parental Attitudes and Academic Achievement," *Journal of Clinical Psychology* 13, no. 4 (1957):328–32.

28. Frank Musgrove, *The Family, Education and Society* (London: Routledge & Kegan Paul, 1966).

29. Torsten Husen, "Home Background and Behavior in the Classroom Situation" (University of Stockholm, 1963).

30. Several authors have made this observation before, including Bernard Mackler, "Blacks Who Are Academically Successful," *Urban Education* 5 (1971):210–37; and Davidson and Greenberg, *School Achievers from a Deprived Background*.

31. Talcott Parsons, "The School Class as a Social System," *Harvard Educational Review* 29 (1959):297–318; Robert Dreeben, *On What Is Learned in School* (Reading, Mass.: Addison-Wesley, 1968); Ray C. Rist, "Student Social Class and Teacher Expectations: The Self-Fulfilling Prophecy in Ghetto Education," *Harvard Educational Review* 40, no. 3 (1970):411–51; Jean Carew and Sarah L. Lightfoot, *Beyond Bias: Perspectives on Classrooms* (Cambridge, Mass.: Harvard University Press, 1977); Cynthia Wallet and Richard Goldman, Home, *School, and Community Interaction: What We Know and Why We Don't Know More*.

32. Dreeben, *On What Is Learned in School*; Rist, "Student Social Class," 411–51; Benjamin Bloom, *Human Characteristics and School Learning* (New York: McGraw-Hill, 1976); Bronfenbrenner, *The Ecology of Human Development*; Jean Anyon, "Social Class and School Knowledge," *Curriculum Inquiry* 11, no. 1 (1981):30–42.

33. Hoge and Luce, "Predicting Academic Behavior from Classroom Behavior"; Cooper, "Pygmalion Grows Up."

34. See Kay P. Torshen, "The Relation of Classroom Evaluation to Students' Self Concepts and Mental Health" (Ph.D. diss., University of Chicago, 1969). Torshen found that there is a definite and, indeed, overwhelming relationship between the grades a student receives in the classroom and that student's mental health. As she suggests, "grades can affect personality even if they do not represent accurate evaluations of cognitive performance." This fact is especially significant in light of research evidence relating to teachers' subjective attitudes toward students and teachers' powers of evaluation of those same students. See especially the work of Gerry Rosenfeld, *Shut Those Thick Lips: A Study of Slum School Failure* (New York: Holt, Rinehart, & Winston, 1971); Rist, "Student Social Class"; Carolyn Persell, *Education and Inequality: The Roots and Results of Stratification in American Schools* (New York: Free Press, 1977); James E. Baugh, "The Experiences of Black Students in a White University: Case Study of Participants in an Educational Opportunity Program" (Ph.D. diss., University of Wisconsin, 1973), and Joan I. Roberts, *Scene of the Battle: Group Dynamics in Urban Classrooms* (New York: Anchor Books, 1971).

2. Research Methods

1. Elizabeth J. Bott, *Family and Social Network* (London: Tavistock Publications, 1957), chaps. 1 and 2; Robert Hess and Gerald Handel, *Family Worlds: A Psychosocial Approach to Family Life* (Chicago: University of Chicago Press, 1959), chap. 1.

2. See the discussion by Reuben Hill and Donald Hansen, "The Identification of Conceptual Frameworks Utilized in Family Study," *Journal of Marriage and Family Living* 22, No. 4 (1960):302–303. The psychosocial process approach to the study of action in families started with the interactionist conceptualizations of Ernest W. Burgess, "The Family as a

Unity of Interacting Personalities," in Jerold Heiss, ed., *Family Roles and Interaction: An Anthology* (Chicago: Rand McNally & Co., 1968), 28–34; Charles H. Cooley, *Human Nature and the Social Order* (New York: Charles Scribner & Sons, 1902); Kurt Lewin, *A Dynamic Theory of Personality* (New York: McGraw-Hill, 1935). This approach is more recently represented in the theoretical and empirical works of Robert Hess and Gerald Handel, *Family Worlds*; Gerald Handel, "The Psychological Study of Whole Families," *Psychological Bulletin* 63, no. 1 (1965):19–41; Talcott Parsons and Robert F. Bales, *Family, Socialization and Interaction Process* (Glencoe, Ill.: Free Press, 1955); Pierre Bourdieu, "Cultural Reproduction and Social Reproduction," in Richard Brown, ed., *Knowledge, Education, and Cultural Change* (London: Tavistock, 1973), 71–112; Jules Henry, *Pathways to Madness* (New York: Random House, 1971); Wesley Burr et al., "Symbolic Interaction and the Family," in *Contemporary Theories about the Family*, Vol. 2 (New York: Free Press, 1979)42–111; Shelton Stryker, "Symbolic Interaction as an Approach to Family Research," *Marriage and Family Living* 21, no. 2 (1959):111–19; Bernard Cohler and Henry Grunebaum, *Mothers, Grandmothers, and Daughters: Personality and Child Care in Three Generation Families* (New York: John Wiley, 1981); Jerold Heiss, *The Social Psychology of Interaction* (Englewood Cliffs, N.J.: Prentice-Hall, 1982).

Robert Hess and Gerald Handel's work "The Family as a Psychosocial Organization" in Gerald Handel, ed., *The Psychosocial Interior of the Family: A Sourcebook for the Study of Whole Families* (Chicago: Aldine Publishing Co., 1967), 11, further elucidates the individual and interactional aspects of whole family analysis. To them, the family unit is conceived as a group of individuals engaged in interaction between themselves and the extrafamilial world (the wider community). Further, each family is conceived as possessing a discernible pattern and form which is subject to description.

Sociologists and anthropologists have recognized that every family world is phenomenologically unique. See Joyce Aschenbrenner, *Lifelines: Black Families in Chicago* (New York: Holt, Rinehart & Winston, 1975); Virginia H. Young, "Family and Childhood in a Southern Negro Community," *American Anthropologist*, 72, no. 2 (1970):269–88; Henry, *Pathways to Madness*. According to this rather heuristic stance, each family unit is a phenomenon that exists in the consciousness of its members and is usually reified through the family member's own sense of meaning (or interpretation) of the extant properties in the family world. Anthropologists have noted that every family exists (and experiences social realities) in some ways similar to all families, in other ways similar to some families, and in still other ways like no other family. This household uniqueness might be called the family ethos. The ethos may be defined as the predominant ideas, values, and ideals of a culture or subculture which gives it its distinctive character (as individual as a fingerprint, as it were). In addition to its predominant persona there will be various mixtures of family dignity, despair, survival instincts, psychic energy, authenticity, soul, smells, human spirit, and human natures—the kind of stuff that is difficult, if not impossible, to measure scientifically. In short, the ethos is the *essence* of the family. See Raymond McLain and Andrew Weigert, "Toward a Phenomenological Sociology of Family: A Programmatic Essay," in Burr et al., eds., *Contemporary Theories about the Family*, 2: 160–205.

The concepts of family *communication, ritual activity, dispositions*, and *compositional properties* provide a framework for interpreting how the family ethos has developed into its current symbolic configuration. That is, researchers may find measures of the family life theme by analyzing the social reality (meanings as perceived by family members) attached to home communication behaviors (verbal and nonverbal interaction); ritual behaviors (repetitive exigencies of everyday life); dispositions (attitudes, beliefs and values), and compositional properties and setting (which refer to the home physical environment and material culture). Perhaps the concept that best represents the family ethos is Hess and Handel's and Csikszentmihalyi's notion of family "life theme" (see Hess and Handel, *Family Worlds*, chap. 1, and Michael Csikszentmihalyi, "Life Themes: A Theoretical and Empirical Exploration of Their Origins and Effects," University of Chicago, 1977). The family life theme may be defined as "the social/psychological problem or set of problems which the members of the family group wishes to solve above all else and which form the basis for a fundamental interpretation of reality and ways of dealing with that reality," (see Csikszentmihalyi, "Life Themes," p. 3). The family life theme may represent the family ethos in that it highlights the underlying "symbolic order" of the family's senses of reality. This symbolic order includes structures of consciousness and pre-predicated meaning, the meaning of symbols and signs in the home, and the gestalt of orientations, goals and means which constitute a structural dimension in a family's life.

3. Bott, *Family and Social Network*, 10.

4. The interested reader will find a chapter that more fully discusses my field experiences and methods in my doctoral dissertation, "Black Families as Educators: A Qualitative Inquiry" (University of Wisconsin, Madison, 1977; available from University Microfilms).

5. See Henry, *Pathways to Madness*, xv.

6. Oscar Lewis, "The Culture of Poverty," *Scientific American* 214, No. 10 (1966): 19–25.

7. Hess and Handel, 1959, 1967.

8. Barney Glaser and Anselm Strauss, *The Discovery of Grounded Theory* (Chicago: Aldine, 1971), chap. 6.

9. According to Chad Gordon at Rice University, "the Persons Conceptions analytical system is designed to permit computer-aided content analysis of any English language descriptions (written or verbal) of individuals. These may be individual's self- conceptions or their conceptions of other people, and they may be in any form that can be punched onto data processing cards or other machine readable form. Open self-descriptions, diaries, novels, or historical accounts also could be analyzed in a single comparative and theoretically relevant system" (personal communication).

10. See, for example, the discussion by Erving Goffman in his book *Frame Analysis* (Cambridge, Mass.: Harvard University Press, 1974), chap. 1.

3. The Family Life of High Achievers in Two-Parent Homes

1. In the Chivers family, as with all the families in chaps. 4 and 5, not all of the children are as successful in school as is the target child. For example, the older children in the Chivers family have already left home and started families of their own, and are working in service occupations after good-to-fair (not particularly outstanding) educational careers. While this study did not gather data on the achievement levels of all the siblings in a household, my own impressions are that there has been a *general* pattern of achievement values and learning habits in the high achievers' families. The structure and impact of these achievement orientations on the siblings seems to have varied depending on the parents' circumstances and behaviors during each sibling's childhood years. We may, however, safely talk in terms of general tendencies for achievement (or non-achievement) within these family units.

4. The Family Life of High Achievers in One-Parent Homes

1. Eric Erickson, *Childhood and Society* (New York: Norton, 1950).

2. From Chicago Department of Development and Planning, 1975.

5. An Analysis of Dispositions and Life-styles in High Achievers' Homes

1. See Bernard Farber, *Family Organization and Interaction*, 100 and 369.

2. Jean Piaget, *The Moral Judgement of the Child* (New York: Free Press, 1948), 101.

3. See Jay Schvaneveldt and M. Ihinger, "Sibling Relationships in the Family" in Wesley Burr et al., eds., *Contemporary Theories about the Family*, 1 (New York: Free Press, 1979):453–467.

4. This observation appears to discredit the notion that only older parents are "settled" and able to provide the necessary support resources for children. Apparently, the parents'

age does not determine their ability to hold supportive child-care attitudes. Perhaps an argument can be made that parents' overall level of satisfaction with the parental role seems to have shifted downward over the years. Many parents may now be experiencing even greater frustration and unhappiness with themselves and their circumstances due to shifting sex role norms. Many are certainly rejecting their children's needs in favor of their own needs, wants, and desires. Ironically, sometimes their inability to cope with the multiple requirements of modern day parenthood causes these parents to strike out at those who are the closest—their children. The ubiquitous demands of urban life have become overwhelming for many. Parents simply find it increasingly difficult to fulfill their social *responsiblity* (legal or moral) to prepare their progeny for high quality educational and occupational opportunities. Indeed, many parents simply need help in fulfilling these tasks. The plain fact is that very few mothers can effectively nurture and monitor two or more children at the same time in our urban-industrial society.

5. Fathers had adjusted to this household pattern quite successfully. Perhaps their ability to accept this egalitarian position is due to their perception that the wife is not trying to take over their status; rather, "the white man," "society," and/or some personal limitation is seen as the real cause of family problems.

6. See T. E. Smith, "Foundations of Parental Influence Upon Adolescents: An Application of Social Power Theory," *American Sociological Review* 35 (1970):860–872, and Walter R. Allen, "The Antecedents of Adolescent Mobility Aspirations," (Ph.D. diss., University of Chicago, 1975). See also John Scanzoni, "Social Processes and Power in Families," in Wesley Burr et al., eds., *Contemporary Theories about the Family*, 1:295–315.

7. Sociologist Robert F. Winch advanced the proposition that "the relative absence of functions [i.e., purposeful, task-oriented] and associated roles deprives the family of a definite objective with respect to child rearing" (see his *Identification and Its Familial Determinants: Exposition of Theory and Results of Pilot Studies* [Indianapolis: Bobbs-Merrill, 1962], 50). As children become psychically and functionally integrated into the multiple activities of the household, parents are in an excellent position to use their authority to groom the child for social and academic work roles. As developing persons, functioning within particular activity structures, these children go on to be attentive toward (and identify with) the parents' expectations over a wide range of behaviors. When parent-child psychological symmetry is this complete, family integration becomes deepest—even as parents prescribe the substance of parent-child roles.

8. See Bert N. Adams, "Birth Order: A Review," *Sociometry* 35, no. 3 (1972):411–39.

9. See Fred L. Strodtbeck, "Family Interaction, Values and Achievement," in David C. McClelland et al., eds., *Talent and Society* (Princeton, N.J.: Van Nostrand, 1958), 135–94; Melvin Kohn, *Class and Conformity: A Study in Values*, 2d ed. (Chicago: University of Chicago Press, 1977).

10. See David Heise, *Understanding Events: Affect and the Construction of Social Action* (Cambridge: Cambridge University Press, 1979); Urie Bronfenbrenner, *The Ecology of Human Development* (Cambridge, Mass.: Harvard University Press, 1979), 57.

11. See Diana Baumrind, "Current Patterns of Parental Authority," *Developmental Psychology Monographs*, vol. 4, no. 1, part 2 (1971):1–103; also, "Socialization and Instrumental Competence in Young Children" in W. W. Hartup, ed., *The Young Child: Review of Research*, 2 (Washington, D.C.: National Association for the Education of Young Children, 1972), 202–24.

12. Baumrind, in Hartup, *The Young Child*, 203–4.

13. David C. McClelland, *The Achievement Motive* (New York: Appleton-Century-Crofts, 1953).

14. Diana Baumrind and A. E. Black, "Socialization Practices Associated with Dimensions of Competence in Preschool Boys and Girls," *Child Development* 38 (1967):291–328; Diana Baumrind, "Reciprocal Rights and Responsibilities in Parent-Child Relations," *Journal of Social Issues* 34, no.2 (1978):179–196.

15. Other researchers have found that these behavior patterns tend to reduce conflict and friction in the household. See, for example, Martin L. Hoffman, "Power Assertion by the Parent and Its Impact on the Child," *Child Development* 31 (1960):129–143; Boyd C. Rollins and D. L. Thomas, "A Theory of Parental Power and Child Compliance," in Ronald E. Cromwell and David H. Olson, eds., *Power in Families* (New York: John Wiley & Sons, 1975), 38–60.

16. See Elmer Martin and Joanne M. Martin, *The Black Extended Family* (Chicago: University of Chicago Press, 1978).

17. See John McManus, "Ritual and Human Social Cognition," in Eugene d'Aquili et al., eds., *The Spectrum of Ritual: A Biogenetic Structural Analysis* (New York: Columbia University Press, 1979), 216–47; Pierre Bourdieu and Jean C. Passeron, *Reproduction in Education, Society, and Culture* (Beverly Hills, Calif.: Sage Publications, 1977).

18. This formulation is not intended to be exclusive or exhaustive. It does not, for example, capture the hidden learning structure (curriculum) contained in the parents' use of verbal labels during interpersonal discourse in the home. It also ignores the qualitative substance of each activity. As one example, we could not tell from this typology whether a family listens to AM radio or FM radio. This typology merely functions as a means of generally conceptualizing how households may organize their time for communication encounters.

19. Indeed, these parents sometimes encourage the youths to "get an education" in order to be more effective in helping improve these societal conditions. Also a few of these parents themselves will have spent some time in night classes in an effort to further their own education.

20. Some of these youths feel that it is exclusively Blacks and other minorities who have been extremely deprived of access to these basic resources, and they are still working to resolve a serious racial and role identity conflict.

21. Other researchers have also found that boys and girls with this psychological orientation appear to be better able to achieve in school settings. See Edgar Epps, "Correlates of Academic Achievement among Northern and Southern Urban Negro Students," *Journal of Social Issues* 25 (1969):55–70; Chad Gordon, *Looking Ahead: Self-Conceptions, Race, and Family as Determinants of Adolescent Orientation to Achievement*, Arnold and Caroline Rose Monograph series (Washington, D.C.: American Sociological Association, 1972).

22. Other studies have found that whenever the parent is employed outside the home, siblings of both sexes are usually more heavily involved in household maintenance. See Bernard Farber, *Family Organization and Interaction*, 37.

23. Sociologist Robert Levine has observed that in populations with scarce subsistence resources, parents will be preoccupied with the child's capacity for future economic self-maintenance (broadly defined) and that child-rearing customs will reflect this priority. See Robert Levine, "Parental Goals: A Cross-Cultural View," in Hope J. Leichter, ed., *The Family as Educator* (New York: Teachers College Press, 1974), 52–65. Consistent with his observation, parents in this study desired to see the student grow up to be an independent adult with good work habits, capable of home (life) management in adulthood. Winch has observed that children who are highly functional in the family group are more likely to be integrated into it and affected by it. As these high-achieving children work in task-oriented home activities, they are able to increase their ability to accept responsibility for familial and extrafamilial roles. See Winch, *Identification and Its Familial Determinants*.

24. Parents working in skilled and semiskilled occupations are likely to have high aspirations that after graduation the student will find a job that pays well. Students are groomed to aspire to the "decent job," which is itself a status symbol in the community. See Martin and Martin, *The Black Extended Family*.

6. The Family Life of Low Achievers in Two-Parent Homes

1. See James Baldwin, *Notes of a Native Son* (1955), 59.

2. Coleman et al., *Equality of Educational Opportunity*.

8. An Analysis of Dispositions and Life-styles in Low Achievers' Homes

1. Bernard Farber, *Family Organization and Interaction.*

2. Diana Baumrind, "Socialization and Instrumental Competence in Young Children," in W. W. Hartup, ed., *Research on Young Children* (Washington, D.C.: National Association for the Education of Young Children, 1972).

9. The Family and the Bases for Academic Achievement

1. Diana Baumrind, "Socialization and Instrumental Competence in Young Children" in W. W. Hartup, ed., *Research on Young Children* (Washington, D.C.: National Association for the Education of Young Children, 1972).

2. Bert N. Adams, *The Family: A Sociological Interpretation*, 3d edition (Chicago: Rand McNally, 1981).

3. Students in all families can be said to have exhibited a high need for achievement if we define "need for achievement" as the desire and ability to continue schooling despite environmental obstacles. It is interesting to note that no student (or parent) viewed schooling as important solely for the attainment of "knowledge." Rather, schooling was seen as serving the concretely functional purpose of enabling the student to become credentialed. John Ogbu's study of Blacks in Stockton, California, found the same attitude to be prevalent. Both students and parents desired the symbols (e.g., diplomas, degrees, etc.) offered by educational institutions. Most parents believed that life chances are increased when these symbols are obtained. See John Ogbu, *The Next Generation: An Ethnography of Education in an Urban Neighborhood* (New York: Academic Press, 1974). Randall Collins argues that such an attitude is dominant in American society. See Randall Collins, *The Credential Society* (New York: Academic Press, 1979).

4. It should be noted that the quality and quantity of information and activities that flow between home and school will significantly affect the child's school performance. Six key indicators of the quality of family-school contact patterns are apparent: (1) school administration strategies for sending messages to parents and vice versa, (2) the amount of time made available to school children for class instruction, (3) school–sponsored program efforts to work with parents on school-home reinforcement strategies, (4) teachers' sensitivity to students' home learning activities, (5) the degree of direct pedagogic planning between parents and students, and (6) parents' involvement in school organizations.

5. For an exception, see Pierre Bourdieu and Jean–Claude Passeron, *Reproduction in Education, Society, and Culture.*

6. See Mario D. Fantini, "Community Participation: Alternative Patterns and Their Consequences on Educational Achievement," paper presented at the annual meeting of the American Educational Research Association, 1980; Sarah L. Lightfoot, *Worlds Apart: Relationships between Families and Schools* (New York: Basic Books, 1977); Cynthia Wallet and Richard Goldman, *Home, School, and Community Interaction* Sandra S. Tangri and M. Laurie Leitch, "Barriers to Home-School Collaboration: Two Case Studies in Junior High Schools' Final Report to National Institute of Education, 1982.

7. James S. Coleman et al., *Equality of Educational Opportunity*; Christopher Jencks et al., *Inequality* (1972); Bernard C. Rosen, "Family Structure and Achievement Motivation," 1961; William Sewell and V. P. Shah, "Parents' Education and Children's Educational Aspirations and Achievements" (1968).

8. See chap. 2, note 2.

9. See Fred Strodtbeck, "Family Interaction, Values and Achievement"; also, "The Hidden Curriculum in the Middle-Class Home"; Urie Bronfenbrenner, "Some Familial Antecedents of Responsibility and Leadership in Adolescents."

10. The work being done at the Harvard Graduate School of Education may provide such an analysis, but it has yet to be published. See Jeanne Chall and Catherine Snow, The

Contribution of Out-of-School Experiences to the Acquisition of Literacy (progress report to National Institute of Education, 1982).

11. Pierre Bourdieu, "Cultural Reproduction and Social Reproduction" in Richard Brown, ed., *Knowledge, Education, and Cultural Change* (London: Tavistock, 1973).

12. See Willard Waller, *The Sociology of Teaching* (New York: John Wiley & Sons, 1932); Steven T. Bossert, "Consequences of Activity Structures," paper presented at the annual meeting of the American Educational Research Association, Boston, 1980; also, *Tasks and Social Relationships in the Classroom* (New York: Cambridge University Press, 1979); Jane Stallings, "Allocated Academic Learning Time Revisited, or Beyond Time on Task," *Educational Researcher* 9 (1980):11–16; Carl Simpson, "Classroom Structure and the Organization of Ability," *Sociology of Education* 54 (1981):120–32; S. J. Rosenholtz and S. H. Rosenholtz, " Classroom Organization and the Perception of Ability," *Sociology of Education* 54 (1981):132–40.

13. At Claremont Graduate School, we have recently completed a study that gives an unprecedented analysis of such dynamics in Anglo-, Black, and Mexican-American families. The pedagogic efficiency of these instructional dynamics were measured for thirty-two family units. These instructional dynamics served as indicators of the level of the pupil's anticipatory socialization opportunities in the home. We had hypothesized that variations in the breadth of the activity structures and process dimensions of the family unit (as determined by standard scores on Likert-type rating scales) will affect pupils' academic levels in the classroom. We further hypothesized that the extent and direction of this effect is contingent upon the level of support (resource allocation patterns) provided to the pupil by the school social system. Our examination of this last hypothesis was especially important since it addressed issues of (1) equity in the school "support opportunities" provided to racial groups, (2) appropriate strategies for bringing about school reforms in different ethnic communities, and (3) the pedagogic efficiency of specific classroom activities. All of our hypotheses were confirmed by the data we collected in this work. See Reginald M. Clark, *Community Opportunity Structure, Family Interaction, and Children's Cognitive Development*, Technical Report No. D-107 (Chicago: Spencer Foundation, 1982).

10. Families and Futures

1. See H. J. Gans, "The Positive Functions of Poverty," *American Journal of Sociology* 78(1973):275–89.

2. Diana Baumrind, "An Exploratory Study of Socialization Effects on Black Children: Some Black-White Comparisons," *Child Development* 43 (1972):261–267; Jerome Kagan, "The Psychological Requirements for Human Development," in Nathan B. Talbot, ed., *Rearing Children in Modern America: Problems and Prospective Solutions* (Boston: Little, Brown, 1976).

3. See the argument by Raymond McClain and A. Weigert, "Toward a Phenomenological Sociology of the Family."

4. Sociologist William J. Wilson reminds us that effective policy programs for poor Black families will address the unique economic and social circumstances of those families. We presume that Black middle class families must be seen as needing an entirely different balance of economic and social resources. See William Julius Wilson, "Race-Oriented Programs and the Black Underclass" in Clement Cottingham, ed., *Race, Poverty, and the Urban Underclass* (Lexington, Mass.: Lexington Books, 1982), 113–132. Over a decade ago, family sociologist Robert Staples wrote that "The Black family, as a single model for study, does not exist. There are individual family units, whose members are Black, who have both experiences unique to that group and experiences common to many other families, Black and White; [The Black family] is a type of social organization whose form changes from social class to social class, region to region, country to country, and culture to culture." See Robert Staples, ed., *The Black Family: Essays and Studies* (Belmont, Calif.: Wadsworth Publishing Co., 1971), p. 3.

5. See especially the work of Ronald Edmonds, "A Discussion of the Literature and Issues Related to Effective Schooling," in Harriet D. Willis, ed., *What Do We Know about Teaching and Learning in Urban Schools?* (St. Louis, Mo.: Cemrel, 1979); Wilbur Brookover et al., *School Social Systems and Student Achievement* (New York: Praeger, 1979); Jane Stallings, "Report on California Schools with Increasing and Decreasing Reading Scores" (Sacramento: California Department of Public Instruction, 1980); Benjamin Bloom, "The New Direction in Educational Research: Alterable Variables" in *All Our Children Learning* (New York: McGraw-Hill, 1981) 382–385; John Goodlad, *A Study of Schooling* (Los Angeles: Institute for the Development of Educational Activities, 1979); Michael Rutter et al., *Fifteen Thousand Hours: Secondary Schools and Their Effect on Children* (Cambridge, Mass.: Harvard University Press, 1979); Reginald M. Clark, *Community Opportunity Structure, Family Interaction, and Children's Cognitive Development* (Chicago: Spencer Foundation, 1982); Anita A. Summers and B. J. Wolfe, "Which School Resources Help Learning? Efficiency and Equity in Philadelphia Public Schools," *Business Review*, and Robert Benjamin, *Making Schools Work* (New York: Continuum Press, 1981).

Most of the current research makes it clear that class size, higher expenditure levels, and "highly" educated teachers do not necessarily make positive contributions to children's school achievement. The available evidence reveals that effective schools are staffed by energetic, committed teachers and are administered by leaders who believe their children can learn what is available to be taught, who believe it is their responsibility to teach them, who are knowledgeable about the pupil's life-styles, and who do not fear reasonable challenges.

6. See Malcolm P. Douglass, "On the Politics of Reading and the Humanizing Experience," paper presented at the Claremont Reading Conference, Claremont Graduate School, Claremont, 1980; Jonathan Kozol, *Prisoners of Silence: Breaking the Bonds of Adult Illiteracy in the United States* (New York: Continuum Press, 1980).

7. See Max Weber, *The Theory of Social and Economic Organization* (New York: Oxford Univerity Press, 1947).

8. School policies often work against the development of a strong classroom-household learning support system for the child. This may be clearly seen, for example, when some teachers tell parents not to help their children with their homework or talk about classroom lessons (ostensibly because the child must learn to perform on his or her own). If these teachers knew how to utilize the parents in the instructional process, general family discourse processes as well as academic assistance to the child might be enhanced. For an excellent discussion of these issues see David S. Seeley *Education Through Partnership: Mediating Structures and Education* (Cambridge, Mass.: Ballinger, 1981). Research is available which shows that when parents are, in some way, used in the instructional process (as compared to simply being in the PTA), their children experience greater achievement gains. See Dorothy Rich et al., "Families as Educators of Their Own Children," in R. Brandt, ed., *Partners: Parents & Schools* (Alexandria, Va.: Association for Supervisors and Curriculum Development, 1979) 26–40; Joyce L. Epstein, "Student Reactions to Teachers' Practices of Parent Involvement," paper presented at the annual meeting of the American Educational Research Association, New York City, 1982; Henry J. Becker and Joyce L. Epstein, "Parent Involvement: A Survey of Teacher Practices" *Elementary School Journal* 83(1980):85–102; Mary Siders, "How to Grow a Happy Reader," paper presented at the annual meeting of the American Educational Research Association, New York City, 1982.

9. See Jane Stallings, "Allocated Academic Learning Time Revisited, or Beyond Time on Task."

10. School policy toward families should be based on the specific achievement problems and needs of children in that attendance center and on the particular circumstances of their home life. For example, parents who are not yet in the work force and who have the time and the talent to motivate learning, may have different needs (in terms of school support

policies) from the parents who work at night and who do not know how to prepare their children properly for educational settings. Of course, when parents are under extreme stress, are having difficulty coping, and are hurting personally, their children's support needs will be different from those of children whose parents are psychologically healthy.

The author has recently created staff development procedures for use with administrators, staff developers, psychologists, and teachers. The purpose of these one-to-five day programs is to assist groups of administrators and teachers in improving their understanding of family life-styles and their skill in using this knowledge in their instructional planning and decision making. Basically, these programs aim to assist school staff to improve the efficiency and effectiveness of their own instructional programs through better utilization of family and community learning resources. Also, Jane Stallings ("Report on California Schools with Increasing and Decreasing Reading Scores," 1980) has reported a successful training program in teacher skills development. Other good programs are also emerging from the research community and from within school district offices to meet these training needs.

11. Of course, it is difficult to instill moral principles when parents frequently break the family's "official" or formal moral code in preference for one of the dubious informal moral codes of the household. See Bettylou Valentine, *Hustling and Other Hard Work* (New York: Free Press, 1978).

Bibliography

Adams, B. *The Family: A Sociological Interpretation*, 3d. ed. Chicago: Rand McNally, 1981.

———. "Birth Order: A Review." *Sociometry* 35, no. 3 (1972):411–39.

———. "Conceptual and Policy Issues in the Study of Family Socialization in the United States." Paper presented at American Educational Research Association, New York City, 1982.

———. *Kinship in an Urban Setting*. Chicago: Markham, 1968.

Adams, B., and Butler, J. E. "Occupational Status and Husband-Wife Social Participation." *Social Forces* 45 (1967):501–7.

Allen, W. R. "The Antecedents of Adolescent Mobility Aspirations." Ph.D. diss., University of Chicago, 1975.

———. "The Search for Applicable Theories of Black Family Life." *Journal of Marriage and the Family* 40 (1978):117–29.

Alschuler, A., and Irons, R. B. "Motivating Adolescents' Achievements." *Urban Education* 7 (1973):323–40.

Anderson, A. "The Role of Literacy in the Non-School and School Environments of Lower Class Children." Research in progress.

Anderson, Carolyn S., "The Search for School Climate: A Review of the Research." *Review of Educational Research* 52, no. 3 (1982):368–420.

Anderson, L. W. "Time and School Learning." Ph.D. diss., University of Chicago, 1973.

Anyon, J. "Social Class and School Knowledge." *Curriculum Inquiry* 11, no. 1 (1981):3–42.

Aschenbrenner, J. *Lifelines: Black Families in Chicago*. New York: Holt, Rinehart & Winston, 1975.

Atkinson, J. W. *An Introduction to Motivation*. Princeton, N.J.: Van Nostrand, 1964.

———. *Motivation and Achievement*. New York: Halsted Press, 1964.

Baldwin, J. *Notes of a Native Son*. New York: Bantam Books, 1955.

Bandura, A., et al. "A Comparative Test of the Status Envy, Social Power, and Secondary Reinforcement Theories of Identificatory Learning." *Journal of Abnormal and Social Psychology* 67 (1963):527–34.

———. "Social Learning Theory of Identificatory Processes." In D. A. Goslin, ed., *Handbook of Socialization Theory and Research*, 213–62. Chicago: Rand McNally, 1967.

Banfield, E. *The Unheavenly City*. Boston: Little, Brown, 1970.

Bank, S., and Kahn, M. D. "Sisterhood-Brotherhood is Powerful: Sibling Sub-Systems and Family Therapy." *Family Process* 14, no. 3 (1975):311–37.

Barker, R. *Ecological Psychology: Concepts and Methods for Studying the Environment of Human Behavior*. Stanford, Calif.: Stanford University Press, 1968.

Baugh, J. E. "The Experiences of Black Students in a White University: Case Study of Participants in an Educational Opportunity Program." Ph.D. diss., University of Wisconsin, 1973.

Baumrind, D. "Reciprocal Rights and Responsibilities in Parent–Child Relations." *Journal of Social Issues* 34, no. 2 (1978):179–96.

———. "An Exploratory Study of Socialization Effects on Black Children: Some Black-White Comparisons." *Child Development* 43 (1972):261–67.

———. "Socialization and Instrumental Competence in Young Children." In W. W. Hartup, ed., *The Young Child: Reviews of Research*, 2:202–224. Washington, D.C.: National Association for the Education of Young Children, 1967.

———. "Current Patterns of Parental Authority." *Developmental Psychology Monograph* 4, no. 1 (1971):1–103.

———. "Authoritarian vs. Authoritative Parental Control." *Adolescence* 3 (1968):253–72.

Baumrind, D., and Black, A. E. "Socialization Practices Associated with Dimensions of Competence in Preschool Boys and Girls." *Child Development* 38 (1967):291–328.

Bean, F. D., and Frisbie, W. P., eds. *The Demography of Racial and Ethnic Groups*. New York: Academic Press, 1978.

Becker, G. S. *Human Capital: A Theoretical and Empirical Analysis, with Special Reference to Education*. New York: National Bureau of Economic Research, Columbia University Press, 1964.

———. *A Treatise on the Family*. Cambridge, Mass.: Harvard University Press, 1981.

Becker, Henry, and Epstein, Joyce L. "Parent Involvement: A Survey of Teacher Practices." *Elementary School Journal* 83, no. 2 (1982):85–102.

Bell, N. W., and Vogel, E. F.1 "Toward a Framework for Functional Analysis of Family Behavior." In N. W. Bell and E. F. Vogel, eds., *A Modern Introduction to the Family*, 1–34. Glencoe, Ill.: Free Press, 1968.

Bell, R. B. "Lower Class Negro Mothers and Their Children." *Integrated Education* 2 (1964–65):23–27.

———. "Lower Class Negro Mothers' Aspirations for Their Children." *Social Forces* 43, no. 4 (1965):493–501.

Bell, R. Q. "Retrospective Attitude Studies of Parent–Child Relations." *Child Development* 29 (1958):323–38.

Benjamin, Robert. *Making Schools Work: A Reporter's Journey through Some of America's Most Remarkable Classrooms*. New York: Continuum Publishing, 1981.

Benson, C. S., et al., "A New View of School Efficiency: Household Time Contributions to School Achievement." In J. W. Guthrie, ed., *School Finance Policies and Practices: The 1980's, A Decade of Conflict*, 169–204. Cambridge, Mass: Ballinger, 1980.

Berger, P., and Luckmann, T. *The Social Construction of Reality: A Treatise in the Sociology of Knowledge*. New York: Doubleday, 1967.

Bernstein, B. "Language and Social Class." *British Journal of Sociology* 11 (1960):271–76.

Billingsley, A. "Black Families and White Social Science." *Journal of Social Issues* 26 (1970):127–42.

———. "Family Functioning in the Low–Income Black Community." *Social Casework* 50 (1969):562–72.

———. *Black Families in White America.* Englewood Cliffs, N.J.: Prentice-Hall, 1968.

Billingsley, A., and Billingsley, A. T. "Negro Family Life in America." *Social Service Review* 39 (1965):310–19.

Blalock, H. M., Jr. *Black-White Relations in the 1980's: Toward a Long-Term Policy.* New York: Praeger Publishers, 1979.

Blau, P., and Duncan, O. D. *The American Occupational Structure.* New York: John Wiley & Sons, 1967.

Blau, Z. S. "Exposure to Child-Rearing Experts: A Structural Interpretation of Class-Color Differences." *American Journal of Sociology* 69, no. 6 (1964):596–608.

———. "Maternal Aspirations, Socialization, and Girls in the White Working Class." *Journal of Youth and Adolescence* 1 (1972):35–57.

Blood, R., and Wolfe, D. "Negro-White Differences in Blue Collar Marriages in a Northern Metropolis." *Social Forces* 48, no. 1 (1969):59–63.

———. *Husbands and Wives: The Dynamics of Married Living.* New York: Free Press, 1960.

Bloom, B. *Human Characteristics and School Learning.* New York: McGraw-Hill, 1976.

———. "New Directions in Educational Research and Educational Practice." In B. Bloom, *All Our Children Learning,* 382– 85. New York: McGraw-Hill, 1981.

Blyth, W. A. S. "Some Relationships Between Homes and Schools." In M. Craft, ed., *Linking Home and School,* 3–13. London: Longmans, 1972.

Bond, H. M. *Black American Scholars: A Study of Their Beginnings.* Detroit, Michigan: Balamp, 1972.

Bossard, J. H. S., and Boll, E. S. *Ritual in Family Living: A Contemporary Study.* Philadelphia: University of Pennsylvania Press, 1950.

Bossert, S. T. "Consequences of Activity Structures." Paper presented at American Educational Research Association, Boston, 1980.

———. *Tasks and Social Relationships in Classrooms: A Study of Classroom Organization and its Consequences.* Washington, D.C.: Arnold M. and Caroline Rose Monograph Series, American Sociological Association, 1979.

Bott, E. J. *Family and Social Network.* London: Tavistock Publications, 1957.

Boudon, Raymond. *The Logic of Social Action: An Introduction to Sociological Analysis.* London: Routledge & Kegan Paul, 1979.

Bourdieu, P. "Cultural Reproduction and Social Reproduction." In R. Brown, ed., *Knowledge, Education, and Cultural Change.* London: Tavistock, 1973.

Bourdieu, P., and Passeron, J. C. *Reproduction in Education, Society and Culture.* Beverly Hills, Calif.: Sage Publications, 1977.

Brandt, R. S. *Partners: Parents & Schools.* Alexandria, Va.: Association for Supervision and Curriculum Development, 1979.

Bransford, J. D., et al. "Cognition and Adaptation: The Importance of Learning to Learn." In John H. Harvey, ed. *Cognition, Social Behavior, and the Environment,* 93–110. Hillsdale, N.J.: Lawrence Erlbaum Associates, 1981.

Braun, C. "Teacher Expectations: Sociopsychological Dynamics." *Review of Educational Research* 46, no. 2 (1976):185–213.

Bronfenbrenner, U. *The Ecology of Human Development*. Cambridge, Mass.: Harvard University Press, 1979.

————. "Some Familial Antecedents of Responsibility and Leadership in Adolescents." In L. Petrullo and B. M. Bass, eds., *Leadership and Interpersonal Behavior*, 239–71. New York: Holt, Rinehart & Winston, 1961.

Brookover, W., et al. *School Social Systems and Student Achievement*. New York: Praeger, 1979.

Brookover, W., and Shiler, T. "Self–Concept of Ability and School Achievement." *Sociology of Education* 37, no. 3 (1964):271–78.

Brophy, J., and Good, T. *Teacher–Student Relationships: Causes and Consequences*. New York: Holt, Rinehart & Winston, 1977.

Bryan, J. H., and London, P. "Altruistic Behavior by Children." *Psychological Bulletin* 73 (1970):200–11.

Burgess, E. W. "The Family as a Unity of Interacting Personalities." In L. S. Cottrell et al., eds. *Ernest W. Burgess on Community, Family, and Delinquency: Selected Writings*. Chicago: University of Chicago Press, 1973.

Burr, W. "Symbolic Interaction and the Family." In W. Burr, ed., *Contemporary Theories About the Family, Vol. 2*, 42–111. New York: Free Press, 1979.

Burr, W., et al., eds. *Contemporary Theories about the Family*, vol. 1 and 2. New York: Free Press, 1979.

Bush, D. M. and Simmons, R. G. "Socialization Processes Over the Life Course." In M. Rosenberg and R. H. Turner, eds., *Social Psychology: Sociological Perspectives*, 133–164. New York: Basic Books, 1981.

Caplovitz, D. *Making Ends Meet: How Families Cope with Inflation and Recession*. Beverly Hills, Calif.: Sage Publications, 1979.

Caplow, T. *Two Against One: Coalition in Triads*. Englewood Cliffs: N.J.: Prentice-Hall, 1969.

Carew, J., and Lightfoot, S. L. *Beyond Bias; Perspectives on Classrooms*. Cambridge, Mass.: Harvard University Press, 1977.

Cervantes, L. F. "Family Background, Primary Relationships, and the High School Dropout." *Journal of Marriage and the Family* 27, no. 2 (1965):218–29.

Chall, J., and Snow, C. "The Contribution of Out of School Experiences to the Acquisition of Literacy." Progress Report to National Institute of Education, 1982.

Chicago Board of Education: Bureau of Administrative Research. *High School Dropout Report, 1966–67 to 1974–75*. Chicago: Chicago Board of Education, 1976.

Chicago Urban League. *The Current Economic Status of Chicago's Black Community*. Chicago: Chicago Urban League, 1977.

Chilman, G. S. "Child-Rearing and Family Relationship Patterns of the Very Poor." *Welfare in Review* 3, no. 1 (1965):9–19.

City of Chicago. *Chicago's Black Population: Selected Statistics*. Chicago: Department of Development and Planning, 1975.

Clark, K. B. *Dark Ghetto: Dilemmas of Social Power*. New York: Harper & Row, 1965.

——. *Prejudice and Your Child*, 2nd ed. Boston: Beacon Press, 1963.

Clark, R. M. "Black Families as Educators: A Qualitative Inquiry." Ph.D.diss., University of Wisconsin, 1977.

——. *Community Opportunity Structure, Family Interaction, and Children's Cognitive Development*. Technical Report no. D–107. Chicago: Spencer Foundation, 1982.

——. "The Dance Party as a Socialization Mechanism for Black Urban Pre-Adolescents and Adolescents." *Sociology and Social Research* 58, no. 2 (1974):124–54.

——. "Significant Concepts for Analyzing How Home Life Affects Literacy Development." Claremont Reading Conference 45th Yearbook, Claremont, Calif., 1981.

——. "The Quality of Family Pedagogic Life—What is That? Or, Understanding How Learning Happens in Domestic Units." Claremont Graduate School, 1982.

Cloyd, J. S. "Small Group as Social Institution." *American Sociological Review* 30, no. 3 (1965):394–402.

Cochran, M., et al., *The Ecology of Urban Family Life*. Summary Report to the National Institute of Education, 1982.

Cohen, E. "Parental Factors in Educational Mobility." *Sociology of Education* 38, no. 5 (1965):404–25.

Cohen, M. "Effective Schools: Accumulating Research Findings" *American Education* (January-February, 1982):13–16.

Cohler, B., and Grunebaum, H. *Mothers, Grandmothers, and Daughters: Personality and Child Care in Three Generation Families*. New York: John Wiley Publishers, 1981.

Coleman, J. S., et al., *Equality of Educational Opportunity*. Washington, D.C.: U.S. Office of Education, 1966.

Collins, R. *The Credential Society*. New York: Academic Press, 1979.

Conklin, M. E. and Dailey, A. R. "Does Consistency of Parental Educational Encouragement Matter for Secondary School Students?" *Sociology of Education* 54, no. 4 (October, 1981):254–262.

Conyers, J. E., and Epps, E. G. "A Profile of Black Sociologists." In J. E. Blackwell and M. Janowitz, eds., *Black Sociologists: Historical and Contemporary Perspectives*, 231–52. Chicago: University of Chicago Press, 1974.

Cooley, C. H. *Human Nature and the Social Order*. New York: C. Scribner & Sons, 1902.

Cooper, H. "Pygmalion Grows Up: A Model for Teacher Expectation, Communication and Performance Influence." *Review of Educational Research* 49, no. 3 (1979):389–410.

Coopersmith, S. *The Antecedents of Self Esteem*. San Francisco: W. H. Freeman, 1967.

Craft, M., ed. *Linking Home and School*, 2nd ed. Atlantic Highlands, N.J.: Humanities Press, 1972.

Crain, R., and Weisman, C. *Discrimination, Personality and Achievement: A Survey of Northern Blacks*. New York: Seminar Press, 1972.

Crandall, V. G. "Achievement Behavior in Young Children." In W. W. Hartup &
N. S. Smothergill, eds., *The Young Child: Review of Research*. Washington,
D.C.: National Association for the Education of Young Children, 1967.

Cromwell, R. E., and Olson, D. H., eds. *Power in Families*. New York: John
Wiley, 1975.

Csikszentmihalyi, M. "Life Themes: A Theoretical and Empirical Exploration of
Their Origins and Effects." University of Chicago, 1977.

Csikszentmihalyi, M., and Rochberg–Halton, E. *The Meaning of Things: Domestic Symbols and the Self*. Cambridge: Cambridge University Press, 1981.

Dave, R. H. "The Identification and Measurement of Environmental Process
Variables That Are Related to Educational Achievement." Ph.D. diss., Chicago: University of Chicago, 1963.

Davidson, H. H., and Greenberg, J. E. *School Achievers from a Deprived Background*. New York: Associated Educational Services, 1967.

Davies, Don, ed., *Communities and Their Schools*. New York: McGraw-Hill,
1981.

Deutsch, M. "The Disadvantaged Child and the Learning Process." In A. H.
Passow, ed., *Education in Depressed Areas*, 163–79. New York: Teachers
College Press, 1967.

Doty, E. T. "The Significance of Family Ritual and Ceremony in the Life Organization of Children." M.A. thesis. University of Chicago, 1923.

Douglass, M. P. "On the Politics of Reading and the Humanizing Experience."
Paper presented at Claremont Reading Conference, Claremont, Calif., 1980.

Drake, S. C., and Cayton, H. R. *Black Metropolis: A Study of Negro Life in a
Northern City*. New York: Harcourt Brace, 1945.

Dreeben, R. *On What Is Learned in School*. Reading, Mass.: Addison-Wesley,
1968.

Drew, D. "A Profile of the Jewish Freshman: 1980." Higher Education Institute,
1981.

Drews, E. M., and Teahan, J. E. "Parental Attitudes and Academic Achievement." *Journal of Clinical Psychology* 13, no. 4 (1957):328–32.

Dreyer, Philip. "Parent-Child Attachement and Children's Competence: A Life-
cycle Perspective." Paper presented at American Educational Research Association, New York City, 1982.

Duncan, O. D. "Inheritance of Poverty or Inheritance of Race?" In D. P. Moynihan, ed., *On Understanding Poverty*, 85–110. New York: Basic Books, 1969.

————. Featherman, D. L., and Duncan, B. *Socioeconomic Background and
Achievement*. New York: Seminar Press, 1972.

Dunmore, C. "Social–Psychological Factors Affecting the Use of an Educational
Opportunity Program by Families Living in a Poverty Area." Ph.D. diss., Wal-
tham, Mass., Brandeis University, 1967.

Edmonds, R.; Billingsley, A.; Comer, J.; Dyer, J. M.; Hall, W.; Hill, R.; McGe-
hee, N.; Reddick, L.; Taylor, H. F.; and Wright, S. "A Black Response to
Christopher Jencks' [Inequality] and Certain Other Issues." *Harvard Educational Review* 43, no. 1 (1973):76–91.

Edmonds, R. "A Discussion of the Literature and Issues Related to Effective
Schooling." In H. D. Willis, ed., *What Do We Know about Teaching and
Learning in Urban Schools?* St. Louis, Mo.: Cemrel, 1979.

Epps, Edgar G. "Correlates of Academic Achievement among Northern and Southern Urban Negro Students." *Journal of Social Issues* 25, no. 3 (1969):55–70.

————. "Ethnic Families as Developers of Children's Aspirations, Expectations and Self-Esteem in the United States." Paper presented at American Educational Research Association Annual Meeting, Boston, 1980.

————. *Family and Achievement: A Study of the Relation of Family Background to Achievement Orientation and Performance Among Negro High School Students.* Ann Arbor: Institute for Social Research, University of Michigan, 1969.

————. "Impact of School Desegregation on Aspiration, Self–Concept and Other Aspects of Personality." *Law and Contemporary Problems* (1975):300–13.

————. [issue editor] "Motivation and Academic Achievement of Negro Americans." *Journal of Social Issues* 25, no. 1 (1969):5–11.

Epstein, Joyce L. "Student Reactions to Teachers' Practices of Parent Involvement." Paper presented at the annual meeting of the American Educational Research Association, New York City, 1982.

Erickson, E. *Childhood and Society.* New York: Norton, 1950.

————. *Identity, Youth and Crisis.* New York: Dutton, 1968.

Etzkowitz, H., and Schaflander, G. M. *Ghetto Crisis: Riots or Reconciliations?* Boston: Little, Brown, 1969.

Evans, F. B., and Anderson, J. G. "The Psychocultural Origins of Achievement and Achievement Motivation: The Mexican-American Family." *Sociology of Education* 46, no. 4 (1973):396–416.

Fantini, M. D. "Community Participation: Alternative Patterns and Their Consequences on Educational Achievement." Paper presented at American Educational Research Association Annual Meeting, Boston, 1980.

Fantini, M. D. and Cardenas, R., eds. *Parenting in a Multicultural Society.* New York: Longman, 1980.

Farber, B. *Family Organization and Interaction.* San Francisco: Chandler, 1964.

————. "Sponsored and Unsponsored Independence." In B. N. Adams and T. Weirath, eds., *Readings in the Sociology of the Family.* Chicago: Markham, 1971.

Farquhar, R. H. "Some Influences on Achievement and Intelligence: An Essay Review." *Administrators Review* 8 (1965):1–4.

Featherman, D. T., and Hauser, R. M. *Opportunity and Change.* New York: Academic Press, 1978.

Foote, N. N., and Cottrell, L. S. *Identity and Interpersonal Competence: A New Direction in Family Research.* Chicago: University of Chicago Press, 1955.

Foster, Herbert L. *Ribbin', Jivin', and Playin' the Dozens.* Cambridge, Mass.: Ballinger, 1974.

Fraser, E. D. *Home Environment and the School.* London: University of London Press, 1959.

Frazier, E. F. *The Negro Family in the United States.* Chicago: University of Chicago Press, 1939.

Freeberg, N., and Payne, D. "Parental Influence on Cognitive Development in Early Childhood: A Review." *Child Development* 38, no. 1 (1967):65–87.

French, J. R. P., and Raven, B. H. "The Bases of Social Power." In D. Cartwright, ed., *Studies in Social Power*. Ann Arbor: University of Michigan Press, 1960.

Frisbie, W., et al. "Patterns of Marital Instability Among Mexican Americans, Blacks and Anglos." In W. Frisbie, ed., *The Demography of Racial and Ethnic Groups*, 143–163. New York: Academic Press, 1978.

Fuller, B., et al. "The Organizational Context of Individual Efficacy." *Review of Educational Research* 52, no. 1 (Spring, 1982):7–30.

Fusco, G. C. *School-Home Partnership in Depressed Urban Neighborhoods*. Washington, D.C.: U.S. Government Printing Office, 1964.

Gagne, R. M. *The Conditions of Learning*. New York: Holt, Rinehart & Winston, 1977.

Gans, H. J. "The Positive Functions of Poverty." *American Journal of Sociology* 78, no. 2 (1973):275–89.

Gasson, R. M., et al. *Attitudes and Facilitation in the Attainment of Status*. Washington, D.C.: American Sociological Association, 1972.

Gecas, V. "The Influence of Social Class on Socialization." In W. Burr et al., eds., *Contemporary Theories about the Family*, Vol. 1, 365–403. New York: Free Press, 1979.

Getzels, J. W. "Socialization and Education: A Note on Discontinuities." In H. J. Leichter, ed., *The Family as Educator*, 44–51. New York: Teachers College Press, 1974.

Ginsberg, H. *The Myth of the Deprived Child: Poor Children's Intellect and Education*. Englewood Cliffs, N. J.: Prentice-Hall, 1972.

Glaser, B., and Strauss, A. *The Discovery of Grounded Theory*. Chicago: Aldine, 1971.

Glidewell, J. C. "Socialization and Social Structure in the Classroom." In M. L. Hoffman and L. W. Hoffman, eds., *Review of Child Development Research*, 221–56. New York: Russell Sage Foundation, 1966.

————. "The Psychosocial Context of Distress at School." In Bar-Tal and L. Saxe, eds., *Social Psychology of Education*, 165–203. New York: John Wiley, 1978.

Glueck, S., and Glueck, E. *Family Environment and Delinquency*. Boston: Houghton Mifflin, 1962.

Goffman, E. *Asylums*. Chicago: Aldine, 1962.

————. *Frame Analysis*. Cambridge, Mass.: Harvard University Press, 1974.

Goodacre, E. J. *Teachers' and Their Pupils' Home Background*. London: National Foundation for Educational Research, 1968.

Goodlad, J. I. *A Study of Schooling*. Los Angeles: Institute for the Development of Educational Activities, 1979.

Gordon, C. *Looking Ahead: Self-Conceptions, Race, and Family as Determinants of Adolescent Orientation to Achievement*. Arnold and Caroline Rose Monograph Series. Washington, D.C.: American Sociological Association, 1972.

Gordon, I. J. [issue editor] "Parents as Teachers: Symposium." *Theory into Practice* 11 (1972):145–201.

Gordon, M. *Human Nature, Class, and Ethnicity*. New York: Oxford University Press, 1978.

Gottlieb, D. "Poor Youth: A Study in Forced Alienation." *Journal of Social Issues* 25, no. 2 (1969):91–120.

Gottlieb, D., and Campbell, J., Jr. "Winners and Losers in the Race for the Good Life: A Comparison of Blacks and Whites." *Social Science Quarterly* 49, no.3 (1968):593–602.

Gouldner, A. W. "Anti-Minotaur: The Myth of Value-Free Sociology." *Social Problems* (1962):199–213.

Greeley, A. "Catholic High Schools and Minority Students." In A. M. Greeley, *Minority Students and Catholic Secondary Schools.* New Brunswick, New Jersey: Transaction Books, forthcoming.

Greenberg, J. W., and Davidson, H. H. "Home Background and School of Black Urban Ghetto Children." *American Journal of Orthopsychiatry* 42, no. 5 (1972):803–10.

Greer, C. *The Great School Legend.* New York: Basic Books, 1972.

Gurin, P., and Epps, E. G. *Black Consciousness, Identity, and Achievement: A Study of Students in Historically Black Colleges.* New York: John Wiley, 1975.

Gutman, H. *The Black Family in Slavery and Freedom, 1750–1925.* New York: Pantheon Books, 1976.

Haley, A. *Roots.* New York: Doubleday, 1976.

Hamilton, K. *Goals and Plans of Black Women: A Sociological Study.* New York: Exposition Press, 1975.

Handel, G. "The Psychosocial Study of Whole Families." *Psychological Bulletin* 63, no. 1 (1965):19–41.

————. *The Psychological Interior of the Family: A Sourcebook for the Study of Whole Families.* Chicago: Aldine, 1967.

Hannerz, U. *Soulside: Inquiries into Ghetto Culture and Community.* New York: Columbia University Press, 1969.

Hare, B. R. "The Relationship of Social Background to the Dimensions of Self-Concept." Ph.D. diss., University of Chicago, 1975.

Harris, D. B., et al. "The Relationship of Children's Home Duties to an Attitude of Responsibility." *Child Development* 25, no. 1 (1954):29–33.

Harris, Yenell Y. *Community Information in Education 1980.* Washington, D.C.: National Center for Education Statistics.

Hauser, R. M., and Featherman, D. T. *The Process of Stratification.* New York: Academic Press, 1977.

Hawkins, D. "Childhood and the Education of Intellectuals." *Harvard Educational Review* 36, no. 4 (1966):477–83.

Heilbrun, A. B., and Walters, D. B. "Underachievement as Related to Perceived Maternal Child-Rearing and Academic Conditions of Reinforcement." *Child Development* 39 (1968):913–21.

Heise, D. *Understanding Events: Affect and the Construction of Social Action.* Cambridge: Cambridge University Press, 1979

Heiss, J. "Social Roles." In M. Rosenberg and R. H. Turner, eds., *Social Psychology: Sociological Perspectives.* 94–129. New York: Basic Books, 1981.

Henry, J. *Pathways to Madness.* New York: Random House, 1971.

Herzog, E., and Sudia, C. "Children in Fatherless Families." In B. Caldwell and H. Ricciuti, eds., *Child Development and Social Policy,* 141–232. Chicago: University of Chicago Press, 1973.

———. "Social Stereotypes and Social Research." *Journal of Social Issues* 26, no. 3 (1970):109–25.

Herzog, E., and Lewis, H. "Children in Poor Families: Myths and Realities." *American Journal of Orthopsychiatry* 40, no. 3 (1970):375–87.

Hess, R. D. "Maternal Attitudes of the Pupil: Some Social Class Comparisons." In A. H. Passow, ed., *Developing Programs for the Educationally Disadvantaged*, 111–29. New York: Teachers College Press, 1968.

———. "Social Class and Ethnic Influences on Socialization." In P. Mussen, ed., *Carmichaels' Manual of Child Psychology*, 457–577. New York: John Wiley, 1970.

Hess, R. D., et al. "Early Experience and the Socialization of Cognitive Modes in Children." *Child Development* 36, no. 4 (1965):869–86.

———. *The Cognitive Environments of Urban Preschool Children*. Chicago: University of Chicago, 1968.

Hess, R. D., and Handel, G. *Family Worlds: A Psychosocial Approach to Family Life*. Chicago: University of Chicago Press, 1959.

———. "The Family as a Psychosocial Organization." In G. Handel, ed., *The Psychosocial Interior of the Family: A Sourcebook for the Study of Whole Families*, 10–24. Chicago: Aldine, 1967.

Hill, R., and Hansen, D. A. "The Identification of Conceptual Frameworks Utilized in Family Study." *Journal of Marriage and Family Living* 22, no. 4 (1960):299–311.

Hill, R. B. *The Strengths of Black Families*. New York: Emerson Hall, 1971.

Hirschi, T. *Causes of Delinquency*. Berkeley: University of California, 1969.

Hobbs, N. "Families, Schools, and Communities: An Ecosystem for Children." *Teachers College Record* 79 (1978):756–66.

Hoffman, L., and Lippitt, R. "The Measurement of Family Life Variables." In P. Mussen, ed., *Handbook of Research in Child Development*, 945–1014. New York: John Wiley, 1961.

Hoffman, M. L. "Power Assertion by the Parent and Its Impact on the Child." *Child Development* 31 (1960):129–143.

Hoge, R., and Luce, S. "Predicting Academic Behavior from Classroom Behavior." *Review of Educational Research* 49, no. 3 (1979):479–96.

Hooper, D., and Roberts, J. *Disordered Lives: An Interpersonal Account*. London: Longmans, 1966.

Howell, Frank M. and McBroom, Lynn W. "Social Relations at Home and at School: An Analysis of the Correspondence Principle." *Sociology of Education* 55, no. 1 (January, 1982):40–52.

Hsu, F. K. *Kinship and Culture*. Chicago, Ill.: Aldine, 1971.

Hughes, H. M., ed., *Life in Families*. Boston: Allyn & Bacon, 1970.

Husen, T. "Home Background and Behavior in the Classroom Situation." (From author) University of Stockholm, 1963.

Jackson, P. *Life in Classrooms*. New York: Holt, Rinehart & Winston, 1968.

Jarrett, R. L. "Adolescent Dating and Ego Development in an Academic High School." M.A. thesis. University of Chicago, 1978.

Jeffers, C. *Living Poor: A Participant Observer Study of Priorities and Choices*. Ann Arbor, Mich.: Ann Arbor Publishers, 1967.

Jencks, C., et al. *Inequality: A Reassessment of Family and Schooling in America.* New York: Basic Books, 1972.

———. *Who Gets Ahead?* New York: Basic Books, 1979.

John–Steiner, V., and Smith, T. "The Educational Promise of Cultural Pluralism." In H. D. Willis, ed., *What Do We Know About Teaching and Learning in Urban Schools?* St. Louis, Mo.: Cemrel, 1979.

Johnson, C. S. *Growing Up in the Black Belt: Negro Youth in the Rural South.* Washington, D.C.: American Council on Education, 1941.

———. *Shadow of the Plantation.* Chicago: University of Chicago Press, 1934.

Jones, L. W. "The Social Unreadiness of Negro Youth." In A. H. Passow, M. Goldberg, and A. J. Tannenbaum, eds., *Education of the Disadvantaged*, 108–15. New York: Holt, Rinehart & Winston, 1967.

Jones, P. A. "Home Environment and the Development of Verbal Ability." *Child Development* 43, no. 3 (1972):1081–86.

Kagan, Jerome. "The Psychological Requirements for Human Development." In N. B. Talbot, ed., *Raising Children in Modern America: Problems and Prospective Solutions.* Boston: Little, Brown, 1976.

Kahl, J. "Educational and Occupational Aspiration of Common Man Boys." *Harvard Educational Review* 23, no. 3 (1953):186–203.

Kandel, D. B. "Race, Maternal Authority and Adolescent Aspiration." *American Journal of Sociology* 76, no. 6 (1971):999–1020.

Kandel, D. B., and Lesser, G. *Youth in Two Worlds.* San Francisco: Jossey-Bass, 1972.

Kantor, D., and Lehr, W. *Inside the Family: Toward a Theory of Family Process.* New York: Harper & Row, 1975.

Kimball, W. L. "Parent and Family Influences on Academic Achievement Among Mexican-American Students." Ph.D. diss., UCLA, 1968.

Kohn, Melvin. *Class and Conformity: A Study in Values*, 2d ed. Chicago: University of Chicago Press, 1977.

Komarovsky, M. *Blue–Collar Marriage.* New York: Random House, 1962.

Kozol, J. *Prisoners of Silence: Breaking the Bonds of Adult Illiteracy in the United States.* New York: Continuum Press, 1980.

Kriesberg, L. *Mothers in Poverty: A Study of Fatherless Families.* Chicago, Ill.: Aldine, 1970.

———. "Rearing Children for Educational Achievement in Fatherless Families." *Journal of Marriage and the Family* 29, no. 2 (1967):288–301.

Kroeber, A. L., and Parsons, T. "The Concepts of Culture and of Social System." *American Sociological Review* 23, no. 5 (1958):582–83.

Kronus, S. "Race, Ethnicity, and Community." In David Street, ed., *Handbook of Contemporary Urban Life*, 202–232. San Francisco: Jossey-Bass, 1978.

Krystall, E. R., and Epps, E. G. "The Father Absence Effect on Adolescent Aspirations: Myth or Reality?" *Journal of Social and Behavioral Sciences* 13, no. 3 (1968):9–17.

Ladner, J. A. *Tomorrow's Tomorrow: The Black Woman.* New York: Doubleday, 1971.

Leichter, H. J., et al. "The Role of the Family in Promoting Children's Acquisition of Literacy for Learning." Research in progress, 1982.

Leichter, H. J., ed. *The Family as Educator*. New York: Teachers College Press, 1974.

Leithwood, K. A., and Montgomery, D. J. "The Role of the Elementary School Principal in Program Improvement." *Review of Educational Research* 52, no. 3 (Fall, 1982):309–339.

Leontiev, A. N. *Activity, Consciousness, and Personality*. Englewood Cliffs, N.J.: Prentice-Hall, 1978.

LeVine, R. "Culture, Personality, and Socialization: An Evolutionary View." In D. Goslin, ed., *Handbook of Socialization Theory and Research*. Chicago: Rand McNally, 1969.

———. "Parental Goals: A Cross–Cultural View." In H. J. Leichter, ed., *The Family as Educator*, 52–65. New York: Teachers College Press, 1974.

Lewin, K. *A Dynamic Theory of Personality*. New York: McGraw-Hill, 1935.

Lewis, H. *Blackways of Kent*. Chapel Hill: University of North Carolina Press, 1955.

———. "Child-Rearing Among Low-Income Families." In L. Ferman, et al., eds., *Poverty in America*, 343–53. Ann Arbor: University of Michigan Press, 1968.

———. "Culture, Class and Family Life Among Low–Income Urban Negroes." In A. M. Ross and H. B. Hill, eds., *Employment, Race and Poverty*, 149–72. New York: Harcourt, Brace & World, 1967.

Lewis, O. "An Anthropological Approach to Family Studies." *American Journal of Sociology* 55, no. 5 (1950):468–75.

———. "The Culture of Poverty." *Scientific American* 214, no. 10 (1966):19–25.

———. *Five Families: Mexican Case Studies in the Culture of Poverty*. New York: Basic Books, 1959.

Liebow, E. *Tally's Corner: A Study of Negro Streetcorner Men*. Boston: Little, Brown, 1969.

Lightfoot, S. L. *Worlds Apart: Relationships between Families and Schools*. New York: Basic Books, 1977.

Litwak, E., and Meyer, H. J. "The School and the Family: Linking Organizations and External Primary Groups." In S. D. Sieber and D. E. Wilder, eds., *The School in Society*, 425–435. New York: Free Press, 1973.

Lyman, S. M. *The Black American in Sociological Thought*. New York: Putnam, 1972.

Mack, D. E. "Where the Black–Matriarachy Theorists Went Wrong." *Psychology Today* 4 (1971):86–8.

Mackler, B. "Blacks Who Are Academically Successful." *Urban Education* 5 (1971):210–37.

Mackler, B., and Giddings, M. "Cultural Deprivation: A Study in Mythology." In R. A. Dentler, et al., eds., *The Urban R's: Race Relations as the Problem in Urban Education*, 208–14. New York: Praeger, 1967.

Mannheim, K. *Ideology and Utopia: An Introduction to the Sociology of Knowledge*. New York: Harcourt, Brace & World, 1936.

Mannino, F. V. "Family Factors Related to School Persistence." *Journal of Educational Sociology* 35, no. 5 (1962):193–203.

Marjoribanks, K. *Families and Their Learning Environments: An Empirical Analysis*. London: Routledge & Kegan Paul, 1979.

———. *Ethnic Families and Children's Achievements*. London: George Allen & Unwin, 1981.

Martin, B. "Parent–Child Relations." In F. D. Horowitz, ed., *Review of Child Development Research, Vol. 4*. University of Chicago Press, 1975.

Martin, E., and Martin, J. M. *The Black Extended Family*. Chicago: University of Chicago Press, 1978.

McAllister, R. J., et al. "Patterns of Social Interaction among Families of Behaviorally Retarded Children." *Journal of Marriage and the Family* 35 (1973):93–100.

McClelland, D. C. *The Achievement Motive*. New York: Appleton-Century-Crofts, 1953.

McCord, J., and McCord, W. M. "Cultural Stereotypes and the Validity of Interviews for Research in Child Development." *Child Development* 32, no. 3 (1961):171–85.

McCubbin, H., et al. "Family Stress and Coping: A Decade Review." *Journal of Marriage and the Family* 42 (1980):855–71.

McLain, R., and Weigert, A. "Toward a Phenomenological Sociology of Family: A Programmatic Essay." In W. Burr et al., eds., *Contemporary Theories about the Family*, Vol. 2, 160–205. New York: Free Press, 1979.

McManus, J. "Ritual and Human Social Cognition." In Eugene d'Aquili et al., eds., *The Spectrum of Ritual: A Biogenetic Structural Analysis*, 216–47. New York: Columbia University Press, 1979.

Mead, G. H. *Mind, Self and Society*. Chicago: University of Chicago Press, 1934.

Mead, M. "Early Childhood Experience and Later Education in Complex Cultures." In M. Wax et al., eds., *Anthropological Perspectives on Education*, 67–90. New York: Basic Books, 1971.

———. "Socialization and Enculturation." *Current Anthropology* 4, no. 2 (1963):184–88.

Mehan, H. *Learning Lessons: Social Organization in the Classroom*. Cambridge, Mass.: Harvard University Press, 1979.

Meltzer, H. "Economic Security and Children's Attitudes to Parents." *American Journal of Orthopsychiatry* 6, no. 4 (1936):590–608.

Merton, R. K. "Insiders and Outsiders: A Chapter in the Sociology of Knowledge." *American Journal of Sociology* 78, no. 1 (1972):9–47.

Miller, G. W. *Educational Opportunity and the Home*. London: Longman Group, 1971.

Miller, H. *Rich Man, Poor Man*. New York: Crowell, 1971.

Mills, C. W. *The Sociological Imagination*. New York: Oxford Press, 1959.

Milner, E. "A Study of the Relationship Between Reading Readiness in Grade-One School Children and Patterns of Parent-Child Interactions." *Child Development* 22, no. 2 (1951):95–122.

Moles, O. C., Jr. "Child Training Practices among Low–Income Families." *Welfare in Review* 3, no. 6 (1965):1–11.

Monane, J. *Sociology of Human Systems*. New York: Appleton-Century-Crofts, 1967.

Moore, W., Jr. *The Vertical Ghetto*. New York: Random House, 1969.

Morrow, W. R., and Wilson, R. C. "Family Relations of Bright High Achieving and Under Achieving High School Boys." *Child Development* 32, no. 2 (1961):501–10.

Mosteller, F. and Moynihan, D. P., eds. *On Equality of Educational Opportunity.* New York: Vintage Books, 1972.

Moynihan, D. P. *The Negro Family: The Case for National Action.* Washington, D.C.: Office of Policy Planning and Research, U.S. Department of Labor, 1965.

Musgrove, F. *The Family, Education, and Society.* London: Routledge & Kegan Paul. New York: Humanities Press, 1966.

Myrdal, G. *An American Dilemma: The Negro Problem and Modern Democracy.* New York: Pantheon Books, 1944.

National Black Child Development Institute. *The Status of Black Children in 1980.* Washington, D.C.: NBCDI, 1982.

National Urban League. *State of Black America, 1978.* New York: National Urban League, 1978.

Newson, J., and Newson, E. *Four Years Old in an Urban Community.* Chicago: Aldine, 1968.

————. *Seven Years Old in the Home Environment.* New York: John Wiley & Sons, 1968.

Nichols, R. C. "Parental Attitudes of Mothers of Intelligent Adolescents and Creativity of Their Children." *Child Development* 35, no. 4 (1964):1041–49.

Nishi, S. M. "Japanese American Achievement in Chicago: A Cultural Response to Degradation." Ph.D. diss., University of Chicago, 1963.

Nye, F. I., and Berardo, F. M. *Emerging Conceptual Frameworks in Family Analysis.* New York: Macmillan, 1960.

Nye, F. I., et al. *Role Structure and Analysis of the Family.* Beverly Hills, Calif.: Sage Publications, 1976.

Ogbu, J. *The Next Generation: An Ethnography of Education in an Urban Neighborhood.* New York: Academic Press, 1974.

————. *Minority Education and Caste.* New York: Academic Press, 1978.

Parsons, T. "The Social Structure of the Family." In R. N. Anshen, ed., *The Family: Its Function and Destiny.* New York: Harper, 1959.

————. "The School Class as a Social System." *Harvard Educational Review* 29 (1959):297–318.

Parsons, T., and Bales, R. F. *Family, Socialization and Interaction Process.* Glencoe, Ill.: Free Press, 1955.

Parsons, T., et al. *Working Papers in the Theory of Action.* Glencoe, Ill.: Free Press, 1953.

Patterson, G. W. "Mothers: The Unacknowledged Victims." *Monographs of the Society for Research in Child Development,* vol. 45. no. 5. Chicago: University of Chicago Press, 1980.

Pavenstadt, E. "A Comparison of the Child-Rearing Environment of Upper-Lower and Very-Lower Class Families." *American Journal of Orthopsychiatry* 35, no. 1 (1965):89–98.

Pearce, Diana. "Women, Work, and Welfare: The Feminization of Poverty" in Karen Wolk Feinstein, ed. *Working Women and Families,* Sage Yearbooks in Women's Policy Studies, Vol. 4. Beverly Hills, Calif.: Sage Publications, 1979.

Perlman, H. "The Role Concept and Social Casework: Some Explorations." *Social Service Review* 35, no. 4 (1961):371–81.

Persell, C. *Education and Inequality: The Roots and Results of Stratification in America's Schools.* New York: Free Press, 1977.

Peters, M. F. "The Black Family-Perpetuating the Myths: An Analysis of Family Sociology." *Textbook Treatment of Black Families* 23, no. 4 (1974):349–57.

Piaget, J. *The Moral Judgment of the Child.* New York: Free Press, 1948.

Piefer, A. "Black Progress: Achievement, Failure and an Uncertain Future." *Carnegie Corporation of New York Annual Report* (1977):1–14.

Propper, A. "The Relationship of Maternal Employment to Adolescent Roles, Activities, and Parental Relationships." *Journal of Marriage and the Family* 34 (1972):417–21.

Pullis, M., and Caldwell, J. "The Influence of Children's Temperament Characteristics on Teachers' Decision Strategies." *American Educational Research Journal* 19, no. 2 (1982):765–781.

Radin, N. L. "Some Impediments to the Education of Disadvantaged Children." In P. H. Glasser and L. N. Glasser, eds., *Families in Crisis.* New York: Harper & Row, 1970.

Rainwater, L. "Crucible of Identity: The Negro Lower-Class Family." *Daedalus* 95, no. 1 (1966): 172–216.

———. *Behind Ghetto Walls: Black Families in a Federal Slum.* Chicago: Aldine, 1970.

———. *What Money Buys? Inequality and the Social Meaning of Income.* New York: Basic Books, 1974.

Ramirez, M., and Castaneda, A. *Cultural Democracy, Bicognitive Development and Education.* New York: Academic Press, 1974.

Raul, L. "Parental Antecedents of Identification." *Merrill–Palmer Quarterly* 6, no. 2 (1960):77–82.

Reid, C. R. *Environment and Learning: The Prior Issues.* Rutherford, N.J.: Fairleigh Dickinson University Press, 1977.

Reid, I. D. *In a Minor Key: Negro Youth in Story and Fact.* Washington, D.C.: Amarican Council on Education, 1942.

Reiss, D. *The Family's Construction of Reality.* Cambridge, Mass.: Harvard University Press, 1981.

Richardson, B. B. "Racism and Child-Rearing: A Study of Black Mothers." Ph.D. diss., Claremont Graduate School, 1981.

Rist, R. C. "Student Social Class and Teacher Expectations: The Self-Fulfilling Prophecy in Ghetto Education." *Harvard Educational Review* 40, no. 3 (1970):411–51.

Robbins, L. C. "The Accuracy of Parental Recall of Aspects of Child Development and Child Rearing Practices." *Journal of Abnormal and Social Psychology* 65, no. 3 (1963):261–70.

Rodman, H. "On Understanding Lower Class Behavior." *Social and Economic Studies* 8, no. 4 (1959):441–50.

———. "The Lower Class Value Stretch." *Social Forces* 42, no. 2 (1963):205–15.

———. "Talcott Parsons' View of the Changing American Family." *Merrill–Palmer Quarterly* 11, no. 2 (1965):209–28.

Rollins, B. C., and Thomas, D. L. "A Theory of Parental Power and Child Compliance." In R. E. Cromwell and D. H. Olson, eds., *Power In Families.* New York: John Wiley & Sons, 1975.

————. "Parental Support, Power, and Control Techniques in the Socialization of Children." In W. R. Burr et al., eds., *Contemporary Theories about the Family*, Vol. 1, 317–64. New York: Free Press, 1979.

Rose, A., ed. *Human Behavior and Social Processes*. Boston: Houghton Mifflin, 1962.

————. "A Systematic Summary of Symbolic Interaction Theory." In A. Rose, ed., *Human Behavior and Social Processes*, 3–20. Boston: Houghton-Mifflin, 1962.

Rosen, B. C. "Race, Ethnicity, and the Achievement Syndrome." *American Sociological Review* 24 (1959):47–60.

————. "Family Structure and Achievement Motivation." *American Sociological Review* 26, no. 4 (1961):574–85.

————. "The Achievement Syndrome: A Psychocultural Dimension of Social Stratification." *American Sociological Review* 21, no. 2 (1956):203–11.

Rosen, B. C., and D'Andrade, R. "The Psycho-Social Origins of Achievement Motivation." *Sociometry* 22, no. 3 (1959):185–218.

Rosenberg, M., and Simmons, R. *Black and White Self-Esteem: The Urban School Child*. Washington, D.C.: Arnold M. and Caroline Rose Monograph Series, American Sociological Association, 1971.

Rosenfeld, G. *Shut Those Thick Lips: A Study of Slum School Failure*. New York: Holt, Rinehart & Winston, 1971.

Rosenholtz, S. J., and Rosenholtz, S. H. "Classroom Organization and the Perception of Ability." *Sociology of Education* 54 (1981):132–40.

Rosenshine, B. "Teaching Functions in Instructional Programs." Preprint, University of Illinois, 1982.

Rubin, L. *Worlds of Pain: Life in the Working Class Family*. New York: Basic Books, 1976.

Rutter, M., et al. *Fifteen Thousand Hours: Secondary Schools and Their Effects on Children*. Cambridge, Mass.: Harvard University Press, 1979.

Sarbin, T. R. "Role Theory." In G. Lindzey, ed., *Handbook of Social Psychology*, 223–59. Cambridge, Mass.: Addison-Wesley, 1954.

Sarbin, T. R., and Allen, V. L. "Role Enactment, Audience Feedback, and Attitude Change." *Sociometry* 27 (1964):183–94.

Scanzoni, J. H. "A Note on the Sufficiency of Wife Responses in Family Research." *Pacific Sociological Review* 8, no. 2 (1965):109–15.

————. "Inconclusiveness in Family Sources of Achievement." *Pacific Sociological Review* 9, no. 2 (1966):108–14.

————. *The Black Family in Modern Society*. Boston: Allyn & Bacon, 1977.

————. "Social Processes and Power in Families." In W. Burr, et al., eds., *Contemporary Theories about the Family, Vol. 1*. 295–315. New York: Free Press, 1979.

————. *Opportunity and the Family*. New York: Free Press, 1970.

Schaefer, E. S. and Edgerton, M. "Paternal Modernity in Child-Rearing and Educational Attitudes and Beliefs." Paper presented at Eastern Conference on Child Development, New Orleans, April 1981.

Schlegal, A. *Male Dominance and Female Autonomy*. New York: HRAF Press, 1972.

Schultz, D. A. *Coming up Black: Patterns of Ghetto Socialization.* Englewood Cliffs, N.J.: Prentice-Hall, 1969.

Schvaneveldt, J., and Ihinger, M. "Sibling Relationships in the Family." In W. Burr, et al., eds., *Contemporary Theories about the Family*, Vol. 1, 453–467. New York: Free Press, 1979.

Schwartz, M. "The Northern United States Negro Matriarchy: Status Versus Authority." *Phylon* 26 (1965):18–24.

Scott, R., and Sattell, L. "School [and] Home: Not Either-Or." *Merrill- Palmer Quarterly* (1969):335–45.

Scott-Jones, D. "Relationships Between Family Variables and School Achievement in Low-Income Black First Graders." Paper presented at American Educational Research Association, Boston, 1980.

Sears, R., et al. *Patterns of Child Rearing.* Evanston, Ill.: Row, Peterson, 1957.

Sewell, W., and Shah, V. P. "Parents' Education and Children's Educational Aspirations and Achievements." *American Sociological Review* 33, no. 2 (1968):191–209.

Shaw, M. C., and White, D. L. "The Relationship Between Parent–Child Identification and Academic Underachievement." *Journal of Clinical Psychology* 21, no. 1 (1965):10–13.

Shibutani, Tamotsu, and Kwan, Kim M. *Ethnic Stratification: A Comparative Approach.* New York: Macmillan, 1965.

Sieber, S. D. "The Integration of Field Work and Survey Methods." *American Journal of Sociology* 78, no. 6 (1975):1335–59.

Siegel, P. "On the Cost of Being a Negro." *Sociological Inquiry* 35, no. 1 (1965):41–57.

Sigel, I. E., and McGillicuddy-DeLisi, A. V. *Parental Distancing, Beliefs and Children's Representational Competence within the Family Context.* Princeton, N. J.: Educational Testing Service, 1980.

Silverstein, B., and Krate, R. *Children of the Dark Ghetto.* New York: Praeger, 1975.

Simmel, G. *The Sociology of George Simmel.* Glencoe, Ill.: Free Press, 1950.

Simpson, C. "Classroom Structure and the Organization of Ability." *Sociology of Education* 54 (1981):120–132.

Simpson, R. "Parental Influence, Anticipatory Socialization and Social Mobility." *American Sociological Review* 27, no. 4 (1962):517–522.

Slaughter, D. "Parental Potency and the Achievements of Inner City Black Children." *American Journal of Orthopsychiatry* 40, no. 3 (1970):433–440.

————. "Relation of Early Parent-Teacher Socialization Influence to Achievement Orientation and Self-Esteem in Middle Childhood Among Low-Income Black Children." In J. C. Glidewell, ed., *The Social Context of Learning and Development*, 101–131. New York: Gardner Press, 1977.

Smith, M. B. "Competence and Socialization." In J. A. Clausen, ed., *Socialization and Society*, 270–326. Boston: Little, Brown, 1968.

————. "School and Home: Focus on Achievement." In A. H. Passow, ed., *Developing Programs for the Educationally Disadvantaged*, 87–107. New York: Teachers College Press, 1968.

Smith, T. E. "Foundations of Parental Influence upon Adolescents: An Application of Social Power Theory." *American Sociological Review* 35 (1970):860–872.

Solomon, D., et al. "Dimensions of Achievement-Related Behavior Among Lower-Class Negro Parents." *Genetic Psychology Monographs* 79 (1969):163–190.

Sommer, R. *Personal Space: The Behavioral Basis of Design.* Englewood Cliffs, N.J.: Prentice-Hall, 1969.

Sprey, J. "Conflict Theory and the Study of Marriage and the Family." In W. Burr et al., ed., *Contemporary Theories about the Family*, Vol. 2, 130–159. New York: Free Press, 1979.

Stack, C. B. "The Kindred of Viola Jackson: Residence and Family Organization of an Urban Black American Family." In N. Whitten, and J. Szwed, eds., *AfroAmerican Anthropology: Contemporary Perspectives*, 303–311. New York: Free Press, 1970.

————. *All Our Kin: Strategies for Survival in a Black Community.* New York: Harper & Row, 1974.

Stallings, J. "Allocated Academic Learning Time Revisited, or Beyond Time on Task." *Educational Researcher* 9 (1980):11–16.

————. "Report on California Schools with Increasing and Decreasing Reading Scores." Sacramento: California Department of Public Instruction, 1980.

Staples, R. E. "Toward a Sociology of the Black Family: A Theoretical and Methodological Assessment." In C. E. Broderick, ed., *A Decade of Family Research and Action*, 131–35. Minneapolis: National Council on Family Relations, 1972.

————. *The Black Family: Essays and Studies.* Belmont, Calif.: Wadsworth, 1971.

Staples, R. E., and Mirande, A. "Racial and Cultural Variations Among American Families." *Journal of Marriage and the Family* (1980):887–903.

Stodolsky, S. S., and Lesser, G. "Learning Patterns of the Disadvantaged." *Harvard Educational Review* 37, no. 4 (1967):546–593.

Strodtbeck, F. L. "Family Interaction, Values, and Achievement." In D. C. McClelland et al., eds., *Talent and Society*, 135–194. Princeton, N.J.: Van Nostrand, 1958.

————. "The Hidden Curriculum in the Middle-Class Home." In A. H. Passow, M. Goldberg and A. J. Tannenbaum, eds., *Education of the Disadvantaged*, 224–620. New York: Holt, Rinehart & Winston, 1967.

Stryker, S. "Symbolic Interaction as an Approach to Family Research." *Marriage and Family Living* 21, no. 2 (1959):111–119.

————. "The Interactional and Situational Approaches." In H. Christensen, ed., *Handbook of Marriage and the Family*, 125–170. Chicago: Rand McNally, 1964.

Sugarman, B. H. "Social Class and Values as Related to Achievement and Conduct in School." *Sociological Review* 14 (1966):287–301.

Sullivan, H. S. "A Note on Formulating the Relationships of the Individual and the Group." *American Journal of Sociology* 44 (1939):932–937.

Sullivan, T. A. "Racial–Ethnic Differences in Labor Force Participation: An Ethnic Stratification Perspective." In F. D. Bean and W. P. Frisbie, eds., *The*

Demography of Racial and Ethnic Groups, 165–187. New York: Academic Press, 1978.

Summers, A. A., and Wolfe, B. J. "Which School Resources Help Learning? Efficiency and Equity in Philadelphia Public Schools." *Business Review* (February, 1975):4–21.

Sutherland, R. L. *Color, Class and Personality*. Washington, D.C.: American Council on Education, 1942.

Suttles, G. D. "Urban Ethnography: Situational and Normative Accounts." In A. Inkeles et al., eds., *Annual Review of Sociology*, Vol. 2, 1–18. Palo Alto, Calif.: Annual Reviews, Inc., 1976.

Taichert, L. C. *Childhood Learning, Behavior and the Family*. New York: Behavioral Publication, 1973.

Tangri, S. S. and Leitch, L. "Barriers to Home-School Collaboration: Two Case Studies in Junior High Schools." Final Report to the National Institute of Education, 1982.

Thernstrom, S. et al., *Harvard Encyclopedia of American Ethnic Groups*. Cambridge, Mass.: Harvard University Press, 1980.

Thomas, J. A. "Issues in Educational Efficiency." In J. W. Guthrie, ed., *School Finance Policies and Practices: The 1980's, A Decade of Conflict*, 145–167. Cambridge, Mass.: Ballinger, 1980.

Thomas, W. I., and Znaniecki, F. *The Polish Peasant in Europe and America*. New York: Alfred A. Knopf, 1927.

Thompson, D. C. *Sociology of the Black Experience*. Westport, Conn.: Greenwood Press, 1974.

Torshen, K. P. "The Relation of Classroom Evaluation to Students' Self–Concepts and Mental Health." Ph.D. diss., University of Chicago, 1969.

Turner, C. R. "Some Theoretical and Conceptual Considerations for Black Family Studies." *Black Lines* 2, no. 1 (1972):13–27.

Turner, R. "Some Family Determinants of Ambition." *Sociology and Social Research* 46, no. 4 (1962):397–411.

U.S. Bureau of the Census. Current Population Reports, Special Studies, Series P-23, No. 54. *The Social and Economic Status of the Black Population in the United States, 1974*. Washington, D.C.: Government Printing Office, 1975.

U.S. Commission on Civil Rights. *Social Indicators of Equality for Minorities and Women*. Washington, D.C., 1978.

Valentine, B. *Hustling and Other Hard Work: Lifestyles in the Ghetto*. New York: Free Press, 1978.

Veroff, J. "Theoretical Background for Studying the Origins of Human Motivational Dispositions." *Merrill-Palmer Quarterly* 1, no. 1 (1965):1–18.

Vygotsky, L. S. *Mind in Society: The Development of Higher Psychological Processes*. Cambridge: Harvard University Press, 1978.

Waller, W. *The Sociology of Teaching*. New York: John Wiley & Sons, 1932.

Wallet, C., and Goldman, R. *Home, School, and Community Interaction: What We Know and Why We Don't Know More*. Columbus, Ohio: Merrill Publishing, 1979.

Walters, J., and Stinnett, N. "Parent–Child Relationships: A Decade Review of Research." In C. B. Broderick, ed., *A Decade of Family Research and Action*, 99–140. Minneapolis, Minn.: National Council on Family Relations, 1972.

Walters, J., et al. "Perceptions Concerning Development of Responsibility in Young Children." *Elementary School Journal* 57 (1957):209–216.

Ware, W., and Garber, M. "The Home Environment as a Predictor of School Achievement." *Theory Into Practice* 11, no. 3 (1972):190–95.

Warner, W. L., Junker, B. H., and Adams, W. A. *Color and Human Nature: Negro Personality Development in a Northern City.* Washington, D.C.: American Council on Education, 1941.

Wax, R. H. "Reciprocity in Field Work." In R. Adams and J. Preiss, eds., *Human Organization Research*, 90–98. Homewood, Ill.: Dorsey Press, 1960.

_____. *Doing Field Work: Warnings and Advice.* Chicago: University of Chicago Press, 1971.

Waxman, H. C. and Walberg, H. J. "The Relation of Teaching and Learning: A Review of Reviews of Process-Product Research." *Contemporary Education Review* 1, no. 2 (Summer, 1982):103–120.

Weber, M. *The Theory of Social and Economic Organization.* New York: Oxford University Press, 1947.

Webster, S. "Some Correlates of Reported Academically Supportive Behaviors of Negro Mothers toward Their Children." *Journal of Negro Education* 34 (1965):114–120.

Weiss, J. "The Identification and Measurement of Home Environment Factors Related to Achievement Motivation and Self Esteem." Ph.D. diss., University of Chicago, 1969.

Weiss, V., and Monroe, R. "A Framework for Understanding Family Dynamics: Part I." *Social Casework* 40 (1959):3–9.

White, B., et al. *Experience and Environment: Major Influences on the Development of the Young Child.* Englewood Cliffs, N.J.: Prentice-Hall, 1973.

Whiting, J. W. M., and Ayres, B. C. "Inferences from the Shape of Dwellings." In K. Chang, ed., *Settlement Archaeology*, 117–133. Palo Alto, Calif.: National Press Books, 1968.

Wicker, A. W. *An Introduction to Ecological Psychology.* Monterey, Calif.: Brooks/Cole, 1979.

_____ "Processes Which Mediate Behavior-Environment Congruence." *Behavioral Sciences* 12 (1972):265–277.

Wilkinson, D. "Toward a Positive Frame of Reference for Analysis of Black Families: A Selected Bibliography." *Journal of Marriage and the Family* 40, no. 4 (1978):707–708.

Williams, T. M. "Child-rearing Practices of Young Mothers." *American Journal of Orthopsychiatry* 44, no. 1 (1974):70–75.

Williams, T. R. "Abilities and Environments." In W. Sewell et al., eds., *Schooling and Achievement in American Society*, 61–101. New York: Academic Press, 1976.

_____. "Abilities and Environments: Another View." Preprint, 1979.

Willie, C. V., ed. *The Family Life of Black People.* Columbus, Ohio: Merrill, 1970.

Willie, C. V. *A New Look at Black Families*, 2d ed. Bayside, N.Y.: General Hall, 1981.

Wilson, A. "Residential Segregation of Social Classes and Aspirations in High School Boys." *American Sociological Review* 24 (1959):836–845.

Wilson, W. J. "The New Black Sociology: Reflections on the 'Insiders' and 'Outsiders' Controversy." In J. E. Blackwell and M. Janowitz, eds., *Black Sociologists: Historical and Contemporary Perspectives*, 322–381. Chicago: University of Chicago Press, 1974.

————. *The Declining Significance of Race*, 2d ed. Chicago: University of Chicago Press, 1980.

Winch, R. F. *Identification and Its Familial Determinants: Exposition of Theory and Results of Pilot Studies*. Indianapolis: Bobbs-Merrill, 1962.

Winterbottom, M. R. "The Relation of Need for Achievement to Learning Experience and Mastery." In J. W. Atkinson, ed., *Motive in Fantasy, Action and Society*, 435–478. Princeton, N.J.: Van Nostrand, 1958.

Wolf, R. M. "The Measurement of Environments." In *Invitational Conference on Testing Problems*, 93–106. New York: Educational Testing Service, 1964.

————. "The Identification and Measurement of Environmental Process Variables Related to Intelligence." Ph.D. diss., University of Chicago, 1964.

Woodson, C. G. *The Miseducation of the Negro*. New York: A.M.S. Press, 1972.

Yanagisako, S. J. "Family and Household: The Analysis of Domestic Groups." *Annual Review of Anthropology* 8 (1979):161–205.

Yarrow, M. R. "The Measurement of Children's Attitudes and Values." In P. Mussen, ed., *Handbook of Research Methods in Child Development*. New York: John Wiley, 1960.

Young, V. H. "Family and Childhood in a Southern Negro Community." *American Anthropologist* 72, no. 2 (1970):269–88.

Zablocki, B. D., and Kanter, R. M. "The Differentiation of Life-Styles." In A. Inkeles, et al., eds., *Annual Review of Sociology*, Vol 2. Palo Alto, Calif.: Annual Reviews, Inc., 1976.

Zajonk, R. B. "Birth Configuration and Intelligence." *Science* 192 (1976):227–92.

Zimmerman, C. C. *Successful American Families*. New York: Pageant Press, 1960.